GAMBLING AND
THE PUBLIC INTEREST

GAMBLING AND THE PUBLIC INTEREST

Peter Collins

PRAEGER

Westport, Connecticut
London

Library of Congress Cataloging-in-Publication Data

Collins, Peter, 1945–
    Gambling and the public interest / Peter Collins.
        p. cm.
    Includes bibliographical references and index.
    ISBN 1–56720–585–2 (alk. paper)
    1. Gambling. 2. Gambling—Law and legislation. I. Title.
HV6713.C64 2003
363.4′2—dc21   2002044976

British Library Cataloguing in Publication Data is available.

Library of Congress Catalog Card Number: 2002044976
ISBN: 1–56720–585–2

First published in 2003

Praeger Publishers, 88 Post Road West, Westport, CT 06881
An imprint of Greenwood Publishing Group, Inc.
www.praeger.com

Printed in the United States of America

∞™

The paper used in this book complies with the
Permanent Paper Standard issued by the National
Information Standards Organization (Z39.48–1984).

10 9 8 7 6 5 4 3 2 1

For Sarah
With Love

Contents

Preface

I hope that this book will be of interest and use to all who are concerned in whatever context—whether as legislators or regulators, as gambling industry professionals or campaigners against gambling, as lawyers or lobbyists, as academic students of commercial gambling or citizens—with the fundamental question "What should the law be regarding gambling?"

Because this is the fundamental question that the book addresses, its central preoccupations are jurisprudential, and the book is composed principally of discussions about what is or would be desirable rather than of descriptions about what is or has been the case. As such, the focus is on arguments and important questions rather than on information and clear-cut answers. For this reason, it is more important that the conclusions of the book be challenging than that they be irresistible.

Another reason why the conclusions offered must often be tentative is that the academic study of gambling behavior and the gambling business is relatively young. There is a great deal—especially in the areas of economics and psychology as they apply to gambling—about which we are as yet uncertain. It is also true that many disagreements about what the law governing gambling ought to be reflect disagreements about matters of moral principle rather than matters of empirical fact. When people dispute issues of principle, argument may compel them to be clear and consistent, to attend accurately to relevant facts, and to give sensitive consideration to alternative moral visions, but the result will be persuasive rather than probative, and in the end the disputants may have to agree to differ.

This is not, however, to suggest that anyone's opinion about what laws governments should pass about gambling is as good as anyone else's. In this, as in other areas, some opinions are better than others because it is true of some opinions, but not of others, that they make use of concepts that are lucid, subtle, and powerful; are informed by a great deal of factual knowledge of many different sorts; are grounded in value judgments that are cogently defended; and exhibit a high degree of logical coherence both internally and with subject matters external to them.

Indeed, one of the reasons why studying the gambling industry is both unusually interesting and unusually difficult is that it requires some mastery of at least the elementary concepts and conclusions of a diversity of disciplines, including philosophy, politics, economics, psychology, medicine, ethics, and law. In this book, therefore, I have attempted to present these necessary elements of those disciplines in a manner accessible to nonspecialists—which is, after all, the only manner in which most of them are accessible to me. I hope, however, that I have done this without perpetrating distortions of the kind that would rightly outrage specialists.

I have also felt it important to ground my discussions in the real world of practice where they have their most insistent application, namely, the worlds of business and politics. It is a fundamental premise of the book that legal and highly regulated gambling industries, especially when they deliver significant benefits for the public purse, are, for better or worse and whether openly or tacitly, a partnership between the public and private sectors in which both parties have a common interest in the overall profitability of the industry as well as in ensuring that the business is reasonably well thought of by the general nongambling public. Consequently I have tried to anchor my more academic discussions in the real concerns of both regulators and business professionals. The book will have served a useful purpose if it enables each side in this partnership to better understand the concerns and perspectives of the other.

For all these reasons, this is an ambitious project that I could not have begun to attempt had I not been extremely fortunate, over the past eight years since I began to study the gambling industry, in the help I have received from a large number of academics in disciplines other than my own, from regulators, from executives in the gambling industry, and from other professionals. This help has come from all over the world—from Africa and Asia and South America, as well as from Europe, Australasia, and North America. Unsurprisingly, I cannot do justice to all the debts I have incurred, and I can only acknowledge (in chronological order) some of the more conspicuous ones. I should like to record my gratitude, therefore, to

Kerry Capstick-Dale, who in 1995 first found for me the consultancy employment that required me to make a serious study of the gambling industry, who has ever since been a collaborator of extraordinary talent in gambling-related work for the public and private sectors in South Africa, and who now manages the public education and public affairs component of the South African National Responsible Gambling Programme;

Peter Bacon and his colleagues at Sun International South Africa who had the foresight to recognize that academics with an interest in the application of economics and public policy studies to the gambling business could be commercially useful to them and who consequently invested in the education in gambling matters of myself and a number of colleagues from South African academia, to which they also contributed greatly with their own knowledge and expertise;

Brian Kantor, whose original insights into the economics of the gambling business are at the heart of the thinking developed in this book and to whom I owe great and manifold debts of other sorts as colleague and dean of the Commerce Faculty at University of Cape Town until 2001;

Derek Auret, Chris Fismer, and others in the South African regulatory community who have in many different ways provided moral and material support as well as furnishing me with rich insights into the many different problems that governments have to address and solve in relation to developing and implementing policy with regard to gambling;

Bill (William R.) Eadington, the doyen of gambling studies internationally, to whose seminal work in gambling studies all students of the subject must be deeply indebted, who encouraged me to apply for and to accept my present position at the University of Salford, U.K., which has given me the time and the incentive to undertake this project, and who remains a most valued mentor;

David Ford and Jan McMillen, Australian experts on, and regulators of, gambling, who afforded much encouragement when I was first studying gambling policy in the South African context and who have since been unfailingly generous and refreshingly forthright in sharing the fruits of their experience and reflections;

Michael Harloe, who has nurtured my endeavors at Salford and whose reading of the early chapters issued in great encouragement to persevere;

Kath Milhench, who continues to be an exceptionally valued colleague at Salford and whose organizational abilities are indispensable to the working of the University's Centre for the Study of Gambling and Commercial Gaming;

Alan Budd, Tom Kavanagh, and their colleagues who have spearheaded the current proposed reforms to British gambling law and who have been unfailingly congenial and helpful whether we were agreeing or disagreeing;

Peter Byrne, who has been a constant source of support as chair of the Centre's Advisory Board and from whose practical knowledge of the industry I have profited greatly;

Anthony Jennens, whose knowledge of property and planning matters in relation to gambling has only been surpassed in its usefulness by his knowledge of addiction counseling;

Robert Dudley, literary agent, who first proposed this project to me and then persuaded the Greenwood Publishing Group to commission it;

Hilary Claggett of Praeger Publishers, who allowed herself to be persuaded and has subsequently nurtured the project through to completion with diligence, sensitivity, and imagination;

The copy editor, who did a first-rate job translating my English into American, eliminating errors, and rectifying infelicities;

The staff of Impressions Book and Journal Services, Inc., who ensured that the production of the book proceeded with efficiency and swiftness;

To most of these people, in addition to their specific contributions to the present book, I owe the more general debt of gratitude for friendship.

Chapter 1

Introduction

This is a book about the relationship of the gambling industry to government. There is no other industry in the United States or in any other more or less free-market economy where the profitability of companies is so overwhelmingly dependent on what the law permits, requires, and prohibits.

Usually, in free markets, the profitability of a company depends on how successful it is in supplying customers with goods and services that they want on better terms than are offered by competitors. If you sell chocolate or run a restaurant, the law will restrict what you can do to some extent. There are trade descriptions laws, hygiene laws, antitrust laws, et cetera, but how much money you make depends overwhelmingly on your company's ability to compete successfully for the public's business. Of course, gambling companies—that is, companies that sell the chance to win money by buying lottery tickets, making bets, or playing games for money—also have to compete for customers, but in the gambling industry, government is far more intrusive. Throughout the United States, as almost everywhere else in the world, government regulates some or all of the following:

- What gambling products and services may be offered
  - to whom
  - by whom
  - at what price (at what odds)
  - in what areas
  - in what venues
  - at what times, and
- How these products and services may be marketed

Moreover, throughout the United States and almost everywhere else in the world, the gambling industry is expected to contribute special economic benefits to the jurisdictions in which it operates. This may consist of promoting earnings from tourism, funding good causes, or paying abnormally high taxes over and above normal corporate, personal, and property taxes.

All this means that the profitability of a gambling company depends to an enormous extent on what the law says rather than simply on what the public wants. The impact of government regulation on profitability works in two contrary directions. On the one hand, the effect of extensive regulation is to constrain the size of the market for gambling products in any particular jurisdiction and therefore to artificially limit the total potential income of gambling companies. Abnormally high taxation also reduces profits. On the other hand, regulation also often makes it easier for companies to make profits because whether inadvertently or by design, regulation restricts competition.

This is seen clearly where governments limit the number of lotteries or casinos that may be operated in their jurisdiction, so that the result is a local monopoly or oligopoly. As we shall see, this enables gambling companies to make abnormally large profits by offering worse odds than they would have to if they were in fiercer competition for customers. Alternatively, it enables companies to cut costs by providing inferior services. But regulation also restricts competition by creating higher barriers to entry for new gambling companies than for new entrants into other industries. Thus typically the law requires that would-be providers of gambling services prove that they are honest, competent, and well backed financially, something not required for someone wishing to start a business selling used cars or life insurance. These measures also tend to favor the emergence of a monopoly or oligopoly industry, enabling operators to charge more than they could in a freer market.

The reasons why the gambling industry is so highly regulated are largely historical, and one of the main topics to be considered in this book is how good these reasons are.[1] As we shall see in more detail, gambling in the past and in most societies has usually been seen as an activity that is socially undesirable and that governments should prohibit or at least discourage. However, because gambling has always been a popular activity, prohibition has usually meant that the gambling business has gone underground and that the provision of gambling services has fallen into the hands of professional criminals. Notoriously, this is how Las Vegas came to be the gambling capital of the United States.[2] Legalization has then followed typically because on the one hand, it has proved extremely difficult (as with alcohol in the United States in the 1920s and with marijuana today) to enforce prohibition against an activity that many people regard as a harmless and legitimate form of recreation. On the other hand, legalization has enabled governments to swell the public purse by capturing a substantial share of the income from gambling businesses.

With legalization, gambling becomes very big business. It is estimated that annually gamblers lose about $250 billion worldwide and in the United States alone about $70 billion.[3] This means that the total amount staked annually by players betting on horse races and other sporting events, on machines and tables in casinos and elsewhere, on lotteries, and over the Internet will be approximately six times these amounts. Obviously, this means that gambling companies have a massive interest in how the regulation of gambling affects their profitability.

However, the earnings from this huge and growing industry do not all go to the shareholders and workers in the companies that provide commercial gambling services. Almost everywhere in the world, where gambling is not primarily an export business, gambling—like alcohol and tobacco—is subject to abnormal rates of taxation, so that government itself has a substantial economic interest in a profitable gambling industry.

On the other hand (and again like alcohol and tobacco), gambling has the potential to do significant harm to people who gamble too much, and this risk generates costs for government and others who have the responsibility for trying to minimize the incidence of, and damage caused by, excessive gambling. This means that governments have an interest, from the point of view of their own revenues as well as from the point of view of getting reelected, in seeing that the benefits that accrue from having a legal gambling industry outweigh the costs. One reason why gambling policy is so controversial is that many people in the United States and elsewhere argue that the benefits do not outweigh the costs.[4] It should also be noted that it is not only governments and gambling companies who have a powerful interest in arguments about what the law should permit, require, and prohibit in relation to gambling. People who earn all or part of their living working on the prevention and treatment of problem gambling (including researchers such as myself) also have an economic interest in the controversy, although this is often not acknowledged.

Given this concatenation of powerful and often conflicting vested interests, it is not surprising that the subject of gambling and its relation to the law is one that elicits strong and antagonistic passions. But controversy about gambling and public policy acquires additional depth and intensity because for many people, gambling is a moral issue. At one extreme there are those who simply think that gambling is immoral and that the law ought to do whatever it can to prevent people from gambling.[5] At the other extreme there are those for whom gambling is a major source of pleasure and excitement.[6] These enthusiasts are likely to think that the law has no business interfering with the pursuit of enjoyment by adults in a free society. In between are all those who view gambling with varying degrees of benevolence or distaste and believe that gambling should be permitted, subject to more or less strict regulation. These various attitudes reflect different moral judgments and, as such, lead to vigorous controversy about what public policy should be in relation to gambling.

Given this explosive mixture of moral passion and financial interest, it is unsurprising that much discussion about gambling and public policy consists not of dispassionate analysis motivated by a desire to increase understanding but of advocacy designed to further the interests of a particular group by causing a particular policy to be adopted. It is also perhaps unsurprising that there is a great deal of muddle in such discussions, with participants unable or unwilling to define clearly what they are talking about and being palpably confused about fundamental matters such as what is a matter of principle and what is a matter of fact. Finally, it is no doubt unsurprising, though regrettable, that under these circumstances there often seems to be a considerable lack of rigor regarding alleged facts and a great deal of self-deception or worse about ulterior motives.[7]

This book aspires to facilitate a discussion of the controversies surrounding gambling and public policy that is free of these deficiencies. In particular, it is my (admittedly ambitious) intention to try to set out, as clearly and comprehensively as possible, a range of public policy options that governments may adopt regarding all the main aspects of gambling activity, and then to examine, as fairly as possible, the most cogent evidence and arguments that can be adduced to support both the case for, and the case against, adopting them. The policy options considered will sometimes be general, for example, the case for and against prohibition or the case for and against using gambling to generate extra tax revenues. They will sometimes be specific, for example, the case for and against compelling the gambling industry to contribute to the prevention and treatment of problem gambling or for and against legalizing gambling via the Internet. It is inevitable that regarding both general and specific issues I shall reach conclusions of my own about what policies would best serve the overarching public interest in particular circumstances, and it is inevitable that some people will disagree strongly with these conclusions. My hope is that where disagreements arise, I will have been sufficiently clear in defining my terms, in identifying what seem to be the relevant empirical facts, and in articulating and defending the moral principles that I believe should govern public policy in this area, that it will be easy for those who disagree with my conclusions to say precisely where they think my reasoning has gone wrong. In this way, debate about gambling and the public interest may be conducted with objectivity, honesty, and mutual respect undeformed by either the mere rationalization of self-interest or the base attribution of motive that regrettably characterizes too much of what is written even in supposedly scholarly contexts.[8]

A methodological theme that will run through all the arguments is the importance of distinguishing between three types of claim or judgment originally categorized in the philosophical writings of Hume and Kant. The three types are analytic claims, where the truth or falsity of what is claimed depends on the meaning of terms; empirical claims, where truth or falsity depends on the facts of experience, on the way the world as a matter of fact is regardless of how we might like it to be; and normative claims, which appeal to norms or principles or ideals and purport to tell us how the world ought to be regardless of how it in fact is.[9]

All three types of claim—analytic, empirical, and normative—play a vital role in arguments about gambling. When people say, for example, that playing the lottery is not gambling, or that governments' using money derived from lotteries to fund public interest projects is not taxation, they are making analytic claims that rely on the definition of terms, and the right response is "It all depends on what you mean by 'gambling' and 'taxation.' " In fact, analysis of the terms involved will reveal that for all practical purposes relevant to the formulation of good public policy, lotteries are indeed a form of gambling, and when government appropriates a portion of the revenues that lotteries raise, it is indeed engaging in a form of taxation. This is not an arbitrary matter, nor is insisting on clear definitions a matter of nit-picking. On the contrary, as these examples indicate, what we are dealing with, and what analysis needs to expose, is a dishonest attempt to avoid what are thought to be the negative connotations of the words "gambling" and "taxation" for public relations purposes. The same dishonest process, as we shall see, is at work in the attempts by the operators of casinos to claim that their business is not "gambling" but "gaming." On the other hand, it is equally important to be clear that from the fact that lotteries and casino games are forms of gambling it by no means necessarily follows that they are immoral activities, whatever the popular prejudices that may be associated with this term. Nor, of course, does it follow from the fact that governments use lotteries as a way of raising taxes that governments are behaving improperly. Analysis of the concepts involved again shows that in both cases the negative conclusions do not follow from the premises.

The importance of being scrupulous about empirical claims ought to be more obvious than it sometimes seems to be. Its importance in relation to controversies about gambling policy is illustrated by considering an argument often made, which goes as follows: "Where gambling is legal, we find a large number of people who are problem gamblers; therefore gambling should be made illegal so that the incidence of problem gambling will be reduced." Obviously, before we can legitimately draw this conclusion, we need to know whether banning gambling will indeed reduce problem gambling or whether it will merely drive it underground and perhaps to that extent out of sight. This is an empirical matter that requires careful scientific research, and the truth is that we simply do not yet know, because the necessary research has not in fact been done, whether prohibition of gambling—or indeed of alcohol or drugs—does or does not diminish the amount of addictive or otherwise self-damaging behavior.[10]

Finally, it is true that all public policy decisions depend on a commitment to norms and values. We must therefore be explicit about the moral principles that underpin our convictions about what public policy ought to be in relation to gambling. Often people will quite honorably have conflicting moral principles or (more commonly) will attach different degrees of importance to moral principles that support different public policies.

For example, most people believe to some degree in the principle of individual liberty, which says that provided they don't harm others, adults should be allowed to live their lives as seems best to them and should therefore not be prevented by government from spending their time and their money as they choose. Most people also believe that it is the duty of government to protect people from harm. However, some people think the first principle means that government has no business in stopping people from gambling—or taking drugs—even if this means that they run a serious risk of harming themselves. Such people might also argue that governments have no business forcing people to wear seat belts in cars. Other people think that government has a duty to discourage or prohibit gambling in order to protect people from their own vulnerability to folly or weakness and from exploitation by others. These people might argue that prohibiting gambling is no different in principle from making people wear seat belts: if a freedom is being curtailed, it is a trivial freedom, and we are justified in curtailing it out of considerations of the greater good.

It is vital to note that when disagreements about normative questions arise, it is not enough merely to assert our moral convictions: we need also to defend them with rational argument. Examining the similarities and differences between making it compulsory to wear seat belts or illegal to take certain drugs and prohibiting gambling is one way in which we deploy rational argument in defense of our moral principles. In this connection, it should also be noted that people whose moral convictions derive from a deeply held religious faith are not exempt from having to defend their views with arguments, at least to the extent that they wish to participate in the democratic process of formulating public policy through public debate. It is one thing for someone to believe that gambling is immoral and contrary to the will of God. This is a perfectly coherent position that deserves to be scrupulously respected by everyone including those who do not share it. But it is quite another thing to assert that one's own sincerely held moral and religious convictions by themselves justify using the coercive power of the state to compel others who have different moral and religious beliefs to behave as one believes they should. This position is typically indefensible because it commits the fallacy of begging the question and amounts to no more than the intolerant and intolerably antidemocratic claim "My moral and religious principles are better than yours, so you and everyone else should be compelled to act on them." Of course, it may be true that your views on religion and morality are the correct ones and that your convictions will be vindicated, if not in this world, then in the next. However, merely asserting your views does not make them true, and if the rest of us are to be persuaded to act on them, we must be given reasons for believing them that are independent of your say-so.

A final point needs to be made about what we can expect to achieve from the study of controversies about gambling and public policy. This is that we shall not reach the kind of secure (albeit not irrefutable or incorrigible) conclusions that we might hope for if we were reviewing arguments about, for example, the age of the universe or how best to treat a particular disease. This is partly because, as I noted in the preface, research into gambling is in its infancy, which is not the case in medicine or cosmology. Consequently we know too little about the likely effects of different policies in relation to gambling to justify great confidence in our assertions about the desirability of pursuing, say, restrictive or permissive policies in relation to gambling. This is in itself an argument for caution among policy makers. But conclusiveness about what is the best public policy for gambling is also elusive because gambling policy always and rightly reflects the prevailing moral or even aesthetic tastes of the culture and society for which the policy is being considered. Not only will good policy for the United States not necessarily be good policy for Saudi Arabia or China: good policy for Reno may not be good policy for Boston. I describe these as moral or aesthetic *tastes* because it seems to me that if one community says, "We don't like gambling and are going to have as little of it as possible," and another says, "We love gambling and want as much of it as the market will bear," they are each entitled to legislate to promote their preference. This is not the case if one community says we like slavery or child prostitution or gladiatorial contests to the death and the rest of us condemn them. With gambling, as with issues of sexual morality, there is a place for moral and cultural relativism, which is not the case where fundamental issues of human rights or the infliction of suffering are concerned.

In any event, it is indisputably the case that whatever gambling policy a society adopts will depend on the broader view it takes of the proper role of government in regulating the conduct of its citizens and the narrower view it takes of what it wants its policy in relation to gambling to accomplish. It will be helpful to characterize at the outset the most important of the general positions that governments have historically adopted in respect of their gambling policy. These are the following:

- Gambling is a vice. It is the business of government to promote virtue and to eradicate vice. Therefore it is the business of government to stamp out gambling.

- Gambling is undesirable. However, the moral and material costs of enforcing the prohibition of gambling are unacceptably high. Therefore government should do what it can to contain and discourage gambling.

- Gambling is a harmless pastime for most people. Government should therefore treat it as a normal part of the entertainment industry except to the extent that special measures are needed to keep the industry crime free and to deal with the dangers of addiction.

- Gambling is a good way for governments to raise money for public interest projects. Therefore an abnormally large share of gambling revenues should accrue to government, and gambling should either not be discouraged or should be encouraged.

- Gambling is a good way for a jurisdiction to earn money from foreigners. Therefore gambling should be treated as an export business—like tourism.

The first of these views has been the dominant one in most societies throughout most of history. It continues to prevail in Islamic countries and, until recently, in China. It is also the view that informs public policy in Utah in the United States. Even in democracies where gambling is permitted, significant minorities continue to be attracted to versions of this view.

The second view is the one that was explicitly enshrined in British law in 1968. De facto, it characterizes the policy of many states in the United States where gambling, especially via a state lottery, is tolerated, but gambling machines and betting are either prohibited or severely restricted.

The third view is probably the commonest view in the countries of the so-called West, that is, in North America, in Europe, and in Australasia. Typically it requires companies and individuals who wish to work in the gambling industry to undergo stringent probity checks to ensure that they are "fit and proper persons." It has inspectors whose job it is to ensure that the games are honest. There are strict regulations to prevent minors from gambling, and regulators typically impose measures for preventing and treating problem gambling.

The fourth view is adopted by almost all governments in relation to national or state lotteries if they have them. It is also the dominant view governing casino policy in much of America where gambling is not an export business, in most of Europe, and in Canada, Australia, and South Africa. Note that this kind of policy does not necessarily consist in having high gambling taxes. Governments often use casino developments for projects of regional development and urban renewal, and typically they look to the benefits in terms of new investment and new employment. Projects of this sort can be seen in Deadwood, South Dakota, in Windsor, Canada, and in Cape Town, South Africa, to mention only a few of the more successful ones.

The fifth view is the one that enabled Monte Carlo to become the gambling capital of Europe in the nineteenth century and is at the heart of government policy in Nevada. It is the policy that is necessary if gambling resorts are to be developed as in Atlantic City, Biloxi, Sun City, and Macao, as well as Monte Carlo and Las Vegas. It is also the policy that underpins attempts by governments in the Caribbean and elsewhere to license Internet gambling.

Of course, not all these views are mutually exclusive, and it is particularly common for countries and states to try to combine the third and fourth views by having a gambling industry that is both highly regulated and highly taxed.[11]

It is interesting and, on the face of it, surprising that there is no historical or contemporary example of a jurisdiction adopting what one might think of as the most natural view, at least for the governments of societies committed to capitalism and free markets. This would be to say that it is not for government to pass judgment on the desirability of its citizens' spending their own time and money pursuing pleasure in whatever way they choose. Nor is it for governments to interfere in commercial transactions between willing buyers and willing sellers. The government's role is solely to prevent citizens from wrongfully harming one another (not from harming themselves) and to ensure that transactions between citizens are conducted without recourse to force or fraud. If governments were to take this view, they would effectively be saying that trade in commercial gambling services should be treated no differently from trade in other goods and services, where the interests of the consumer are protected mainly by the forces of competition and where otherwise the principle of caveat emptor—let the buyer beware—applies. There are cases—Albania is one, Moscow at one time was another—where a free market in the supply and consumption of gambling services has grown up, but this happens as a consequence of an absence of public policy rather than because government has consciously decided that a free market in commercial gambling services is the right policy to pursue.

It is not obvious why decisions about gambling should not be left to the free choice of adult citizens. The main reasons advanced are the following:

- Gambling is a vice or otherwise peculiarly undesirable.
- Gambling is peculiarly conducive to criminal activity.
- Gambling has a peculiar role to play in the economy.
- Gambling is peculiarly dangerous to those who engage in it.

These issues supply the structure for the principal material covered in this book. Chapter 2 begins by defining the phenomenon of gambling, what it is and what are its principal attractions. In particular I will discuss the question of whether commercial gambling is best thought of as a "vice" industry or simply as a part of the entertainment industry. To address these issues will require both conceptual and phenomenological analysis of the kind in which philosophers specialize.

Chapter 3 considers the arguments for and against the view that gambling should be banned. Because the issue here is essentially about what governments should do, it is an issue in political theory. In particular it is about what the relationship should be between public policy and private morality in societies that are committed to the principles of individual liberty and democratic decision making. The ultimate issues here are issues of profound moral principle in which it is far from obvious that prohibitionists hold all the moral high ground, leaving libertarians or permissivists to rely on rather cynical, pragmatic considerations only.

Chapter 4 considers the various ways in which the law seeks to protect players and the general public from abuses by commercial gambling companies. This is a matter of having good laws and regulations and good public administration. Chapter 5 considers the question of how the gambling industry relates to the rest of the economy. This requires an accurate understanding of the relevant economic principles. Chapter 6 addresses the question of problem gambling and addictive gambling. This will require some consideration of the medical and psychological evidence about normal and abnormal gambling behavior.

This material will, I hope, supply readers, whatever their interests, with the bulk of the evidence and argument necessary for forming rational conclusions about what, in the particular circumstances of their own society, would constitute good public policy in relation to gambling.

Thus far everything said will have been primarily related to land-based commercial gambling, that is, to purchasing lottery tickets, making bets, and playing games for money that take place in physical venues located in the jurisdiction where the supplier and consumer of gambling services are present. We need to consider what difference it makes from the point of view of public policy now that commercial gambling transactions can easily be conducted via the Internet, through television, or with cell phones. The principles of good law and good regulation will presumably stay the same, but many peculiar practical difficulties might seem to arise in relation to enforcement, given current and anticipated technological developments. These technological developments and the practical issues they raise for good public policy may in turn reverberate into fresh questions concerning the regulation of land-based gambling. Chapter 7 therefore deals with interactive gambling and related technological issues.

The whole book proceeds on the assumption that whether gambling is or is not an immoral activity is an issue that can be set aside for the purposes of formulating good policy in relation to the gambling industry. I believe this to be correct but recognize that for most people who are opposed to gambling, their opposition is grounded in a deep-seated sense that gambling is an immoral activity and that it would be better if people didn't do it, even if it is not desirable to use the force of law to prevent them. The view that if something is wicked, even though not obviously or directly harmful to others, then the government should be doing something about it, is one that it is difficult to dissolve. Moreover, the view that gambling is somehow corrosive of the moral character of a community has a direct bearing on the question of whether gambling is at least indirectly harmful to others in a way that is legitimately within government's concerns. Even leaving aside these considerations, the view that gambling is immoral deserves to be discussed in its own right. I therefore devote a final chapter to this topic.

My overall conclusions about gambling and public policy may prove disappointing given the fierce moral passions that the subject generates. These are that gambling is not typically, in my view, a major force for either economic good or economic harm. Also, although I recognize that the distress caused by excessive gambling in individual cases can be as appalling as with any other addiction, I do not think this is a major social evil in comparison with, say, drugs, domestic violence, AIDS, or even reckless driving. In the great scheme of things, I think that gambling and what government does about it are of rather limited moral and social importance.

On the other hand, gambling policy has great practical importance, which derives from the fact that commercial gambling has the capacity for redistributing large sums of money. It is not necessary to subscribe to Marxism to believe that much interest in gambling policy is related to the natural desire that many different kinds of people have to arrange for some of this money to be redistributed toward themselves and their favorite causes. It is consequently of substantial practical importance for public policy to ensure that the people who benefit from the distribution of resources that gambling policy brings about are the ones that government most wishes to benefit.[12]

If this book serves no other purpose than to assist governments in achieving this end, the inquiry that it undertakes will have been worthwhile. I add as an appendix, by way of demonstrating the practical application of all this argumentation, a critical assessment of the policy options that are currently being considered in the U.K. in relation to the reform of gambling law and, in particular, the introduction of American-style casinos and of legal interactive gambling. This will, I hope, be interesting in its own right and also serve as a concrete case study.

NOTES

1. The precontemporary (i.e., pre-1990s) history of gambling is well recounted in J. L. Ludovici, *The Itch to Play: Gamblers in High and Low Life* (London: Jarrolds, 1962). For a history rich in sociological insight about gambling in the United States, see John M. Findlay, *People of Chance: Gambling in American Society from Jamestown to Las Vegas* (New York: Oxford University Press, 1986). A short and up-to-date historical account of gambling in America is given in Richard A. McGowan, *Government and the Transformation of the Gaming Industry* (Northhampton, Mass.: Edward Elgar, 2001).

2. For a good history of Las Vegas, see Barbara Land, *A Short History of Las Vegas* (Las Vegas: University of Nevada Press, 1999).

3. Warwick Bartlett, *First Annual Review of the Global Betting and Gaming Market, 2000–01* (West Bromwich, U.K.: Global Betting and Gaming Consultants, 2001).

4. For example, see Robert Goodman, *The Luck Business: The Devastating Consequences and Broken Promises of America's Gambling Explosion* (New York: Simon and Schuster, 1995). This book contains much useful material, but it is unfortunate that like much of what is written about the social and economic impacts of the gambling industry by both pro- and antigambling authors, Goodman's crusading passion undermines confidence in his objectivity and sense of perspective. The subtitle does not sound as if it is heralding a text that will be characterized by scrupulous scholarly balance and judiciousness.

5. A comprehensive exposition of this view that has stood the test of time surprisingly well is B. Seebohm Rowntree, *Betting and Gambling: A National Evil* (London: Macmillan, 1905).

6. A good discussion of this issue by a gambling enthusiast is found in David Spanier, *Easy Money: Inside the Gambler's Mind*, 2d ed. (Harpenden, U.K.: Oldcastle Books, 1995), chaps. 10–11.

7. It is sometimes difficult to resist the conclusion that reports prepared by, and capitalizing on, the reputation of big accounting consultancies almost invariably reach

the conclusions that their funders want them to reach. This is usually pro-gambling. It is also, however, depressingly easy to predict what the empirical findings of antigambling scholars will purport to show. In both cases, it would not be appropriate to single out individual studies. However, the whole issue is discussed in Richard A. McGowan, "The Ethics of Gambling Research: An Agenda for Mature Analysis," *Journal of Gambling Studies* 13, no. 4 (1997): 274–89. This paper initiated a discussion including papers from B. Gambino, "Method, Method, Who's Got the Method? What Can We *Know* about Compulsive Gamblers?"; J. Fahrenkopf, "Pursuing 'An Agenda for Mature Analysis' "; B. P. Horn, "The Courage to Be Counted"; and R. A. Yaffee and V. J. Brodsky, "Recommendations for Research and Public Policy in Gambling Studies"; all these, together with a reply by McGovern, are in *Journal of Gambling Studies* 13, no. 4 (1997): 291–319.

8. A particularly unfortunate example of this occurs in a recent and supposedly peer-reviewed special issue of *Managerial and Decision Economics*, in which J. W. Kindt seeks to undermine findings by two of the most distinguished academics in the field of gambling studies by accusing them and the publications they are associated with of having improper links with the gambling industry. Even if this were true, which it is not, it would not throw any light one way or another on whether the empirical findings they report are in fact true. See J. W. Kindt, "The Costs of Addicted Gamblers," *Managerial and Decision Economics* 22 (2001): 17–63.

9. The locus classicus for this distinction is Immanuel Kant, *Kritik der Reinen Vernunft* (Critique of pure reason), 2d ed., trans. Paul Guyer and Allen W. Wood (Cambridge: Cambridge University Press, 1998), 136–46.

10. The view that seems to me most plausible is that the increased availability of gambling opportunities that accompanies legalization does indeed tend to increase problem gambling. But the greater attention that this problem receives when gambling is legal and the greater resources that are put into treatment and especially prevention tend to reduce the overall incidence of, and damage caused by, problem gambling. For further discussion, see chapter 5 in this volume. A particularly good study supporting the first hypothesis is R. Ladouceur et al., "Prevalence of Problem Gambling: A Replication Study," *Canadian Journal of Psychiatry–Revue Canadienne de Psychiatrie* 44, no. 8 (1999): 802–4. It is regrettably harder to find good evidence of effective treatment programs, but reports of help lines set up in response to worries about legal gambling describe substantial activity, some of which is presumably effective. See M. Griffiths, A. Scarfe, and P. Bellringer, "The U.K. National Telephone Helpline: Results of the First Year of Operation," *Journal of Gambling Studies* 15, no. 1 (1999): 83–90; and C. MacDougall, *Problem Gambling Helpline: Annual Narrative Report, 1997–98* (Halifax, Canada, 1998).

11. For a comprehensive account of casino law around the world, see Anthony N. Cabot et al., eds., *International Casino Law*, 3d ed. (Reno, Nev.: Institute for the Study of Gambling and Commercial Gaming, 1998).

12. See Anthony N. Cabot, ed., *Casino Gaming: Policy, Economics, and Regulation* (Las Vegas, Nev.: UNLV International Gaming Institute, 1996). The generally helpful economic discussion in Anthony N. Cabot and William N. Thompson's chapter "Gam-

bling and Public Policy" seems to me to be marred by an a priori assumption that what's good for gamblers is good for the community, and hence that any interference with market forces is a priori undesirable. Consequently the authors seem uncritically hostile to monopoly and oligopoly casinos even though these may serve the overall public interest better than a proliferation of casinos. See chapter 5 in this volume.

Chapter 2

What Is Gambling?

The standard definition of gambling identifies it as an activity where

- Two or more parties place at risk something of value (the stakes)
- In the hope of winning something of greater value (the prize)
- Where who wins and who loses depends on the outcome of events that are unknown to the participants at the time of the bet (the result)[1]

This definition is intended to provide the necessary and jointly sufficient conditions for saying of any activity that it constitutes gambling. This means that if any of the conditions are not met, the activity is not gambling, and if all three are met, then the activity is gambling. Thus this definition covers all forms of gambling, whether undertaken privately or offered commercially. The definition, however, requires some further discriminations if it is not to be misleading.

First, the definition covers a number of activities that people often don't think of as gambling. In particular, it includes, in addition to betting on events and playing casino games for money, activities such as purchasing lottery tickets, participating in prize draws, and taking part in newspaper competitions. Sometimes these activities are not thought of as gambling because they involve such small stakes. More commonly, they are thought not to be gambling because they are organized, at least in part, to promote good causes and therefore avoid being morally reprehensible. However, it should be no part of the definition of gambling that it involve high stakes or be somehow sinful. As we shall see in chapter 8, whether gambling is wicked or not requires argument and cannot be a matter of definition.

Contemporary debates about gambling and public policy are principally concerned with commercial gambling where a company offers to provide gambling opportunities as a for-profit business. An important distinction within commercial gambling is made between gambling in which the play by the house is automatic, and gambling where the suppliers of gambling services pit their judgment against their customers. The paradigm for the first sort of gambling is the mechanical play of a roulette wheel or a gambling machine. With a roulette wheel or gambling machine, the amount that the house will win over time is determined by the ratio of results in which the house wins to those in which the player wins. The paradigm for the second type of gambling is betting on horse races or other sporting events where the bookmaker relies on being able in the long run to make better judgments about probabilities than the punter.

Commercial gambling operations naturally prefer to rely on certainties rather than on their own judgment and seek to eliminate the possibility of being outplayed. Totalizer, or pari-mutuel, bets on horse races eliminate this possibility. So do the rules and strategies that casinos adopt to prevent card counting at blackjack. In the case of games such as poker where almost everything depends on the skill of the players, the house usually charges a fee to all players for hosting and administering the game.

This distinction is important for regulation because it reveals the true nature of commercial gambling activity. It might be argued that since commercial gambling operations typically depend on mathematical facts that ensure that the company cannot lose in the long run, these companies are not, in fact, gambling because they are not in fact taking risks. In other words, the companies are not gambling because they do know the outcome. This sounds like cheating in normal contexts where gambling occurs. Nor is this suggestion really mitigated by the consideration that the commercial companies do not know the outcome of particular wagers and indeed sometimes do lose to players who walk away with their winnings.

Occasionally, in the history of gambling regulation, governments have taken the view that house advantage somehow constitutes fraud and have sought to make it illegal.[2] This is difficult to enforce and, if effectively enforced, would obviously make it impossible for commercial gambling companies to operate. However, seeking to eliminate house advantage is also to misconstrue the character of commercial gambling operations. What commercial gambling companies are selling, for better or for worse, are certain kinds of pleasure. What is distinctive is that they charge for supplying this service most commonly by imposing odds and other conditions that ensure that over the long run the house will win. This is why casino operators genuinely view card counting as cheating: it involves obtaining the pleasure of play and not paying for it. If this is so, however, it raises the question of whether the companies should be required to post their prices (i.e., the size of the house advantage for each game) in the same way that other retailers are required to show prices.

Later in the chapter, we will return to the question of what exactly it is that gambling companies sell when we consider whether gambling is more properly thought of by governments and others as vice or as entertainment. Meanwhile three other questions about what is and what is not "gambling" need to be addressed.

The first is whether people buying and selling shares on the stock market are gambling. It is, of course, true that some people use the stock market as a medium for gambling and choose their share purchases by using a pin (the so-called dartboard portfolio). However, the stock market is first and foremost an instrument for investment that enables people to participate in the creation of wealth. This means that over time, investors may be expected to make a profit, which is precisely the opposite of what may be expected for the majority of gamblers who bet with commercial gambling operations. Also, investing in the stock market is not a zero-sum game in which one person's winnings are another's losses, even though it is true of any individual transaction that either the buyer or the seller will turn out to have got the better deal. Rather, buying and selling shares and associated financial products are exchanges in which a willing seller of a risky investment sells to a willing buyer. What is exchanged is a risk that at the agreed price is unacceptably high to the seller and acceptably low to the buyer. What this shows is that whether an activity is gambling or not depends in part on what its point is. The point of buying shares of stock is not normally to "try your luck" or to "pit your wits against an opponent for money." It is always part of the point of gambling that players are doing one or both of these things.

The difference between gambling and investing on the stock market needs to be stressed because on the whole, attempts to liken "playing the market" to gambling are intended either to discredit the business of buying and selling shares or to make commercial gambling more respectable. Also, as we will see in chapter 6, one of the causes and symptoms of problem gambling is the illusion that commercial gambling is a form of investment instead of a form of recreation for which one pays.

A second suggestion, less frequently made perhaps because it does not plausibly serve any propaganda purposes, is that buying insurance policies to protect one's financial interests in the event of premature death or other possible calamity is a form of gambling. The difference here, however, is that both parties to the transaction desire the same result, for example, that the client will not die prematurely or suffer the calamity provided against. The purpose of the transaction is to enable the clients to purchase not the hope of winning money for themselves or their heirs but a measure of peace of mind in the face of (remotely) possible disaster.

Having said this, it should be mentioned that the distinction between gambling, investing, and insuring may become somewhat blurred in the case of certain spread betting transactions in financial markets where the spread bet enables the trader to obtain a form of insurance against the possibility of regular transactions going awry. It is, however, a good maxim in formulating definitions that simply because there are disputed areas between the borders of concepts, it does not follow that there is no clearly identified territory on either side. Besides, as I will argue further, it is crucial to gambling that the primary purpose of the activity be a form of play.

This consideration leads to a third and, in some ways, more difficult question, namely, whether certain types of professional gamblers are really gambling. The first-rate poker player who plays only against people of far less expertise comes close to being in the position of casino owners who know that in the long run they are bound to win. Or perhaps professional gamblers are more like other professional players of games. People often play pool and bridge and golf for money. Some people make a living from what they win by betting on their own prowess at these games. It seems that there is a continuum running between being a successful gambler at gambling activities that require a substantial degree of skill and being someone who plays games professionally, in the same way as other sporting professionals do, particularly those who depend on winning prizes. For many purposes, it makes better sense to understand such people as practicing a profession or plying a trade rather than as gambling.

What this consideration also raises is the relative role of skill and chance in gambling. It is sometimes thought that chess is a game of pure skill, while poker is a game of chance, because in poker you are dependent on the cards you draw, whereas in chess what is crucial is the position of the pieces, and once the game has started, this is entirely a function of the players' choices. This is misleading in two respects. First, there are elements of luck in chess such as whether your opponent is for some extraneous reason off form or whether you make good moves "by accident," that is, without realizing what advantages they will secure for you. Second, the skill in poker and many other card games consists precisely in being able to play your cards well whatever they are and perhaps especially in being able to play bad cards well. (Some people think this is an important lesson for the conduct of real life.)

There are no games of pure skill, but perhaps there are also no games of pure chance, where the outcome is wholly determined by luck, and skill has no role to play at all.[3] For example, you improve your chances, albeit infinitesimally, by avoiding the number nineteen in your selection of numbers. This is because nineteen features in the birth date of the overwhelming majority of lottery players, and many players use their birth date to select their numbers. This means that you are more likely to win less (because you will have to share the prize) if your number comes up with a nineteen in it. And even with gambling machines powered by random number generators that guarantee a particular percentage advantage to the house, and even more so with casino games such as blackjack played according to rules that guarantee a small advantage to the house, prudent play will enable some players to lose less over a longer period of play than others.

What all three of these examples bring out is that the standard definition of gambling is defective to the extent that it makes no mention of the purpose of gambling. This is, as the etymology of the word makes clear, gambling is always connected with the playing of games. Now, what constitutes a game is itself a difficult and philosophically highly interesting question. There may be no such thing as the "essence" of a game understood as some characteristic or set of characteristics that all games necessarily share. No less a philosophical authority than Wittgenstein addressed the question of what a game is and concluded as follows:

Consider ... the proceedings that we call "games." I mean board-games, card-games, ball-games, Olympic games, and so on. What is common to them all?—Don't say: "There *must* be something common, or they would not be called 'games' "—but *look and see* whether there is anything common to all.—For if you look at them you will not see something that is common to *all*, but similarities, relationships, and a whole series of them at that. To repeat: don't think, but look!—Look for example at board-games, with their multifarious relationships. Now pass to card-games; here you may find correspondences with the first group, but many common features, and others appear. When we pass next to ball-games, much that is common is retained, but much is lost.—Are they always amusing? Compare chess with noughts-and-crosses [tic-tac-toe]. Or is there always winning and losing, or competition between players? In ball-games there is winning and losing; but when a child throws his ball against the wall and catches it again, this feature has disappeared. Look at the parts played by skill and luck; and at the differences between skill in chess and skill in tennis. Think now of games like ring-a-ring-a-roses; here is the element of amusement but how many other characteristic features have disappeared! ... I can think of no better expression to characterise these similarities than "family resemblances."[4]

It may thus be a mistake to look for characteristics that are common to all gambling activities and constitute their essence, because there is no essential characteristic common to all games. Instead we should look at the ways in which some games and some gambling activities resemble each other in some respects but not in others, as do members of the same family.

Wittgenstein's observation, and particularly his injunction "don't look for the meaning, look for the use," will help us to clear away a tiresome piece of casuistry that has until recently infected most writing about gambling. This is the question of whether commercial "gambling" is more properly described as commercial "gaming." Etymologically, the two words are more than synonyms: they are different versions of the same word. However, the archaic "gaming" is thought by the casino industry to be free of the negative associations that adhere to "gambling." Hence the absurd pretense that casino companies are not in the gambling business. Hence the names of the American Gaming Association, the Nevada Gaming Board, and so forth.

In fairness, it may be that casino companies have merely been catering to the preferences of their customers who may like to nurture the pretense that what they are doing is playing games rather than gambling. But if anything in modern usage is distinctive about gambling rather than gaming, it is that gambling always implies playing for money; and what casinos indubitably do is to organize the playing of games for money, and they charge a fee for providing this service, usually in the form of a percentage of the money staked. The folly of casino companies' pretending that they are not in the gambling business consists not merely in the fact that the usage is misleading; it is also bad public relations. So even in terms of the casino companies' own objectives, such usage is counterproductive. By insisting on the use of "gaming" rather than "gambling," casino companies give the impression that they have something to hide. The verbal conceit makes them look cute and evasive and, in particular, reinforces the view that they are being deceitful whenever they come to talk about problem gambling.

A far better strategy from a public relations point of view is for casino companies to say, "Yes, certainly we're in the gambling business. Gambling affords the vast majority of the people who do it a great deal of harmless pleasure. As with many other activities, a small minority of people engage in it to excess and damage themselves in the process. We do all that we reasonably can to prevent excessive gambling and to help those for whom gambling becomes a problem." It is encouraging that recently the CEO of Caesar's took this kind of line in explaining why he was now using the word "gambling" rather than "gaming" in his advertising.[5]

Wittgenstein notwithstanding, it does seem essential to the nature of games that their primary purpose is providing enjoyment to the players.[6] Games may also be instructive in the arts of war or of living well; they may be organized commercially as spectator sports, and they may be practiced professionally, in which case the enjoyment of players may be incidental. But nothing would count as a game unless it was at least capable of being played for pleasure alone as part of the many activities that count as play and not as work or other utilitarian activity that serves some extrinsic purpose.

This is of considerable importance for the question of how governments should treat gambling because it shows that what they are concerned to regulate is the way people play. This in turn raises the crucial question of whether governments should regard themselves as dealing with a vice or a recreation.

Gambling used to be treated as a vice to be discouraged, if it could not be eradicated, by legal and religious sanction. Today those in the commercial gambling business insist that gambling is simply a branch of the entertainment business.

To what extent is gambling similar to, and different from, other activities that used to be thought of as vices, activities that are usually prohibited to the young, and some people in most societies think should be prohibited to adults, too? Vices were traditionally understood as forms of wickedness that did damage not to others but to the (immortal) soul of those who engaged in them.[7] As such, the concept of vice originally depended on a religious concept of the soul. But in secular culture, the idea of vice retains the sense of being something that you should not engage in because of the harm you will do to yourself rather than to others. When people were more accepting of the idea that government has an obligation to ensure that its citizens live virtuously—and in particular to facilitate the saving of immortal souls—it seemed natural that government should ban vices even though this meant creating a category of victimless crime. More recently people have come to accept either that it is impractical for government to ban vices or that the project of using government for the enforcement of morals is itself morally illegitimate.

These activities include smoking tobacco and drinking alcohol; using and selling other psychotropic drugs, ranging from cannabis and ecstasy to cocaine and heroin; and trading in pornographic material and commercial sex. All these activities used to be collectively designated "vices" and as such were disapproved of even when indulged in moderation. Most of them—the partial exception is moderate drinking—continue to be viewed as vices not only by the more puritanical adherents of major religions but also by large numbers of people who on secular grounds think it would be better if people did not participate in these activities. Historically, most of these activities (though not, until fairly recently, smoking) have been treated by governments as vices in contexts where it was widely accepted that a major function of government is "the removal of wickedness and vice"—as the general intercession in the Book of Common Prayer expresses it.

It should be remembered, however, that going to the theater has also often been treated as a vice, with actors being regarded as engaged in an essentially immoral profession, and the provision of theatrical entertainment being vigorously circumscribed by laws. All this shows that perceptions of what constitutes a vice change substantially as societies change, whether vice is perceived as defiance of the will of God, or simply as a form of self-damaging behavior that the law should at least discourage, if not prohibit. It also shows that societies are typically inconsistent in their attitude to different alleged vices and what their government should do about them.

Naturally those who work in the gambling industry do not wish to be thought of as being in a similar line of business as purveyors of drugs or pornography or even of alcohol and tobacco. They wish to be seen as participants in the leisure or entertainment industry, and they believe that just as going to the theater was once but is no longer considered to be depraved, so going to a betting shop, visiting a casino, or buying a lottery ticket should now be treated as a normal part of the pursuit of fun. Surveys in North America, Europe, Australia, and South Africa offer some support for the view that a majority of people no longer regard gambling as immoral but see it simply as a form of entertainment that gives some people pleasure and, like all other forms of enjoyment, does no harm provided it is not engaged in to excess. On the other hand, people commonly accept that gambling is dangerous at least in the same way as alcohol is.[8]

It is worth asking at this point what exactly the entertainment is that purveyors of commercial gambling services are selling. A number of distinct forms of pleasure need to be identified here, and they form a useful basis for categorizing gambling activities.[9] These include the following:

- The pleasure of playing games (gambling as condiment). Table games clearly emerge from the practice of spicing up ordinary competitive card, dice, and board games by playing for money. Machine gambling offers the enjoyment associated with spicing up the playing of solitary games that do not offer the chance of winning money: pinball, solitaire, computer games. The pleasure here is primarily in the play, and the gambling is, as it were, a condiment. If the playing were not intrinsically pleasurable, losing would be unmitigatedly disagreeable. In terms of the pleasure of play, it makes no difference whether the games are predominantly of skill (poker) or luck (roulette), whether they are played with others (bingo) or alone (solitaire, computer games), or whether betting is essential to the play (blackjack) or incidental (bridge).

- The pleasure of fantasizing about being rich (gambling as soft financial pornography). The lottery offers the clearest example of this form of pleasure. People buy a ticket (or plan to buy a ticket) and spend the rest of the week daydreaming and discussing with friends and family what they will do with the money when they win. Big jackpot machines, premium bonds, accumulator bets, and pools also offer fuel for this kind of fantasy, where for a comparatively small stake, players have the remote chance of winning a huge prize.

- The pleasure of being intoxicated (gambling as psychotropic drug). Although much less is known about the physiology of gambling than of drugs, which can be tested on animals,[10] it seems clear that for some gamblers there are pleasurable sensations of a psychophysical sort similar to the high that psychotropic drugs induce. The principal ingredients in the high are fear and hope. This is the aspect of gambling analogous to riding a roller coaster or bungee jumping and presumably involves an adrenaline rush. However, there is an important difference between gambling and other adrenaline-producing entertainments. On a roller coaster, the fear is of dying, and the hope is to survive. But participants know that the risks are not real and that they are taking part in a simulation. The pleasure to be derived in this way from gambling requires that the chances of both winning and losing are real. To compensate for this, the stakes are not normally very high: the worst that can happen is that one will lose one's money, not one's life—unless one is playing Russian roulette.

- The pleasures of escape (gambling as theater). Racecourses, bingo halls, betting shops, and casinos all offer places where people can escape from loneliness, boredom, stress, and even the strain of having to take life and money seriously all the time. They offer escape from these things into places that are congenial, convivial, stimulating, and even glamorous. This offers the attractions of both being a spectator at the theater and a performer in the drama.

Obviously, the immoderate pursuit of any of these pleasures may be damaging to the well-being of the individual. People may spend too much time and money playing games of any sort, including, notoriously, golf. People may become obsessed with fantasies of wealth to the point where their obsession damages their lives, as illustrated in the supposed case of the couple who got divorced because they couldn't agree how they would spend their lottery winnings if they won. People can certainly pursue the thrill of risk associated with gambling to the point where they raise the stakes beyond what they can tolerably afford to lose. And the fantasy associated with the theatrical aspect of gambling can become so dominant that people lose contact with reality. In general, however, the provision of these forms of pleasure may be reasonably considered a part of the entertainment industry and deserving to be treated as such.

The question of whether the pleasure of gambling could reasonably be considered immoral, and therefore whether gambling is a vice, is treated in chapter 8. The different question of whether, even if gambling is a vice, government should be trying to prevent people from engaging in it, is treated in the next chapter. The question of whether gambling, because of its historical associations with organized crime, needs to be more strictly regulated than other businesses to keep it crime free is examined in chapter 4. And finally, what should be done by governments to address the fact that gambling is clearly for some people a dangerous activity is discussed in chapter 6. These questions do not bear directly on the question of what gambling is and what it is that people are doing when they gamble. To conclude our discussion of these questions, we need finally to ask, "What other activities is gambling most like?"

This, as I have indicated, is the question that underpins all the others. What you think public policy about gambling should be will depend on whether you think gambling is most relevantly similar to going to the movies, ingesting cocaine, watching soap operas, eating candy, playing golf, consuming pornography, smoking, having a massage, attending a ball game, visiting a brothel, riding a roller coaster, shopping, or having a drink.

All these activities clearly afford people pleasure for which they are willing to pay. They are also all activities in which some people overindulge either periodically or habitually and thereby do damage to themselves and those close to them. Gambling has some affinities ("family resemblances") to all of them, though the resemblance is stronger in some cases than in others.

Some of these activities are pure recreation—golf, watching television—which may have a tendency to cretinize but otherwise have a low propensity to do substantial, or at least obviously substantial, harm. Even if gambling is mainly a recreation, it clearly has a propensity to do obvious harm, and government cannot ignore this. Some activities are as potentially dangerous as gambling but are for the most part necessary and normal parts of people's lives. This is true of shopping, of having sex, and of eating. Here prohibition is not even a conceivable government option. Gambling does not fall into this category, whatever its advocates implausibly say about the urge to gamble being intrinsic to human nature.

The truth is that, in modern Western democracies at least, the activity that commercial gambling most resembles is drinking alcohol. There are three principal points of resemblance.

First, both activities are considered vices in many religions, but also by many who rely solely on secular, human considerations and point to the generally deleterious effect the activities have on the quality of life of both individuals and society as a whole.[11] On the other hand, this is not a majority view, even among those who do not drink or gamble themselves. Nor, probably, is it the majority view even of religious believers.

Second, it seems certain that excessive gambling, like excessive drinking, can lead to addiction, understood as a condition in which addicts indulge to the point where they do themselves significant damage but also experience severe difficulty in giving up or cutting down their indulgence. However, unlike cigarette smokers, most gamblers and drinkers do not become addicts: instead, they find in gambling and drinking sources of harmless enjoyment. Moreover, it can plausibly be claimed, for gambling as for liquor, that indulgence, far from being antisocial, actually facilitates sociability.

Third, gambling and drinking are clearly hugely popular across a wide diversity of people, and the people who enjoy them are prepared to spend a great deal of money to secure these pleasures. This is why they are amenable to being taxed at abnormally high rates and why prohibition is such a politically difficult option.

The theme of whether gambling is properly considered as being similar to other activities is one to which we shall regularly recur in contexts as varied as tax policy and the prevention and treatment of addiction. Meanwhile it is a sound strategy in thinking about anything to do with gambling and public policy to ask, "Is this similar, and if not, why is it different from what we think and do about public policy in relation to liquor?"[12] The answers will perhaps usually, but not necessarily always, favor a higher degree of permissiveness regarding gambling than we are accustomed to. Sometimes, as for example with the requirement that the industry should take at least some responsibility for limiting the harm caused by problem gambling, comparing gambling and liquor may cause us to think that similar obligations should also be imposed on the liquor industry.

NOTES

1. The *Oxford English Dictionary* has: "Gamble: To play games of chance for money." According to I. Nelson Rose, "Gambling, under the common law, is any activity in which: (1) a person pays something of value, called consideration; (2) the outcome is determined at least in part by chance; and (3) the winnings are something of value" (I. Nelson Rose, *Gambling and the Law*. Hollywood, Calif.: Gambling Times, 75). In some ways the *OED* definition is more illuminating because it retains the essential connection between gambling and play.

2. The almost wholly unsuccessful U.K. Betting and Gaming Act of 1960 sought to prevent commercial casino games by requiring that for a gambling game to be legal, every chance in the game must be equal, all money must be returned to the players, and no one must be required to pay to participate. See J. L. Ludovici, *The Itch to Play: Gamblers in High and Low Life* (London: Jarrolds, 1962), 224.

3. It is a source of some astonishment that books continue to appear that promise to teach readers how to beat the casino, not only with strategies for playing games such as blackjack but also with methods for winning on slot machines. If everything depended on pure luck, the authors of these books would have nothing plausible to write about. The doyens of this genre who offer serious and accurate insight into best playing strategies for the games they discuss are David Sklansky and Mason Malmuth. See especially their *Gambling for a Living: How to Make $100,000 a Year* (Las Vegas, Nev.: Two Plus Two Publishing, 1997). Another way of winning about which people write books is by exploiting the system of "complimentaries"—the free inducements or "lagniappes" given to good gambling customers. See, for example, Max Rubin, *Comp City: A Guide to Free Las Vegas Vacations* (Las Vegas, Nev.: Huntington Press, 1994). Alas, Las Vegas has of late become much more prudent in the use of complimentaries.

4. Ludwig Wittgenstein, *Philosophical Investigations*, trans. G. E. M. Anscombe (Oxford: Basil Blackwell, 1963), 31–32.

5. See "Promotions/Marketing," *Casino Chronicle* 19, no. 34 (28 June 2002).

6. See also J. Smith and V. Abt, "Gambling as Play," *Annals of the American Academy of Political and Social Science* 474 (1984): 122–32.

7. For a thoroughgoing exposition of this view, see B. Seebohm Rowntree, *Betting and Gambling: A National Evil* (London: Macmillan, 1905).

8. The earlier American survey evidence is discussed in Anthony N. Cabot, *Casino Gaming: Policy, Economics, and Regulation* (Las Vegas, Nev.: UNLV International Gaming Institute, 1996), 5–7. The more recent evidence was gathered by the National Opinion Research Center at the university of Chicago and submitted to the National Gambling Impact Study Commission (1999). It is published at www.norc.uchicago.edu. The U.K. evidence is reported in the U.K. government-commissioned *Gambling Review Report* (2001) published in London and at www.gamingreview.gov.uk. Evidence of a backlash against what is perceived to be too much gambling in Australia can be found in the Productivity Commission, *Inquiry into Australia's Gambling Industries* (1999) published in Canberra and at www.pc.gov.au.

9. Scholars have used many different principles of classification in categorizing games. The French sociologist Roger Caillois identifies four categories: games based on *agon* (competition), games based on *alea* (chance), games based on *mimicry* (make-believe), and games based on *ilinx* (exhilaration) (Roger Caillois, *Les jeux et les hommes* [Paris: Gallimard, 1958], 21–34). Rainer Buland categorizes games according to the different kinds of decisions or "exercises of freedom" they involve (Rainer Buland, "Die Einteilung der Spiele nach ihren Freiheitsaspekten," in *Homo Ludens: Internationale Beitrage des Institutes fur Spielforschung und Spielpadagogik an der Hochschule Mozarteum Salzburg*, vol. 7 [Munchen: Verlag Emil Katzbichler, 1997], 259–80). The chance-skill dichotomy is also used by Richard A. McGowan in *Government and the Transformation of the Gaming Industry* (Cheltenham, U.K.: Edward Elgar, 2001), 18–20. I am not persuaded that any of these categorizations are as useful as one based on the different types of satisfaction that players seek from the games they play—which, of course, has affinities with the insights of Caillois.

10. For a discussion of the physiology of gambling and its relevance to the question of whether gambling is or is not like other addictive drugs, see Jeffrey Gray, "The Concept of Addiction," annexure G to the (U.K.) Gambling Review Report, presented to Parliament by the Department of Culture, Media, and Sport, July 2001—commonly referred to as the "Budd" report after the chair of the review body that prepared it and on which Professor Gray served.

11. The views of the world's main religions on gambling are described in Cabot, *Casino Gaming*, 19–37.

12. For an account of the empirical similarities and differences in the relevant addictions, see H. R. Lesieur, S. B. Blume, and R. Zoppa, "Alcoholism, Drug Abuse, and Gambling," *Alcoholism: Clinical and Experimental Research* 10 (1986): 33–38.

Chapter 3

Should Gambling Be Legal?

In this chapter, I review the principal arguments for and against the view that gambling should be illegal and conclude that gambling should not be illegal.

Whether gambling should be legal is a question for public policy and as such is a question the answer to which requires a combination of normative and empirical judgments. This means that the answer we give will depend in part on the political principles and social ideals to which we subscribe, as well as on what we think as a matter of fact will be the likely consequences of adopting one policy rather than another.

My argument against prohibition differs from many that are made in this area in that I stress that there are strong *moral* objections to be raised against those who maintain that gambling should be prohibited by law. These moral considerations would, I believe, be decisive against prohibition even if the more commonly urged pragmatic objections to banning gambling—notably the extreme difficulty of doing so—could be overcome. In a book of this sort, this discussion of prohibition is important in its own right, but it is also necessary, I believe, to treat it fairly comprehensively, because the view that people take on the desirability or otherwise of prohibition provides the principles that inform all other matters of public policy in relation to gambling, including all questions relating to how commercial gambling should be regulated. The arguments for and against the legalization of gambling also constitute the principal arguments for and against proposals that gambling law should be liberalized.

Although the question of whether gambling should be banned has an inescapable moral component—it is a question about what is the *right* thing to do—it is not the same question as the question of whether gambling itself is immoral.[1] As a matter of fact, many people do think that gambling is immoral and is properly accounted a vice. Often they think so because they subscribe to a particular religious creed and believe that gambling is harmful in some way to people's spiritual welfare. Others think that gambling is immoral, not on the basis of any religious beliefs but because they think it a shameful waste of time, energy, and money.

On the other hand, many other people think gambling is not at all immoral. These people typically think that for the vast majority of people who engage in it, gambling is a harmless recreation that, provided it is practiced with moderation, cannot reasonably be judged to be inherently immoral.[2]

For people who think gambling is immoral on religious grounds, the prohibition of gambling is like the prohibitions that many religions impose on certain types of sexual activity, for example, prostitution. For people who think that gambling is immoral because it is a degrading or wasteful way spending time, energy, and money, gambling is perhaps thought of as being like consuming pornography. For people who think gambling in moderation is a harmless pleasure, the most likely comparisons will be with drinking alcohol or going to the movies.

Of course, objections to gambling on moral and religious grounds deserve to be treated with respect and to be debated on their merits. But this is quite different from saying that because some people, even a majority of people, believe gambling as an activity to be immoral, the law should make it a crime to gamble. It is quite possible that a majority of Americans think that it is immoral for adults to engage in private in homosexual activities. It does not follow from this that homosexual practices between consenting adults in private should be illegal. Nor—perhaps more interestingly—does it follow that the people who think such practices are immoral must also be committed to thinking that they should be illegal.

In this chapter, I will begin by considering six arguments that have commonly been adduced to support the view that gambling should be illegal:

- The "enforcement of morals" argument
- The "paternalist" argument
- The "human costs" argument
- The "social costs" argument
- The "democratic consensus" argument
- The "practical difficulties" argument

These arguments form pairs. The first two depend on assumptions about the state possessing moral and psychological knowledge that is superior to that of the individual or the average citizen. The third and fourth depend on empirical claims about how much harm gambling does. The last two have in common that on examination they turn out not to support the prohibition of gambling because the premise on which they rely is in fact false. None of these arguments, in my judgment, supports the prohibition of gambling. Nevertheless, they do indicate the reasons and areas in which the state is justified in treating commercial gambling differently from other service or retail businesses in what is perhaps best called "the pleasure industry." These considerations bear directly on why the gambling industry should be subject to a set of quite specific regulations not required elsewhere and what these regulations should be.

I consider these arguments broadly in the order in which they have as a matter of historical fact emerged as the dominant attitudes of those who believe gambling should be illegal, at least in the developed world.[3] As we shall see, the evolution of the arguments to some extent reflects the increasingly plural character of modern societies where people with widely different sets of beliefs and values have to live together in reasonable harmony under the same government and the same set of overarching laws.

By examining what seems to be wrong with the principal arguments deployed to support the view that gambling should be illegal, I shall be exposing what seem to be the three strongest kinds of reason for believing that gambling should be legal. I will therefore conclude by gathering together and elaborating on these reasons. In particular, I will consider whether gambling should be legalized because this will contribute to the greatest happiness of the greatest number of people; because it would be unfair to discriminate against the majority of gamblers, for whom gambling is a harmless pastime; because it can be a good way of redistributing wealth to the benefit of the poor; and because having liberal gambling laws is part of a commitment to maximizing individual liberty. Although I maintain that the arguments in favor of legalization decisively outweigh the arguments for prohibition, I also believe that there are some good reasons (fewer perhaps than is usually assumed) for restricting the availability of commercial gambling beyond what would be justified if gambling were to be treated simply as a form of entertainment no different from any other sector of the entertainment industry and if the provision of gambling services were to be left entirely to market forces. My reasons for believing both that gambling should be legal and that it should be subject to special regulation derive from a number of value judgments to which I subscribe and which inform my conception of how a morally attractive society will be governed. It is vital that I be open about this, because ultimately what people believe about how government should treat gambling—or the pursuit of any other pleasurable activity that some deem to be undesirable—depends on the social and political principles to which people subscribe. Consequently if debate about these matters is to be honest and constructive, it is essential that people be candid and explicit about the moral judgments that underpin these principles.[4]

THE ENFORCEMENT OF MORALITY

The first argument is the simplest. It runs as follows.

- Gambling is immoral.
- It is the business of government to try to eradicate immorality.
- Therefore it is the business of government to try to eradicate gambling.

This argument is a valid syllogism. This means that if you accept the premises, you are logically obliged to accept the conclusion. In fact, throughout history and in many cultures today, both the premises of this argument and its conclusion have been taken for granted. People have assumed unquestioningly that there are absolute moral laws that govern not only how people should treat one another but also what forms of pleasure may legitimately be indulged in and what forms of pleasure are prohibited. Typically, moral laws of this sort are thought to be enshrined in the teachings of the religion of the society in which they are accepted, and they thus have the authority that comes from being acknowledged as the revealed will of God.

Because of their place in systems of religious belief, moral arguments against gambling and other alleged "vices" are likely to arouse strong emotions and in particular feelings of disgust and indignation at the thought of others gambling. This passion makes it politically difficult to accommodate people who hold moral beliefs of this kind and additionally believe that government should legislate to enforce conformity to them. Such believers regard the failure of government to eradicate vice as evidence that society is collapsing into intolerable decadence and in doing so is defying the revealed will of God. Because they see matters in this way, it is difficult for them to take the view that though gambling is wicked, it should nevertheless not be prohibited by government simply because many people in society do not recognize its wickedness.

However, as we have seen, many people do not accept that gambling is immoral; that is, they deny the first premise of the "enforcement of morals" argument. More important, many people would argue that even if this first premise were true, the conclusion would still not follow because the second premise is not true. Such people deny that it is the business of government to use the power of the state to compel people to behave in a way that those who govern deem to be moral.

Instead such people typically propose that the only justification for interference by the state in the choices that individuals make about how to conduct their lives is when the exercise of such choices threatens to harm others in a way that violates their legitimate rights. This view of the role of government has its origins in the political philosophy of Hobbes and Locke. It is fundamental to the beliefs of the founding fathers of the U.S. Constitution, and as we shall see, it was clearly articulated in the nineteenth century in John Stuart Mill's famous and still influential essay *On Liberty*. It is also the general principle that underpins political creeds that attach fundamental importance to individual freedom of choice. Most Americans, whatever their party allegiance, do subscribe to such an overarching political creed that requires all people to show a high degree of tolerance for others who have beliefs and tastes that differ from their own. Their conception of the kind of society that America should be includes acceptance of the "maximum equal liberty" principle. This asserts that in a well-governed society, all people will enjoy the maximum amount of freedom to decide for themselves how to live their lives in a way that is compatible with everyone else enjoying the same amount of freedom.

It is, of course, inconsistent with this principle to claim that you should be prevented from gambling if you so choose simply because I think gambling is wicked and even though your gambling in no way restricts the freedom of other people or otherwise harms them.

Part of the reason for rejecting the "enforcement of morals" argument in favor of prohibiting gambling is that many people don't think gambling is immoral, and it is therefore difficult to achieve political consensus. The more important reason is that most people think that it is morally wrong for the state to interfere with the essentially private choices of individuals about how they will spend their time and money, providing they are not doing harm to anyone else. In particular, it seems wrong for the state to interfere with these choices that do not harm others solely on the grounds that some people, even many people, deem the activities in question to be immoral.

THE PATERNALIST ARGUMENT

The paternalist argument runs as follows.

- Gambling is bad for people.
- It is the business of government to prevent people from doing things that are bad for them.
- Therefore government should stop people from gambling.

Again, this is a valid syllogism in which the conclusion follows logically from the premises. The argument differs from the "enforcement of morals" argument in that it does not require government to claim absolute knowledge of what is morally right and wrong for everybody or the right to impose codes of moral conduct on individual citizens who don't subscribe to them in the area of private morality where people are not harming one another. This is why in relation to gambling, the paternalist argument is a more acceptable argument than the "enforcement of morals" argument in societies where there is widespread disagreement about moral matters. Typically, such disagreement comes about because the authority of a single religion and of those people—priests, mullahs, rabbis, and so forth—who claim to articulate that authority in matters of morality is no longer widely accepted.

The paternalist argument, however, depends only on there being widespread agreement about what is bad for people. Until quite recently, for example, there was widespread agreement in the West that ingesting marijuana is bad for people and that government should use the power of the state to stop people from obtaining and consuming this drug.

In short, the paternalist argument is about protecting people from themselves, and this suggests that the state is not acting in an authoritarian way to impose what look like subjective moral rules on citizens who may quite rationally and sincerely reject them. Instead the state is being authoritarian out of compassion toward its citizens in cases where these citizens are not the best judges of their own interests. The argument is called a "paternalist" argument because it represents the role of the state toward its citizens as being the same as that of a loving father toward his children.

Although the argument does not require the government to possess ultimate authority with respect to morality, the paternalist argument does claim that government knows best what is good for people and what is bad for them, and it assumes that government has not merely a right but a duty to force people to do what is good for them and to prevent them from doing what is bad for them.

The argument may, of course, encompass the same material as the "enforcement of morals" argument if it is claimed that all activities pronounced by (typically religious) authority to be immoral are also in fact bad for you because, for example, they imperil the future well-being of your immortal soul. A paternalist might thus prohibit gambling on the grounds that it is immoral and will therefore inevitably lead to your being punished by God. But, of course, the paternalist does not need to appeal to either religion or morality. It is enough to claim, as can indeed plausibly be claimed, that people who gamble run the risk of ruining their lives, and therefore the government should prevent them from incurring this risk.

Paternalist arguments are much more acceptable in the United States than arguments that appear to violate the constitutional separation of church and state. Paternalist considerations underlie a great deal of the reasoning on which American legislation relating to psychotropic drugs is founded. However, even in this area, it is doubtful whether prohibition could survive solely on paternalistic claims that taking drugs is bad for people. In fact, the paternalist case, in the case of drugs, is thought to be strongly bolstered by consideration of harm to others.

In the case of gambling, especially in Europe, where paternalism used to be in general more acceptable as a basis for political action than it has been in the United States, the law often sought to protect people from themselves. The poor, in particular, were often thought to require being prevented by law from gambling themselves and their families into starvation, and governments legislated accordingly. At some points in British history, it was thought necessary to prevent the rich from gambling away their fortunes so as to protect the position of the aristocracy at the head of the class system.

Nowadays, however, the paternalist case for prohibiting gambling either generally or to particular sections of the population is considerably weaker. This is partly, perhaps, because in modern societies, thanks to social security, people don't starve. Also, there is greater commitment to the principle of equality, which means that the poor should enjoy not only equality of opportunity but also equality of respect; and this means they should not be patronized by being told that they are too irresponsible to gamble.

However, the main reason why paternalist arguments against gambling are generally repudiated is empirical. It is plausible (though not indisputable) to say that most people who take heroin—or who smoke cigarettes—do themselves significant harm. It is not plausible to make this claim about most people who gamble—or who drink alcohol. As a matter of fact, it seems that the vast majority of people who gamble—who buy lottery tickets, who place bets on horse races and other sporting events, or who gamble on cards, dice, or slot machines—do so without causing themselves any harm. Certainly, they lose money for the most part and in the long run, but that is simply the price that they knowingly and willingly pay for the pleasure they get from gambling. If this is so, then to ban gambling because a small minority of gamblers are reckless would be even less justifiable than to ban cars because a minority of drivers are reckless—less justifiable because reckless gamblers do a great deal less harm to others than do reckless drivers.

Even if this were not so, however, there would still be a strong moral argument against prohibiting gambling on paternalistic grounds. This is that even if governments do in fact know best what is in people's interests, they are still not justified in interfering. In this view, interfering with people's freedom of choice to protect them from harming themselves goes against and goes beyond the legitimate role of government in a free society. This point is made forcibly by John Stuart Mill in *On Liberty*.

The sole end for which mankind are warranted, individually or collectively, in interfering with the liberty of action of any of their number, is self-protection .... The only purpose for which power can be rightfully exercised over any member of a civilised community, against his will, is to prevent harm to others. His own good, either physical or moral, is not a sufficient warrant. He cannot rightly be compelled to do or forbear because it will be better for him to do so, because it will make him happier, because, in the opinion of others, to do so would be wise, or even right. There are good reasons for remonstrating with him or reasoning with him, or persuading him, or entreating him, but not for compelling him, or visiting him with any evil in case he do otherwise. To justify that the conduct, from which it is desired to deter him, must be calculated to produce evil to someone else. The only part of the conduct of anyone, for which he is amenable to society, is that which concerns others. In the part which merely concerns himself, his independence, is of right, absolute. Over himself, over his own body and mind, the individual is sovereign.[5]

The paternalist argument against legalized gambling, then, seems to fail in part because gambling has not been shown to be harmful for the majority of people who engage in it. But even if it were, government would still not be entitled to prevent adult citizens from accepting the risk—or even the certainty—of harm if they judge it to be worthwhile and choose accordingly.

THE HUMAN COSTS ARGUMENT

Mill's view is widely endorsed in the culture of modern, developed, secular, and pluralistic societies such as that of the United States.[6] This means that great importance is attached to the freedom of individuals to choose for themselves what they will believe and how they will live. Correspondingly, there is considerable hostility to attempts by governments to compel people in their private lives to live either as government thinks they ought to or as it thinks would be good for them. Government should not interfere with what consenting adults do in the privacy of their bedrooms, nor should government dictate how people may spend their own time and money in the pursuit of pleasure provided no one else is being damaged. From the logic of these arguments, it seems to follow that government should not interfere with people who want to gamble.

For these reasons, contemporary arguments in favor of prohibiting gambling increasingly rely on claims that legalized gambling does in fact cause unjustifiable harm to people other than those who gamble. There are two main versions of this argument. Both rely heavily on the phenomenon of "problem gambling." The first claims that problem gamblers, that is, people who gamble excessively or compulsively, inevitably cause harm to a large number of people whose lives and well-being are closely bound up with the problem gambler. The most plausible category of people allegedly so harmed are those whose lives are emotionally as well as materially bound up with problem gamblers: their partners, children, parents, and all those who are in any way dependent on a problem gambler. The types of harm that problem gamblers inflict on these people include impoverishment, insecurity, humiliation, depression, domestic distress of all sorts, and perhaps particular emotional devastation if the gambler commits suicide or goes to prison. These forms of harm may be said to constitute the human cost of problem gambling.

The second version of the "harm to others" argument claims that problem gambling has unacceptable social costs—costs, that is, that fall on taxpayers. One of the most important differences between human costs and social costs is that the latter are thought to be quantifiable, while the former are not. Mainly for this reason, the human costs argument and the social costs argument are very different, the former appealing to subjective feelings of compassion, the latter to allegedly objective economic calculations. I shall consequently consider the social costs argument separately in the next section.

The logic of the human costs argument is more complex than the arguments we have considered in the preceding sections. It runs as follows:

- Addictive gambling (like any other addiction) causes extreme distress to the families of the addict and others close to him or her.
- These human costs outweigh any benefits that legalizing gambling might bring—pleasure for nonaddictive players, jobs for employees of gambling companies, taxes for governments, et cetera.

- Legalized gambling inevitably increases the prevalence of gambling addiction.
- It is the duty of governments to protect families and other innocent parties from potential damage by gambling addicts where the human costs outweigh the benefits.
- Therefore it is the duty of government to prevent increases in the prevalence of addictive gambling by not legalizing or by de-legalizing gambling.

The first premise of this argument is unexceptionable. Gambling addiction is as real as drug addiction and alcoholism. It has the same claim to be thought of, and treated as, a psychological illness as these other more familiar conditions. It certainly has horrible consequences for the loved ones and dependents of gambling addicts who, in extreme cases, kill not only themselves but their families as well because they regard suicide as the only escape from the living hell that life has become for all concerned.

Given this, it is easy to see why people are intuitively inclined to accept the second premise as well. To compel nonaddictive gamblers to find other pleasures, employees to find other jobs, and governments to find other sources of revenue seems a small price to pay for saving the loved ones of gambling addicts from the extreme suffering that otherwise faces them.

There is no question that if gambling were as addictive as, say, smoking, and the vast majority of regular gamblers became addicts, and if prohibition were clearly the best way of drastically reducing the number of such addicts, then the case for prohibiting gambling to protect the innocent victims of the addictive gambler's behavior would be irresistible. The trouble is that we know that the first of these conditions is not met—the vast majority of regular gamblers do not become addicts—and there is some reason for thinking that prohibition would merely result (as with drugs) in people becoming addicted through the underground market. The comparison that immediately springs to mind is the prohibition of alcohol in the United States in the 1920s and 1930s.

In other words, the second premise may not be as acceptable as at first appeared. It may be that the evils of prohibition—of having gambling services supplied, like drugs, by organized crime—will be worse, not merely adding massive law enforcement costs but actually making it harder to provide help to addictive gamblers and their families. Moreover, the third premise of the human costs argument is also far from self-evident: it may not be inevitable that legalized gambling increases the incidence of addictive gambling. Legalized gambling may only increase the visibility, rather than the prevalence, of addictive gambling. It may also be that there are ways of regulating gambling so that the incidence of addictive gambling in a legal environment is less than it would be if gambling were illegal. What is certain is that we do not know enough about how the provision of legal gambling affects the incidence of addictive gambling and how prohibition would alter the picture. Neither advocates of legal gambling nor their opponents should pretend that we do.

There is also an issue of proportionality. This relates to the fourth premise, that is, the supposed duty of government to minimize harm for the families of addicts.

Because the human costs argument appeals to widespread feelings of horror and compassion at the plight of the families of addictive gamblers, it is easy to represent those who do not accept it as being callous with respect to the sufferings of gambling addicts and their families. However, we need to ask the question "How much can and how much should government try to do to stop its citizens causing each other distress?" The law forbids spouses to hit each other. Should it try—can it reasonably hope—to stop spouses from shouting at one another, especially, say, in front of their children? If it could do so easily and without unacceptable side effects, no doubt the answer would be yes. But the truth is that to enforce such a prohibition would be accounted an intolerable intrusion into people's private lives. It would have thoroughly undesirable consequences, such as encouraging or requiring neighbors to report on each other. And probably the harm done is comparatively small given all the other evils to which government (and its police) have to attend. In other words, a law to prevent members of families from verbally abusing one another would be considered disproportionate.

Addictive gamblers are a small minority even of regular gamblers, and the damage they do to others is almost certainly considerably less than that caused by, for example, people who drink too much. Consequently, it would seem to be disproportionate to take away the freedom to pursue pleasure as they choose of the vast majority of people who gamble harmlessly in order to pursue a policy that will have substantial social costs and be of dubious effectiveness in minimizing the suffering of the people the policy is designed to help.

THE SOCIAL COSTS ARGUMENT

The social costs argument against gambling is even more complex than the human costs argument. It runs as follows:

- The legalization of gambling brings quantifiable benefits to some people and costs to others.
- The aggregate of these costs and benefits is the cost and benefit to society as a whole.
- Governments should choose from among available policies the one that will result in benefits exceeding costs as much as possible or costs exceeding benefits as little as possible.
- With all policies that permit legal gambling, the ratio of social costs to benefits is less favorable than with the policy of prohibition.
- Therefore government should adopt a policy of prohibiting gambling.

The idea that the case for prohibiting gambling could be demonstrated objectively by calculating the social costs derives from the economic theory of cost-benefit analysis. This theory is based on the general utilitarian theory pioneered by Jeremy Bentham in the nineteenth century and, developed as a branch of economics in the 1970s by E. J. Mishan, holds that it is possible to quantify the total benefits and the total costs likely to attach to any proposed course of action. It will then be possible to compare the net surplus of costs over benefits or of benefits over costs of different courses of action. When this calculation has been made, the right course of action is identified as the one that offers the highest net benefits or the lowest net costs for society as a whole.

In the utilitarian version of this calculation, what needs to be quantified is the pleasure and pain, or, what is perhaps different, the happiness and unhappiness that different courses of action will generate. The pleasure/pain, happiness/unhappiness of each member of society is assumed to be equally important, and the idea is that the right public policy will be the one that leads to the greatest balance of pleasure over pain or to the greatest happiness of the greatest number of people, where each counts for one, and none counts for more than one.

In the economic version of this procedure, cash values are attached to each of the costs and each of the benefits in all the proposed courses of action, and the right course of action is identified as the one that, overall, leaves society richer, in other words, with more resources overall to spend on the goods and services that people want to purchase.

In this view, the benefits of legalizing gambling accrue most obviously to people who like gambling. They are now able to indulge their taste without incurring the cost of breaking the law or paying the additional price that is charged by (usually monopolistic) illegal operators. If the costs of gambling include the risk of going to prison or being compelled to pay a large fine, then these costs will for many prove to be what they are intended to be: literally prohibitive. This means that with legalization, gamblers are richer because they can obtain pleasure more cheaply and have more money left over to spend on other things.

The social costs of legalizing gambling arise if legalization is accompanied by new expenditures that now have to be borne by others who would not previously have had to bear them and consequently wind up being poorer than they would have been had gambling not been legalized. Suppose legalization brings an increase in crime, as might happen if legalization meant that more gamblers engage in embezzlement to finance their gambling, or if gamblers prove to be an exceptionally easy target for muggers. Under these circumstances, a demand would arise for additional resources for law enforcement, that is, more policing costs, more trial costs, and more imprisonment costs. This would lead to new demands on the public purse, which taxpayers would have to meet. The same is true if it is found that the legalization of gambling leads to an increase in the amount of disease that needs to be treated at the taxpayer's expense. This is what is claimed by people who say that legalization leads to a substantial increase in pathological gambling.

In principle, it should be possible to work out what the total increased costs to the taxpayer will be as well as how much money will be saved by gamblers, who can now purchase more cheaply the same quantity of pleasure as they could obtain previously through illegal gambling or through more expensive substitute activities. When these two sums are compared, one can say whether there is more or less wealth in society overall.

It should be noted that the obvious thing to do in this situation, which is what almost all jurisdictions in fact try to do, is to tax the activities of gamblers so as to ensure that gambling taxes at least cover the social costs that the availability of legal gambling generates.

Unfortunately there is as yet no clear agreement among economists about how social costs and benefits relating to gambling are properly to be measured. Consequently there are no authoritative measurements. In the absence of appropriately rigorous and accurate analysis there is a strong tendency among both opponents and defenders of the industry to engage in the same fallacious reasoning.

Thus defenders of the industry simply account all the good things that are associated with gambling—for example, employment and increased revenues to the public purse—as social or public benefits, ignoring the fact that the same volume of employment or tax could quite possibly have been secured without gambling. In fact, legalizing gambling has a beneficial effect on employment only if the new employment that occurs in the gambling industry is employment that would not have occurred in some other industry had gambling not been legal. There is in fact some reason to think that the advent of gambling may shift leisure expenditure to less labor intensive activities such as operating gaming machines and away from more labor intensive activities such as running restaurants or manufacturing luxury goods. If that is so, the effect of gambling on employment is negative. Similarly, defenders of gambling overlook the fact that the same tax revenues could have been collected without gambling by a process that might have been less popular but would have been arguably fairer because not "regressive," that is, levied for the most part from those least able to afford it.

Conversely, opponents of gambling tend to exaggerate the social costs by suggesting that there would be no domestic, psychological, social, and economic problems that the state must alleviate through providing welfare and remedial services if gambling was illegal.

Cost-benefit analysis has two other limitations that restrict its usefulness in deciding whether legalizing gambling is good public policy.

First, because cost-benefit analysis is only concerned with whether the total wealth in society increases or decreases, it is not sensitive to questions of distribution. It does not matter to cost-benefit analysis whether those who enjoy the benefits or bear the costs in any sense deserve to be doing so. In particular, cost-benefit analysis also fails to address the question of whether the overall flow of benefits is from richer to poorer or from poorer to richer.

Second, cost-benefit analysis makes the mistake common among economists of assuming that the more choices people have that they can satisfy, the happier they will necessarily be. This will be true only to the extent that people make choices that will in fact maximize their happiness, and of course people often make bad choices in this respect. From the point of view of maximizing the enjoyment in one's life, the decision to spend a lot of time playing gaming machines may be just such a bad choice. As we shall see, there is a powerful argument for legalizing gambling to extend freedom of choice, but this argument derives its power from the conviction that freedom of choice is a good thing in itself, not because maximizing free choice necessarily leads to happiness—which it often does not.

It is true that an argument against the legalization of gambling that claimed that the quantifiable impact of legalization on the well-being of society as a whole will be less beneficial or more costly than other alternative policies would be persuasive if the relevant measurements could in fact be carried out. At present they cannot be, partly because of conceptual confusion in the definition of terms, partly because the relevant data are not available, and partly because many of the costs and benefits are inherently unquantifiable. This is not to deny that good cost-benefit analysis has an important role to play in the determination of public policy toward gambling, even though it cannot be expected to settle the matter finally as long as there are substantial disagreements about matters of moral principle.

THE DEMOCRATIC ARGUMENT

A simple argument for banning gambling would go as follows:

- Governments should pass laws that a majority of people would like to have passed.
- A majority of people would like to have gambling banned.
- Therefore the government should ban gambling.

To find out whether the second premise is true, the government could hold a referendum, as happened recently in California. Alternatively, as has happened in other jurisdictions, parties could run for office on the promise of banning gambling.

It might be thought that in a country committed to democratic government, this would be the end of the matter. If a majority of people want legal gambling, then gambling should be legal; if they do not, then it should be illegal. Moreover, the process can be refined so that people can express themselves, for example, in favor of public lotteries but against casinos, or in favor of one or two or three casinos but no more. And indeed, to a substantial degree, this is what happens. It would certainly seem indisputable that if a majority in a particular community wants no gambling or wants only limited gambling, their government should act on that preference. This is why there is presently no gambling in Utah or Hawaii, and only limited gambling in many other states. The same principle is, at the time of writing, being written into gambling law in the U.K.

There are two points to be made about the democratic argument in relation to the claim that gambling should be illegal. The first is the obvious one that, in fact, where this question is put fairly before the court of public opinion, majorities in most jurisdictions in democratic countries favor legalization in some form and do not favor prohibition.

The second point is one touched on at the beginning of the chapter and in considering whether governments should compel people to conform to moral rules that they don't accept even though there is no danger of illegitimate harm to others. This is that contrary to what is too easily assumed, the first premise of the democratic argument cannot be accepted without substantial qualification. The fact that a majority of people want government to do something does not necessarily mean that government should do it. When majorities in certain parts of the United States, such as California before 1948, supported laws banning sexual relations between members of different race groups, this did not make the antimiscegenation legislation right.

More generally, the political theory that underpins the Constitution of the United States and those of other developed democracies attaches as much importance to freedom and individual rights as to democracy. What this political theory holds is that the less individual conduct is subject to any form of government regulation, the better; and this remains true even where the government proposing the regulation is acting democratically, that is, with popular support. All government, including democratic government, should leave people as free as possible to determine how to live their own lives, and there are some decisions that no government, however strong its democratic mandate, can compel its citizens to make one way rather than another, for example, what religion to subscribe to, what political party to support, and what kind of personal relationships to pursue.

It is not, of course, plausible to argue that there is a right or freedom to gamble that is equal in importance to the right and freedom to worship according to one's conscience, to vote according to one's convictions, and to love according to one's passions. It is not, however, implausible to think that people have a right, and should be free, to pursue pleasure in whatever way seems best to them. It is also not implausible to say that the government has no business interfering with the exchanges of goods and services between willing buyers and willing sellers just because the services involve creating gambling opportunities.

This would provide a further difficulty for the argument that gambling should be banned because most people want it banned even if that were indeed what most people want. Probably this is a line of thought that deserves to be taken more seriously in relation to drugs law.

THE PRACTICAL DIFFICULTIES ARGUMENT

A final possible argument against the legalization of gambling runs as follows:

- There are some negative impacts of legalized gambling potentially so serious that, unless they can be prevented, gambling should not be legalized—for example, gambling by minors, money laundering, the rigging of games by gambling companies, the fixing of races and other sports events by bettors and bookmakers, the proliferation of loan-sharking, begging, prostitution, and drug dealing in the vicinity of gambling establishments, the general sleazification of neighborhoods, et cetera.

- These negative impacts cannot in fact be prevented except by prohibiting all gambling.
- Therefore all gambling should be prohibited.

This argument may link back to the social costs argument to the extent that there is an implicit claim that the financial cost to the state of eliminating these evils would far outweigh any financial benefits that might accrue. It may also link to the democratic argument, which says, for example, "We don't want casinos in our area because we don't want our children growing up in the vicinity of a casino."

Some of what is wrong with this argument as it stands is that it may not take into account that the alternative to legal gambling may not be no gambling but instead a great deal of illegal gambling. This, however, is not a decisive point against the argument. It is, in fact, indubitable that the legalization of gambling results in more gambling overall: large numbers of people who enjoy gambling are simply too law abiding to engage their taste if to do so they must break the law.

The more telling point to be made against this argument is that it depends on an empirical claim that is in fact often false. It is not, in fact, overwhelmingly difficult in practice to regulate the availability of commercial gambling opportunities to ensure that the negative impacts anticipated do not materialize. Indeed, in the case of casinos, so important is it for good business that customers feel safe and comfortable going to and from casinos that casinos themselves typically hire extensive private security to ensure this. Similarly, because casinos are highly sensitive to the potential public outcry if minors are found unattended on their premises, they often take measures to ensure that minors are less likely to be neglected by their parents at a casino than outside a bar, or less likely to be playing truant at a casino than in a shopping mall. It is also more likely that problem gamblers will be identified and helped in a well-regulated gambling industry than in an illegal one. The reason for this, again, is that the gambling businesses have a commercial interest in ensuring that this is so.

However, the issue of practicality might still be crucial in determining whether some specific form of gambling should be prohibited on the grounds that it cannot in practice be properly regulated. This argument is sometimes deployed with considerable plausibility with respect to having gaming machines outside casinos, for example, in supermarkets, mom-and-pop shops, bars, restaurants, gas stations, Laundromats, rail and bus stations, and the like. Collectively, this is known as the "slot route" industry when an operator runs a chain of machines located in different and typically nongambling venues. The practicality argument also plays a part in the view that betting on college football and other college sports should be prohibited partly to avoid encouraging illegal betting by minors and partly because of the dangers of cheating.

Perhaps the most interesting use of the practicality argument in support of the prohibition of a particular form of gambling relates to interactive gambling over the Internet and by cell phone. Many people and many politicians claim that permitting Internet gambling will mean there is "a casino in every living room," that it will be impossible to prevent children from gambling, that customers will be cheated, et cetera. In fact, these supposed regulatory obstacles are less formidable than they at first appear. The real weakness of this kind of argument against Internet gambling is that it backfires. What is really difficult from a practical point of view is preventing people from gambling on the Internet as things are at present.

UTILITY AND THE CASE FOR LEGAL GAMBLING

The positive case for having a legal gambling industry is composed partly of utilitarian considerations about what as a matter of empirical fact will make for the greatest good or happiness of the greatest number of people, and partly of considerations relating to two absolute moral principles, namely, the requirements of justice and the right to liberty. I shall briefly summarize what I take to be the force of each of these considerations.[7]

The most straightforward utilitarian reason for not prohibiting gambling is that gambling obviously gives pleasure to those who engage in it without obviously causing pain to anyone else. In the case of commercial gambling, it also affords substantial and palpable benefits to all those involved in supplying gambling services—the investors and employees of gambling companies. With commercial gambling, we apparently have a straightforward case of willing buyers and willing sellers doing deals that benefit both of them. Buyers pay a price for enjoyment that they judge to be the best use they can make of their money at that particular time. Sellers supply a service at a price that makes it worthwhile to invest the time, energy, talent, and courage necessary to supply the service. On the face of it, there are many winners and no losers, so having a legal gambling industry is conducive to the greatest happiness of the greatest number of people, and therefore, on utilitarian principles, government should allow it.

As we have seen, some people argue that the damage caused by excessive and compulsive gambling is so great that it outweighs these benefits. But the truth seems to be that the harm caused by gambling is comparatively small—compared to the harm caused by alcohol, for example. It is also certain that prohibition will not eliminate the incidence of problem gambling and may not even reduce it. On the other hand, it is certain that all sorts of undesirable consequences flow from having a large illegal gambling industry, which is what has happened almost everywhere where legal gambling has been prohibited or severely restricted.

Nor does it appear that the thought of other people gambling causes such widespread and intense offense and distress that this outweighs the pleasures of the consumers and suppliers of gambling services. Probably in the United States and other liberal democracies, the thought of government interfering with individual free choice causes much greater offense. Besides, it is not practicable and perhaps not proper for government to base decisions about whether to ban activities on people's testimonies about what they feel when they think about other people engaging in such activities.

Nor, of course, can a utilitarian permit what is often unspoken in the antigambling argument, namely, the view that the pain caused to problem gamblers and their families is morally more important than the "trivial" pleasure secured by nonaddictive gamblers or the happiness that is afforded to the sellers of gambling services by their greedy "exploitation" of human weakness. The interests of the wicked and the virtuous must be treated equally by the utilitarian calculus, which is one reason why many philosophers think it is an inadequate moral theory.

I believe the truth about the effects of legalized gambling on the sum total of human happiness to be that whether gambling is legal or illegal makes very little difference. Some evidence for this comes from the fact that the demand for more liberal gambling laws hardly ever comes from consumers and almost invariably comes from suppliers of gambling services. It is suppliers who seek to lobby politicians for liberalization.

Most of the benefits are canceled out by the costs: the more gamblers lose with consequent pain to their dependents, the more employees and investors earn with consequent pleasure to their dependents. Insofar as there are advantages in using gambling to raise taxes, these relate to the fact that gambling taxes are less resented than other taxes, though probably more of them come from the poor, for whom they may be more painful. Either way, taxing gambling at an abnormally high rate does not to alter the total percentage of a society's earnings that governments think it desirable to appropriate.

There are only two unambiguous benefits of legalizing gambling to an economy. The first is where gambling becomes essentially an earner of "foreign" or out-of-state revenues because the availability of gambling attracts foreign or out-of-state visitors. In practice this only happens where, as in Nevada, Atlantic City, Macao, Sun City, and Monte Carlo in the last century, the foreigners who come to gamble do not have the opportunity to engage in the desired form of gambling in their home jurisdiction. This, however, provides the countries and states where the particular forms of gambling have been illegal with a strong incentive to legalize them so as not to have the gambling spending of their own citizens leak away to foreign jurisdictions. The second is where the costs to society of having an illegal industry are as great or greater than the costs of a legal industry, and the benefits in terms of consumer and supplier satisfaction and unresented taxes are smaller.

These two considerations are probably marginal in the case of land-based gambling, though between them, they tell strongly in favor of legalizing and regulating Internet gambling, at least in the medium term.

JUSTICE AND THE CASE FOR LEGALIZING GAMBLING

There are two main ways in which considerations of justice, rather than utility, are appealed to in support of the legalization of gambling. The first appeals to retributive justice, the notion that people should be treated according to what they deserve. The second appeals to distributive or social justice, the idea that society's resources should be fairly (and usually fairly equally) shared out.

The retributive claim consists simply of the assertion that it is not fair for the many who gamble responsibly to be penalized because of the fecklessness of the irresponsible few. The thought here is that if steps are to be taken by governments to limit the harm caused by excessive gambling, they should not be at the expense of the legitimate enjoyment of gambling by the vast majority of gamblers who are not classifiable as having "a problem." Any force this argument may have derives, I think, from our sense of what is proportionate. If the harm caused by problem gambling were much greater and its incidence much more widespread, this argument would be much less persuasive. If we knew—as in fact we do not—that 90 percent of heroin users become addicted and only 10 percent use it as a harmless recreation; if, further, we knew that 90 percent of all heroin addicts are doomed to premature and painful death or indefinite hospitalization; and if, finally, we knew that making the use of heroin a criminal offense would or does substantially reduce the number of addicts, then we would not feel obliged to oppose prohibition on the grounds that it is unfair to the 10 percent of users for whom heroin provides harmless pleasure.

With gambling, as with drinking (but not smoking), the vast majority of consumers are not addicts and are not doing themselves and others serious harm by gambling. Consequently we are disposed to think that prohibition would be unjust or at least disproportionate. If the numbers were to change, so probably would our perception of injustice. It should also be noted that it would be highly unjust to deny or discount the rights of those who gamble and those who cater commercially to the tastes of gamblers simply because we, or a majority of us, disapprove of gambling. People who want the law to prohibit or restrict gambling often seem to me to do this tacitly or unconsciously, particularly when they disapprove of those who make a lot of money by running casinos or bookmaking. The unspoken thought is that these rich and wicked people do not deserve to have their most important interests protected by the law on the same basis as everyone else's. What is wrong with this becomes apparent if we consider a case where moral and religious condemnation is even more widespread. Thus we may disapprove of loose young women who accept money to be photographed with no clothes on. We may also disapprove of dirty old men who pay to look at such photographs. But if there really are such things as human rights possessed by everyone simply by virtue of being human, then loose women and dirty old men have exactly the same human rights as professors and social workers and ministers of religion. So it would be with those who work in the gambling industry and their customers, even if we all thought they are as morally reprehensible as the most vehement moral denouncers of gambling claim.

The argument relating to distributive justice that supports the legalization of gambling depends on the claim that gambling is a good way to raise funds for public interest projects and, in particular, to redistribute funds from the better-off to the worse-off. Thus if gambling enables government to fund projects that are paid for (mainly) by the affluent but benefit (mainly) the poor, then gambling may be said to be contributing to social justice.[8]

Obviously this argument depends on the agreement that it is desirable that government should redistribute from richer to poorer, and this is disputed by economic libertarians, who think that government may only legitimately raise taxes to protect all its citizens equally from violence and deceit. However, all the main political parties in developed democracies such as the United States, in fact, subscribe to policies that make it the responsibility of government (i.e., taxpayers) to minimize poverty and to mitigate the worst of its consequences— such as not being able to feed, clothe, house, educate, and provide health care for yourself and your family. If, therefore, legalized gambling turns out to be a particularly effective way of funding welfare services of one sort or another that would otherwise be unavailable to the poor, there is a case for saying that legalizing gambling furthers the ends of social justice.

Much gambling policy is indeed driven by this kind of consideration. When lottery money, as happens with the U.K. lottery, is distributed to charities (in excess of what would have been donated if there was no lottery), this may well benefit the worst-off in society and, therefore, be benign from the point of view of distributive or social justice. The same can be said when private clubs in Australia use some of their profits from gambling to pay for hospital wings, classrooms, and sporting facilities for the poor of the region where they are located. In parts of the United States, Canada, France, and South Africa, the development of casino gambling has been successfully used for projects of urban renewal and regional development in especially disadvantaged areas.

There are two main difficulties with all these arguments.

The first is that we are really only talking about a particular way for government to raise taxes. All government activities are supposed to further the public interest, that is, the set of interests that we all have over and above our individual and sectional interests. Protecting us from violence at the hands of foreigners indisputably fits into this category, as does enforcing laws prohibiting the use of force and fraud in our dealings with one another. Alleviating poverty is usually accepted as being in the public interest, and though this is less obvious, it may become more plausible if providing social security is thought of as a way of insuring everybody against bad luck. The reason why we think it right to fund all these public interest activities through taxation is because this is both fairer and more efficient than leaving it to the conscience of individuals. Arguably, then, if the money raised by gambling for public interest projects is well spent, it is money that should have been raised by government anyway.

This is the main reason why governments prefer their revenues from gambling not to be singled out and earmarked ("hypothecated") for particular projects but rather to go into the general funds of government, where expenditure can be prioritized in the normal way on the basis of rational judgments about competing claims on the total public purse. On the other hand, governments in democracies have to get elected and hope to get reelected. They cannot, therefore, be indifferent to what their electors want, and what they want is always the same: low taxes and high levels of public services. Some public services—policing, for example—are judged to be so important by the public that they will put up with high taxes to pay for them. Others are sufficiently unpopular with the public that governments are usually compelled to skimp on them. Funding pure research in the sciences and humanities or making art available to the poor or alleviating the distress of people who wreck their lives by gambling too much may all fall into this category.

Under these circumstances, what a relatively high consumption tax on gambling does is to render politically possible public expenditure on activities that people would otherwise categorize as a "waste of public money." This, of course, places a considerable responsibility on those who earmark and spend gambling revenues to select popular projects and to ensure that the money is efficiently spent. Those who are charged with allocating lottery revenues for charitable projects often fail in this.

The politics of taxation as it applies to gambling accounts for the second difficulty in accepting that gambling taxes are a good way of promoting social justice. This is that, as a matter of fact, earmarked gambling revenues typically come from the poorer sections of society and are used to fund projects that benefit or are enjoyed by the less poor. Lottery funds, in particular, are often used to fund scholarships to universities or to subsidize cultural activities such as opera or modern art, which as a matter of fact benefits the better-off in society.

Whether gambling contributes to social justice by securing a redistribution of wealth from richer to poorer depends crucially on how government spends the share of gambling revenues that it collects over and above normal personal, property, and corporate taxes. If, for example, in the United States, extra taxes raised from gambling were devoted entirely to causes such as children with AIDS in Africa, removing land mines, abolishing Third World debt, or simply increasing the foreign aid budget beyond what it would otherwise be, then gambling might be said to be promoting social justice. Similarly, where lotteries—like church raffles or bingo evenings—succeed in generating funds for charities more effectively than simply requesting donations, they may also be mechanisms for redistributing from richer to poorer. Finally, if casino policy in a state or a country is deliberately designed to capture gambling revenues from a more affluent area for creating jobs and providing amenities and services in a relatively deprived area, then again this may be benign from the point of view of (re)distributive justice. In fact, it seems that for reasons embedded in the logic of democratic politics, much of the taxation of gambling—like much general taxation—has the effect of redistributing from rich and poor toward the middle.

What this tells us is that considerations of social justice are not particularly persuasive in deciding whether gambling should be legal or not, but they are crucial for determining whether and how the availability of legal gambling should be restricted and regulated.

FREEDOM AND THE CASE FOR LEGALIZING GAMBLING

I have now examined six reasons often adduced in support of the claim that government should prohibit or restrict the availability of gambling opportunities and found them defective. I have also looked at three reasons for thinking that government should adopt permissive policies toward the availability of gambling, namely, that permissiveness promotes the greatest happiness of the greatest number of people; that it avoids discriminating unfairly against gamblers; and that it facilitates a distribution of wealth that benefits the least advantaged. These arguments, too, I have found to be unpersuasive. This leaves what I take to be the most compelling reason for thinking that gambling should be legal, namely, that this is entailed by a commitment to individual freedom. To use the power of the state to prevent people from gambling runs counter to the political ideal that requires that individuals should be as free as possible to make their own decisions about how to conduct their own their lives. Specifically it is to arrogate to government the right to prescribe how people pursue pleasure. No doubt preventing people from gambling is not so grave an assault on individual liberty as when government seeks to prescribe individual conduct in the areas of personal relations, religious and political belief, or economic activity more generally. Nevertheless it is not trivial. There are at least five good reasons why we should require strong countervailing reasons before we acquiesce to the view that government may legitimately interfere with the right of adult individuals to pursue pleasure in whatever manner seems best to them provided only that the involvement of other adults is consensual and that any harm to third parties is both indirect and minimal. The first four of these reasons in support of the principle already quoted from Mill's *On Liberty* are adduced by Mill himself.

First, if we are not free in this area, we will not be free in others. Mill tells us that the principle he has enunciated for distinguishing where government may and where it may not interfere with the freedom of the individual "requires liberty of tastes and pursuits; of framing the plan of our life to suit our own character; of doing as we like, subject to such consequences as may follow: without impediment from our fellow-creatures so long as what we do does not harm them, even though they should think our conduct foolish, perverse or wrong."[9] This freedom forms part of the freedom that is fundamental to, and unqualified in, a fully free society because "the only freedom which deserves the name, is that of pursuing our own good in our own way, so long as we do not attempt to deprive others of theirs, or impede their efforts to obtain it" (16).

A second reason for thinking this freedom important is that if we allow government, on the occasions when we agree with it, to interfere with other people's tastes and pursuits on the grounds that they are foolish or unhealthy or reprehensible, we will have no defense when government seeks to interfere with our own convictions and preferences simply because others disagree with or disapprove of them. "We must beware," Mill tells us, "of admitting a principle of which we should resent as a gross injustice the application to ourselves" (86).

The third reason that Mill identifies for thinking this freedom important is that my happiness depends, to a significant degree, not merely in my engaging in activities that I in fact enjoy. It also requires that I engage in them of my own free will, that I do them because *I* have chosen to do them. As Mill puts it: "Where, not the person's own character [is] the rule of conduct, there is wanting one of the principal ingredients of human happiness" (56). Being free is a necessary condition for happiness in this quite special and profound way.

Fourth, being free is also, Mill thinks, a necessary condition for progress. Mill adds to his description of freedom in the passage just quoted that it is also "quite the chief ingredient of individual and social progress" (56), and earlier he has told us that happiness for human beings consists in satisfying "the permanent interests of man as a progressive being" (14). The thought here is that human well-being consists of a process of self-fulfillment, which is likely to be different for different individuals. This requires that we live in a society that permits experimentation with a diversity of ways of living no less than with a diversity of beliefs and ideas.

Mill recognizes that opponents will argue: "gambling, or drunkenness, or incontinence, or idleness, or uncleanness are as injurious to happiness, and as great a hindrance to improvement as many or most of those acts prohibited by law" (80). But for all four of the reasons given, he thinks that "with regard to the merely contingent ... injury which a person causes society, by conduct which neither violates any specific duty to the public, nor occasions perceptible hurt to any assignable individual except himself; the inconvenience is one which society can afford to bear, for the sake of the greater good of human freedom" (82).

To this normative judgment, Mill adds an empirical consideration that he takes to be decisive. Even if government, on behalf of public opinion, were justified in proscribing some kinds of behavior in the domain of personal tastes and compelling conformity to others, the evidence of history is that government will botch the job. "The strongest of all the arguments against the interference of government with purely personal conduct, is that when it does interfere, the odds are that it interferes wrongly, and in the wrong place" (83).

However, the fifth and, I believe, strongest reason for thinking that freedom to pursue pleasure in the way that seems best to one is not found in Mill, but it does connect with the idea that if society has to pay a price for tolerating a diversity of lifestyles, it is a price worth paying. The argument here is that not to accord to adults the maximum possible freedom to decide for themselves how to live their own lives is to violate their dignity as autonomous moral agents and to reduce citizens to a condition of permanent infantility. This argument differs from Mill's in that it does not require us to claim that government interference might not in fact result in greater happiness for most of its citizens. It is quite clear that people in government do sometimes know better what is in the interests of its citizens than they do themselves, just as parents are often right in judging that their children are forming romantic attachments that will cause them great unhappiness. But freedom consists in the right to make bad choices as well as good ones, and a society that seeks to protect people from the consequences of bad choices in matters of lifestyle by taking away their freedom to choose at all violates their fundamental rights and assaults their dignity as persons, no less surely than a society that denies them the freedom to worship or to love as seems best to them.

CONCLUSION

The conclusion of all these arguments for the legalization of gambling is not inescapable because ultimately they depend on value judgments that others may not share. If I reflect on what is most important in my conviction that gambling should not be prohibited by law, it comes down to a set of judgments about the kind of society I want to live in. Thus I do not want to live in a society that is highly puritanical in that it frowns on pleasure generally and on many largely harmless pleasures in particular. Nor do I want to live in a society that is highly authoritarian in that it arrogates to itself the right to prescribe what pleasures people may and may not indulge in. I also do not want to live in a society that makes it difficult to be adventurous in the pursuit of pleasure or one that inhibits economic creativity by restricting the forms of entertainment that people may provide on a commercial basis. Above all, I want to live in a society in which I can think for myself and make up my own mind about how I wish to spend my time, money, talents, and energy without being bossed around and frustrated in my designs by the agents of impersonal government. Of course I recognize that I will make some foolish choices, but at the end of my life, I want to be able to say that for better or worse, my choices were *my* choices, and my life was lived as *I* wanted to live it, even though this means that

I have more mistakes to regret than would have been the case if I had been forced to live according to the prescriptions of some external agency, however benign.

If it is pointed out to me that people's overindulgences may lead to ill health or have other negative impacts, such as destitution, that society, through its taxpayers, must try to alleviate, my response is that of course we could have a society in which sufferers from, say, smoking-related diseases were not eligible for state-subsidized health care. However, out of considerations of compassion, I would rather live in a society that seeks to look after even the undeserving poor and even the sick who are entirely responsible for their own diseases. If that means a higher tax burden, so be it.

These value judgments are not unchallengeable. If I became convinced that legalizing any gambling at all would really create extreme and widespread misery, and that prohibition would prevent this, then my commitment to liberty might be trumped in this case. Moreover, if I became convinced that all gambling is as highly dangerous as drinking absinthe or smoking crack cocaine or driving without a seat belt are alleged to be, then I would probably, though reluctantly, support prohibition. In fact, I consider the incidence of dangerously excessive gambling to be fairly small as a proportion of gamblers and the harm caused by excessive gambling to be relatively small compared to the damage caused by inter alia alcohol, drugs, and overeating. In general, I consider the arguments made against legal gambling that emphasize the evils of "problem gambling" to lack a sense of proportion and perspective.

All of this is quite compatible with thinking that nothing serious would be lost in terms of individual freedom if commercial gambling is made subject to some special regulations. It might be thought that gambling, like many other forms of pleasure, should be available only to adults, though this is not as self-evident as it is generally assumed to be. It might be thought that gambling presents special opportunities for various kinds of fraud and that therefore competitive market forces alone will not ensure honest commercial transactions. It might also be thought that gambling should be run as a state monopoly or be otherwise restricted and taxed to ensure the maximum benefits for nongamblers (or for gamblers in their capacity not as consumers of gambling services but as members of the general public). Other special regulations might be justified if gambling is integral to a collective strategy to attract tourists.

Also, my view that gambling should not be prohibited is entirely compatible with the view that the world would be a better place if gambling had never been invented or if gambling were to fall into desuetude as people become educated to enjoy many other pleasures that are richer and subtler than gambling.

What my arguments do show, I believe, is that government has no moral right to ban or restrict the availability of gambling opportunities because it, even with the support of a majority of voters, thinks that people should not want to take advantage of those opportunities. This means that those who oppose the legalization of gambling or the liberalization of gambling law not only have no monopoly on the moral high ground; the ground that they do occupy may itself be shaky and difficult to defend from a moral point of view.

NOTES

1. The issues discussed in this chapter are predominantly issues in political theory because they deal with questions about what governments should and should not do. I have discussed the most important issues of principle at some length in my *Ideology after the Fall of Communism: The Triumph of Liberal Democracy?* 2d ed. (London: Bowerdean, 1993). Among the issues discussed there which are most relevant to the present discussion are the nature and justification of democracy; the relationship between the will of the majority and the rights of individuals; distributive justice and taxation policy; the moral basis for the maximum equal liberty principle; and utility and liberty as competing political ideals.

2. For a historical discussion see J. C. Burnham, *Bad Habits: Drinking, Smoking, Taking Drugs, Sexual Misbehaviour, and Swearing in American History* (New York: New York University Press, 1993). For a discussion of the issue see, for example, E. Black and F. Zehtab, "Vice or Virtue? Gambling in Manitoba," *Policy Options* 16 (1995): 40–43.

3. See in this connection the excellent treatment in Gerda Reith, *The Age of Chance: Gambling in Western Culture, Routledge Studies in Social and Political Thought* (New York: Routledge, 1999).

4. There are a number of books that bring together the main arguments for and against the legalization of gambling, notably: D. Dixon, *From Prohibition to Regulation: Anti-gambling and the Law* (Oxford: Clarendon Press, 1991); C. P. Cozic and P. A. Winters, *Gambling, Current Controversies* (San Diego, Calif.: Greenhaven Press, 1995); and K. Healey, *Gambling, Issues for the Nineties* (Balmain, N.S.W.: Spinney Press, 1997). Some relevant articles include I. N. Rose, "The Rise and Fall of the Third Wave: Gambling Will Be Outlawed in Forty Years," in *Gambling and Public Policy*, ed. W. Eadington and J. Cornelius (Reno, Nev.: Institute for the Study of Gambling and Commercial Gaming, 1994); A. Oddo, "The Economics and Ethics of Casino Gambling," *Review of Business* 18, no. 3 (1997): 4–7; and D. K. Herrmann, "The Decision to Legalize Gambling: A Model of Why (U.S.) States Do What They Do," *International Journal of Public Administration* 22 (1999): 1659–80.

5. J. S. Mill, *On Liberty*, ed. Stefan Collini (1861; Cambridge: Cambridge University Press, 1989), 13.

6. For a contemporary discussion see M. Scriven, "The Philosophical Foundations of Las Vegas," *Journal of Gambling Studies* 11, no. 2 (1995): 61–67. Scriven argues that even if the violation of rights involved in prohibiting gambling could in principle be justified with reference to the harm that gamblers do themselves, the empirical evidence does not, as a matter of fact, support prohibition on these grounds.

7. A discussion of some of these issues as they apply specifically to the introduction of casinos in the United States can be found in R. J. Rychlak, "The Introduction of Casino Gambling: Public Policy and Law," *Mississippi Law Journal* 64 (1995): 291–362.

8. For a discussion of the relevant facts about who does and who does not benefit from the legalizing of casino gambling, see T. J. Repham et al., "Casino Gambling as an Economic Development Strategy," *Tourism Economics* 3, no. 2 (1997): 161–83. See also the discussion of lotteries and casinos in chapter 5 of this volume.

9. Mill, *On Liberty,* 15.

Chapter 4

How Should Gambling Be Regulated?

Let us assume that there is a market for gambling in a jurisdiction where either all or much gambling activity was previously prohibited. Let us further assume that government has decided, perhaps for some of the reasons discussed in the last chapter, that it should not be illegal to try to cater for this market. In other words, the general issue of whether allowing a legal gambling industry to emerge is in the overall public interest or not has been decided in favor of legalization. Government may, nevertheless, think that there are special features of commercial gambling as an activity and as a business that mean it will be in the public interest to impose restrictions of various sorts on how this industry may operate. Government may think, in other words, that from the point of view of public policy, gambling is in important respects different from the rest—or most of the rest—of the pleasure industry. For example, government may think that, in ways that are relevant to its legitimate concerns, what goes on in a casino is not wholly like what goes on in a restaurant or a movie house and that selling lottery tickets is different from selling candy or novels. If so, how should government regulate its gambling industry?

One could ask the same question by imagining that the choice facing government arises when a commercial gambling industry has already emerged in the normal way in response to market forces and government is now, for whatever reason, considering whether this new industry needs to be subject to special regulations. As a matter of fact, in recent history, governments have usually confronted the problem in the context of legalizing a previously illegal industry rather than of trying to rein in one that has hitherto operated as an ordinary part of the leisure business in a free market. But either way, the question confronting government is "What are the principal features of a well-regulated gambling industry?" This is the question that we will address in this chapter.

We will first consider how the gambling industry would operate if it were treated simply as a normal part of the entertainment industry. We will then consider the issue of good regulation in relation to the following five areas that governments typically subject to special regulatory control:

- The nature of the gambling services that may be supplied—the "products," the product mix, and the price
- Qualifications required from people wishing to supply these gambling products and services
- Requirements determining who may and may not purchase gambling products and services
- Where and when these services may be supplied
- How they may, must or must not be marketed

Regulation in these cases is primarily intended to prevent or reduce harm to the public. When government is thinking about ways in which the gambling industry can be harnessed to secure benefits of various sorts for the public, the question it needs to address is "Should the gambling industry be required to contribute a larger share of its earnings to the public purse than is required from other industries through the normal taxation process?"

An affirmative answer to this last question leads governments to use regulations to prohibit, or at least inhibit, competition with state-run lotteries and, often, to limit the number of casinos and other gambling operations that it licenses, as well. Here the intention of government is to use the regulation of the gambling industry to create monopolies or oligopolies and hence monopoly or oligopoly profits. These abnormal profits can then be captured for the public purse through various forms of taxation. We will consider this question of a special taxation regime for the gambling industry in the next chapter.

If government thinks that restrictions on the gambling industry of any of these sorts, for any of these reasons, are in the public interest, they will embody them in special regulations that go beyond the normal government requirements that apply to all businesses, or at least to all relevantly similar businesses. Regulations take the form "You may do this, but only if ... ," and it is usually thought that trading in gambling services requires regulations of this sort. Consequently, we need to examine what special regulations, if any, government should require the industry to conform to.

This question "How should gambling be regulated?" is deceptively simple and misleadingly suggests that there is only one way in which a gambling industry can be well regulated or that there is a single set of desirable regulations and that regulatory dispensations are admirable to the extent that they successfully inscribe and enforce these regulations.

In fact, whether regulations are good regulations or not depends on their appropriateness to the objectives that government is trying to achieve through the regulation of its gambling industry. And, of course, different governments will quite rightly have different objectives.

I noted in the introduction that the main political principles in which regulatory objectives have historically been grounded are

- To secure conformity to behavior that society through its government deems to be moral and to prevent behavior that society deems to be immoral
- To prevent people from harming themselves
- To prevent people from harming others
- To generate relatively unresented taxes
- To promote tourism

What is good and bad regulation will therefore vary depending on the underlying policy objectives that the regulations are intended to further. What is good or bad regulation in Biloxi (which wanted to use gambling to establish itself as an attractive destination resort for tourists) will be significantly different from what is good or bad regulation in Detroit (which is catering mainly for its own local market—and trying to stop them from traveling to Windsor in Canada to gamble). What's good regulation in Canada or Holland, where government owns the gambling industry, will be to some extent different to what's good in the United States, Australia, or France. All these may in turn differ from what is good and bad regulation in the context of the state of Utah, or in many Islamic countries where there are widely and strongly held religious objections to gambling.

Some good gambling regulations will be common to all jurisdictions—for example, those designed to prevent money laundering or to ensure that customers are not cheated—but many will be specific to the perceived problems and opportunities that confront particular communities and their governments. For this reason, the most important first step for any government to take when considering how to regulate the gambling industry is to ask itself what it is trying to achieve and what are its priorities.

In general, governments claim that gambling needs to be regulated for one or more or all of the following reasons:

- To prevent minors from gambling
- To prevent criminals from owning or working in the gambling industry
- To prevent increases in crimes such as prostitution, drug dealing, and loan-sharking as a consequence of having a legalized gambling industry
- To prevent the gambling industry from being used for money laundering
- To protect gamblers from being defrauded by the suppliers of gambling services
- To protect gamblers from having false beliefs about the nature of commercial gambling activities
- To reduce the risk that people will become "problem gamblers" or gambling addicts

On the other hand, much inadequate or ineffectual regulation derives from the fact that legislators have been confused or unrealistic in relation to what they are trying to achieve.

For example, some jurisdictions note that under certain circumstances, gambling can yield abnormally high tax revenues, attract tourists, lead to investment in urban renewal projects, create jobs for the presently unemployed, and so forth, and they conclude that the more gambling of every sort that they legalize, the more of all these good things they will obtain. In fact, this is a muddle because these objectives tend to compete with one another, so that, for example, more money invested on labor-intensive, job-creating projects will mean less money available to be captured in the form of high taxes. Urban renewal projects will probably not be the best for attracting tourists. Or again, because Las Vegas has been successful in using gambling in attracting leisure and business tourists from all over America and indeed the world, many jurisdictions have thought that if they legalize Las Vegas–style casinos, they will get the same benefits. This is unrealistic. In fact, the overwhelming majority of the world's jurisdictions are not suitable for transformation into gambling resorts because, unlike Las Vegas, they do not start off with the massive advantage of being the nearest place where gambling is legal for a very large number potential gambling enthusiasts.

In the same way, governments often get confused about what they are trying to accomplish when they regulate to minimize the negative impacts of gambling. This is seen clearly where governments move to minimize the incidence of problem gambling by, for example, banning the gambling businesses in their jurisdiction from offering Internet gambling. The object of regulating Internet gambling is not to prevent something with allegedly undesirable social consequences from coming into existence. It is to control and reduce the potential for harm of an activity that is already there while perhaps simultaneously securing the economic benefits associated with a successful export business. In fact, the more governments ban the domestic supply of Internet gambling services, the greater the incentives they create for relatively unregulated companies offshore to supply their citizens with gambling services over the Internet. This is analogous to the way in which prohibition drives consumers to make use of services supplied by organized crime.

Good regulation thus depends on good policy, and good policy will vary in accordance with the needs of, and opportunities available to, different communities. One of the best ways for government to start thinking accurately about these issues is to ask, "Whom do we want to benefit, and on whom do we want (or are we willing) to impose costs?" All regulation is designed to secure benefits for some at the expense of others. Health and safety regulations impose costs on businesspeople and seek to secure benefits for their customers and for the general public. Regulations about smoking in public places prevent smokers from behaving as otherwise they might choose with the intention of protecting or catering for the preferences of nonsmokers. And, of course, most taxation—which is the most universal form of regulation—is designed to benefit some at the expense of others.

The principal categories of people whose interests need to be taken account of in examining the impact of regulating the gambling industry are

- Politicians whose election prospects may be influenced by what they do about gambling policy
- Gamblers
- Taxpayers
- Shareholders, employees, and ancillary service providers in the gambling industry
- Civil servants and regulators concerned with the gambling industry
- Those employed by taxpayers to engage in gambling-related work, including police officers, therapists, social workers, lawyers, and academic researchers
- The general public
- Local communities
- The poor
- Children
- Those vulnerable to becoming excessive gamblers
- Criminals

Politicians may be expected to be unambiguously in favor of doing whatever they can to protect and promote the interests of themselves, their administration, and their party. With respect to criminals, it is to be hoped that government will be concerned to frustrate the protection and promotion of their interests. With respect to children, taxpayers, and the general public, government will be disposed to secure their interests as far as possible. With respect to all other groups, the attitude of government is likely to vary between the supportive, the neutral, and the hostile, depending partly on the principles that politicians bring to their work and partly on their judgment about the relative political influence of the groups concerned.

In the case of all gambling regulation, governments need to be much clearer than they often are about whom they are seeking to benefit at the expense of whom and why. It is consequently helpful to look at gambling regulation with reference to these different categories of people on whom the burdens and benefits of the main forms of gambling regulation are intended to fall. This will enable us to see more clearly how effective specific items of regulation are likely to be in achieving their proclaimed objectives. It should be noted in this connection that regulation is almost certainly bad regulation if the primary beneficiaries are regulators for whom a proliferation of unnecessary regulations may mean an increase in their power, status, and earnings.

Another way of assisting governments and others to think clearly about good gambling regulation is to ask, "What other businesses is the gambling industry like and in what respects?"

Let us therefore look again at some of the commercial activities to which trading in gambling services may be compared:

- Selling books and magazines
- Selling theater tickets
- Running a restaurant
- Putting on sporting events
- Providing sexual services for money
- Trading in pornography
- Trading in liquor
- Selling cigarettes
- Selling psychotropic (mind-altering) drugs
- Selling chocolate

For this reason, in looking at various forms of gambling regulation, we will ask, "What assumptions about how the gambling industry is similar to, and different from, other industries underpin this regulation?" and "Are these assumptions warranted?"

To summarize, then, I will relate the discussion of different types of regulation to the following:

- The possible overarching objectives that a government might have in relation to its gambling industry
- The assumptions about why the gambling industry is different that are used or implied to justify subjecting the gambling industry to abnormal regulations
- The categories of people on whom it is intended to confer benefits or impose burdens
- Those who in reality are likely to receive the benefits and bear the costs

In this way, I hope to make plain the rationale behind good gambling regulation and to show why it is desirable to have many of the regulations that are in fact common in the gambling industry. However, as we shall see, regulations sometimes do not have the consequences intended for them or which politicians and regulators point to in justifying them. We will also see that government is frequently inconsistent in its regulation of gambling to the extent that the industry is treated very differently from others that are similar in the relevant respects.

A FREE MARKET IN GAMBLING

It is widely accepted, especially in the United States but increasingly in the rest of the world, that governments should leave the conduct of business for the most part to the operation of free markets. This means that (other things being equal, as they are not, for example, in times of war) people should be allowed to employ their time, talents, and energy in whatever form of work they choose. They should then be able to sell the fruits of their labor in the form of goods and services to anyone willing to buy them at the price at which they are willing to sell. With the money they thus earn, they should then be free in their turn to buy the goods and services that others are offering. In short, in a free market, individuals, not governments, determine who supplies what to whom and on what terms.

In this system, the role of government is limited to what government does everywhere under the common law. In particular, government prevents people from employing force or fraud in the conduct of commercial activity. It protects people from negligence and the rest of society from having to bear incidental costs—what economists call "externalities" such as the costs of pollution—which are inflicted on it by particular commercial activities. Perhaps also, government seeks to ensure that consumers are as informed as possible about the consequences of the decisions they make.

If commercial gambling were treated as simply a normal part of the retail or leisure industry in which gambling companies sell different kinds of pleasure to willing consumers, then government would seek to ensure the following:

- That the business is not used as a front for facilitating criminal activity such as money laundering or drug dealing
- That in the games on which people gamble, nobody cheats
- That debts are honored
- That companies in competition with one another do not use violent or other criminal means to secure commercial advantage
- That advertising and marketing are not deceptive
- That gambling companies pay their taxes in the same way that all businesses are required to pay taxes

Gambling venues would, in addition, be subject to normal health and safety regulations, to normal planning permission rules and environmental regulations, to employment law and laws governing fair trading, such as antitrust laws. And no doubt, to all sorts of other rules and regulations, which, even in the capitalist United States, diminish the clarity of the pure free market vision.

If gambling were treated as a normal business, however, government would not adopt many measures that are, in fact, imposed on the gambling industry by most or all jurisdictions. Among the measures that would not obtain if commercial gambling were treated simply as another normal business are the following requirements:

- That companies prove that their owners and employees are trustworthy
- That companies prove that they have substantial resources
- That companies prove they have the necessary competence to conduct their business

- That measures be put in place to prevent or reduce the likelihood of consumers consuming more than is good for them
- That people under a certain age be prevented from buying the goods and services that the company offers
- That competition among would-be suppliers be restricted by law

In many ways, leaving the gambling industry to essentially the same market forces that govern other industries is an attractive one. The idea that economic activity should be shaped by market forces rather than by government regulation is not simply an article of secular Western faith. It is supported by two powerful general considerations. First, a system that leaves people responsible for their own economic choices shows a greater respect for the fundamental human right to liberty than any system in which government restricts such choices. Second, free markets reward those who are successful in supplying others with the goods and services that they actually want. By doing so, they harness human energy and creativity to the promotion of real human well-being—something that government-managed economies conspicuously (and unsurprisingly) fail to do.

However, the attractiveness of leaving the development of the gambling industry to market forces diminishes substantially when we consider what would, in fact, be likely to happen. If the gambling industry were regulated according to normal market principles only, anyone would be able to place a bet with anyone, on anything, at any commercial as well as any private venue. Anyone could open a business dedicated to supplying gambling opportunities, and gambling services could be supplied in all sorts of existing venues. Anyone would be able to organize a lottery for personal profit. No doubt, specialization would develop as some gambling businesses proved more successful than others in attracting the custom of the public. High-quality service at good prices would be ensured by competition to capture and retain the custom of individual consumers, and consumers would be expected to protect their own interests by shopping around and following the principle of caveat emptor: "Let the buyer beware."

So far, so good, champions of free markets might say. However, if there were indeed a free market in gambling, there could be no state lotteries to fund good causes because these would be in competition with one or more private lotteries, which could offer better prizes because none of their revenue would be going to good causes. Bookmakers could take bets on every conceivable kind of sporting and other event including the future price of stocks and the outcome of school and college sporting events. Casinos of all sizes, offering all sorts of different gambling products as well as all sorts of other services, would proliferate in every large city and small town. There would be slot machines, offering unlimited prizes, wherever people might be expected to have a little time on their hands and a little money in their pocket that they were prepared to risk at unfavorable odds to pass the time and in the hope of winning. Gambling machines would consequently appear in bus and rail stations, in airports, in supermarkets and mom-and-pop stores, in restaurants and bars and clubs of all sorts, in Laundromats and gas stations, in hospitals, in college common rooms, in doctors' waiting rooms and hospitals. Companies would be able to operate slot machines in their offices and factories in the hope of recovering from their workers some of the money they pay them in wages. Increasingly, there would be television channels dedicated to interactive gambling, and lottery games including perhaps Keno would be offered with whatever frequency the market can tolerate via cell phones, and there would be no regulation of Internet gambling products (as is mostly the case at present).

As we shall see, all sorts of arguments are used to justify taking steps to limit the proliferation of gambling opportunities. It is said that machine gambling must only take place in venues from which minors are excluded, or there must not be more gambling than can be effectively regulated, or that we must restrict the availability to reduce the risk of "problem gambling." The truth, however, is, I suspect, that even if we could eliminate the risks of making it easy for minors to gamble, if we could overcome the problems of adequate regulation, and if we could effectively counter the risks of increased problem gambling, most communities would still simply not think it desirable to have gambling machines (in particular) in every conceivable kind of venue. Their objections might be classed as aesthetic, but, as already noted, politicians in a democracy would nevertheless have to respect them.

Before leaving the idea of an unregulated gambling industry, it is worth seeing who would be the principal beneficiaries of such a system. The answer is that the main beneficiaries of such free-market competition would be gamblers. This is because everywhere competition mainly benefits consumers, who, because of competition for their business among suppliers, typically get a greater variety of goods and services to choose from at very low ("competitive") prices.

The other main beneficiaries of a free market in the gambling industry would be those seeking to break into the industry as new entrants. These will be people who think they can compete successfully for new customers or for customers who are currently patronizing existing companies. All regulation, whatever its nature and purpose, is likely to impose some additional costs that act as a barrier to entry. Some regulatory requirements in the gambling industry impose huge costs and constitute major barriers to entry. The kind of costly "probity" investigations that most jurisdictions require for most or all employees in a gambling business and the requirement to demonstrate a deep pocket constitute just such a barrier to entry—which is why all over the world established companies claim to think that probity investigations are important to secure the public interest.

We will return to this issue. Meanwhile it is to be noted that a policy focused on promoting the interests of gamblers by securing for them the best value for money would indeed seek to approximate as closely as possible to the conditions of a free market. However, it is far from obvious that the interests of gamblers ought to be paramount in designing gambling policy and the regulatory environment that goes with it. If instead we think that policy should seek to maximize the interests of the general public, including nongamblers and gamblers considered apart from their taste for gambling, then we will not necessarily favor free markets. A free market in commercial gambling benefits the punters, but not necessarily the public.

REGULATING GAMBLING PRODUCTS

Governments that regulate the gambling industry typically set rules about what games and other activities people may offer and take bets on. They will stipulate the rules according to which table games must be played. They will require every game played on a gaming machine to be individually licensed. They may require that some types of gambling be not offered in the same place as other products or stipulating what the product mix must be between different gambling products must be. They may have rules setting minimums and maximums for stakes and prizes and for the odds that must be offered.

Governments don't do any of this with restaurants. If you have the necessary permissions to open a restaurant, you can put whatever you like on your menu and charge whatever price you think appropriate. Government will, of course, forbid you to serve food that might constitute a health hazard, and you may be penalized if you sell horse meat pretending that it is prime rib. But for the rest, if you offer an unattractive menu, serve unpalatable food, and charge excessive prices, you can expect to be punished by the market (which will ensure that you go broke), but not by government.

Why, then, in regulating the gambling industry should government stipulate how many zeroes you can have on your roulette wheel or stipulate the maximum size of the jackpots your gaming machines may pay out?

There are three strong arguments for claiming that unlike other products, gambling products should be subject to special regulation. The first concerns cheating. The second concerns reducing the risks of compulsive gambling. The third concerns the protection of revenues to the public purse.

First, then, there is a plausible case to be made for thinking that gambling is an activity in which it is abnormally easy for gambling companies to cheat their customers. This is obvious in the case of gambling machines where the player cannot inspect the mechanisms that determine the ratio of winning to losing outcomes nor make sure that the outcome is in fact the product of random number generation. It is also true that there are all sorts of ways for the house to cheat the players in card games. Making clear rules giving the house a small statistical advantage, only which all players understand, makes cheating much more difficult and causes it to fall much more unambiguously into the category of fraud. Similar considerations apply to strict regulation of how bookmakers operate and how lotteries must be conducted.

It is also thought that the regulation of gambling products is desirable to mitigate the incidence of problem gambling. Some gambling products are thought to be more addictive than others, notably those that offer betting opportunities that follow one another in rapid and unbroken succession. On this basis, machine gambling and table games are contrasted with betting on events such as horse races, and both are contrasted with buying a lottery ticket or two once or twice a week. We will consider this further in relation to the whole question of minimizing the incidence of, and damage caused by, problem gambling.

Finally, governments regulate the nature of gambling products to protect their revenues. This is clearest in the case of lotteries where the state has a substantial interest in the profits. To protect the state lottery, governments are likely to forbid other organizations, including charities, to operate lotteries that offer comparably large prizes and might therefore detract from the funds that go to the government's own coffers or to government-sponsored "good causes." Government may well restrict the availability of mixed-stake, unlimited-prize machine gambling to protect its stake in casinos. We will consider the question of using regulation to restrict competition and drive up prices and profits in the next chapter.

Perhaps the closest analogy for the regulating of gambling products is the regulating of medicines that may be sold in a drugstore. On the one hand, customers are likely to lack the knowledge or the means of acquiring the knowledge of what the real properties of various medicines are. On the other hand, some medicines have various kinds of harmful effects, including being addictive. What makes gambling abnormal and therefore justifies abnormal regulation is the exceptional difficulty that customers would otherwise have in making informed choices.

In any event, it seems intuitively reasonable to wish to protect the customers of gambling companies from being easily defrauded by insisting that the games they offer can be officially checked for fairness. It is perhaps surprising that this way of benefiting gamblers does not go further. Very few jurisdictions, for example, require that companies publish the odds against winning in the various games that they offer or post the payout rate of the different gambling machines in their establishments. To require this would be to do no more than to require that customers be told the price of the product or service they are buying before they pay for it. Similarly, jurisdictions do not commonly limit the amount that people can spend on different gambling products (e.g., lottery tickets) in any one day or require them to set themselves limits at the beginning of a session of gambling for what they can lose. Interestingly, both these types of regulation may well come to be judged either necessary or desirable when it comes to regulating Internet gambling.

REGULATING THE SUPPLIERS

Modern commercial gambling, as everyone knows, was developed in the United States by organized crime. Organized crime had always run illegal lottery-type numbers games, been involved in illegal bookmaking, and run gambling in nightclubs and in the back rooms of restaurants. Organized crime was also the first to exploit machine gambling by developing casinos in Las Vegas. Moreover, when criminals ran Las Vegas, the operations were themselves notoriously crooked. This has provided story lines and background in countless movies about gangsters.[1] It is consequently not surprising, therefore, that gambling is popularly thought of as a business that criminals are particularly likely to want to get into. Together with drug dealing and prostitution, gambling is perceived as being part of the traditional core business of organized crime.

It is also not surprising that when under pressure from the federal government, the government of Nevada set about creating a properly regulated legal gambling industry, their first priority was to get the Mafia out of the gambling business in Nevada and to ensure that those who owned and operated casinos were respectable and upright businesspeople. In this way, the practice developed of requiring the owners and most of the employees of casinos to go through a thorough investigation of their background and to meet strict "probity" criteria. In this way, the government of Nevada through its gaming commission could refuse a license to people with unsavory backgrounds already in the industry and hopefully prevent people with criminal associations from getting into the industry in the future.

This requirement that employees and substantial shareholders in casino companies pass a stringent probity test has been adopted in all other U.S. jurisdictions and in most other countries where American-style casino gambling has been introduced. Similar though usually somewhat less stringent tests are also often applied worldwide to employees in other parts of the gambling business such as bookmakers. There are few signs that either government or the industry thinks it would be a good idea to relax or abandon probity requirements.

This is somewhat surprising. After all, there are many other businesses—accounting, banking, stockbroking, bartending, selling insurance or used cars or real estate—that don't require employees to undergo probity checks, though arguably their opportunities to behave fraudulently will be comparable. Also probity checks are time consuming and expensive for applicant companies. In addition, many of the questions that respectable executives have to answer are experienced as impertinent and manifestly irrelevant—for example, about alimony arrangements between former spouses.

More generally, it should be obvious to regulatory authorities that what brings organized crime into commercial activities is not the fact that there are no probity checks on those who want to get into particular businesses but the fact that the particular business is outlawed or perhaps so highly taxed and in other ways legally restricted that there is a profitable market for the illegal supply of the relevant goods and services. Prohibition is what brought organized crime into the liquor business, and the abolition of prohibition through the repeal of the Eighteenth Amendment is what enabled the liquor industry to become crime free. Moreover, the profits from the conduct of an honest gambling operation are so attractive that it would normally be folly for an operator to jeopardize them by compromising its reputation and its license to trade by engaging in illegal activities. When we add to this that gambling companies are typically public companies and therefore subject to the same regulations and scrutiny as applies to all other public companies, it becomes difficult to see why anyone in the industry still welcomes the uniquely strict regulation of who may and who may not work in this industry. It is not even as if probity checks are infallible in eliminating scams from the gambling industry.

The truth is, of course, that rigorous and expensive probity checks constitute a substantial barrier to entry and therefore help to keep competition away from established businesses. They also create reasonably attractive work for regulators, as well as substantial fees for forensic accountants and others.

Given these views, readers will not be surprised to learn that I view the probity requirements, which are currently imposed on would-be employees and substantial shareholders in the gambling industry, as unnecessary, wasteful, and anticompetitive. At the very least, they could be drastically simplified. More constructively, I would think that there is substantial room for far greater interjurisdictional cooperation so that the international community of regulators develop uniform standards, share relevant information, and recognize each other's certification procedures.

Pressure for such international cooperation is likely to be intensified by the need to regulate Internet gambling. In a world where gambling services can be supplied out of everywhere from Liberia to Finland by operators of any nationality, there almost certainly will develop international probity checking processes, registers of accredited operators, and common standards. Perhaps in this area we will look to practices developed for certifying ships and their captains regardless of the flag of convenience under which they sail.

In the gambling industry, the strict regulation of suppliers of gambling services has been overwhelmingly justified with reference to the need to keep gambling crime free. But most jurisdictions in fact add two other requirements before they will license a gambling business. The first is that operators demonstrate competence to run the operations in which they propose to trade. The second is that operators prove they have adequate financial resources to sustain their business.

At first glance, both of these requirements are even more unwarrantably hostile to the spirit and practices of a free-enterprise economy than the requirement that operators prove their honesty. After all, if you want to open a restaurant, nobody expects you to prove that you can cook, and if you want to make a movie, it's likely to be your bankers, not government officials, that you have to convince about the adequacy of your resources.

This view of the matter, though logical, overlooks what is peculiar about the gambling industry. This is not that market forces in conjunction with the common law relating to negligence are inadequate to protect the consumers of gambling services from the incompetence of suppliers. Nor is it that the gambling industry deals with large sums of money that makes it sensible to investigate the financial resources of suppliers. That is an argument for subjecting gambling to whatever special regulations are appropriate to the financial services industries such as banking or insurance. This happens in the U.K., for example, with spread betting and also happens in practice wherever government seeks to reduce the risks of gambling being used for money laundering. The real reason why it makes sense for governments to be especially concerned that its gambling businesses do not collapse owing large amounts of money to customers and other creditors has to do with the peculiar political sensitivity of the gambling industry. This has two components.

First, in countries such as the United States, gambling is likely to have been legalized only in the teeth of some quite intense opposition, and even among supporters of legalization there is likely to be an awareness that gambling brings in its wake some negative social impacts. This means that broad public support for a legalized gambling industry is likely to be unusually fragile, and government therefore has an exceptionally strong interest in ensuring that the gambling industry is as well thought of as possible among the general public. If a casino or a lottery or a bookmaking business goes bankrupt because its employees make regular or serious mistakes or because it runs out of funds to pay its debts, this will obviously seriously damage the reputation of the industry as a whole and may well be held against government by its electors. From a political point of view, therefore, the collapse of a gambling company through incompetence or lack of adequate financing is not like the collapse of a local theater because its actors give dismal performances or its managers can't raise the money to pay them. We shall see that government has a similarly exceptional political concern that the gambling industry should enjoy good public relations with respect to the harm that gamblers may be thought to do to themselves through gambling too much. This is clearly different from the concern that governments might have about, for example, the fast-food business and those who eat too much. The difference consists in the public perceptions, not in the objective dangerousness, of gambling too much as opposed to eating too much. And, of course, democratic politics are largely about public perceptions of reality rather than about reality itself.

The second characteristic of the gambling industry that makes it peculiarly sensitive from a political point of view is that governments typically have an abnormal financial interest in the profitability of the industry. This is so even when government does no more, as with lotteries, than to use gambling to increase tax revenues. It is obviously still more so if the government has awarded, for example, a casino license on the promise that this will provide attractive nongambling local amenities, attract tourists, and generate jobs. It is significant, in this respect, that those who would like to see gambling banned or at least severely restricted frequently deplore the "addiction" of governments to gambling taxes—as if government officials had a sick and sinister interest in raising "dirty" money from gambling as opposed to consuming "clean" money from, say, increased property taxes. The truth is, as we shall see, that governments like gambling taxes because they are comparatively unresented, and this is an entirely proper reason for governments to take account of in formulating their taxation policy.

The truth is, as we have already noted, that the relationship between government and a legalized gambling industry that pays higher taxes than other industries is really one of partnership, even though the partnership is formally conducted at arm's length. This means that both parties to the partnership—government as well as industry—have a strong interest in the commercial success of the business. It also means that both parties—individual gambling businesses as well as government—have a strong interest in a widespread public perception of the industry as reliable and competent as well as socially responsible and honest.

This is the real justification for regulating the suppliers of gambling services so as to ensure that companies wishing to obtain a license be technically competent and financially sound as well as honest. What government is really doing in this respect is carrying out a form of due diligence with respect to companies with whom government is proposing to enter into a partnership, albeit a tacit one.

REGULATING CONSUMERS

An answer often given to the question "Why does the gambling industry need to be regulated (in ways that do not apply to other industries)?" is

- To keep out criminals
- To ensure that the games are fair
- To protect the vulnerable, especially children

Quite often these objectives of legislation are spelled out explicitly. Almost invariably, where they are not explicit, these objectives are implicit in the laws and regulations that govern the gambling industry. There is a fourth objective of gambling regulation, which is sometimes not only spelled out but vigorously implemented in jurisdictions such as California and Switzerland, which have a strong tradition of fostering participatory democracy through referenda. This fourth objective is to give expression to the wishes of the local community.[2]

This objective, together with the objective of protecting the vulnerable, generates the principal regulatory restrictions that governments commonly impose on who may gamble. There are three main classes of such people: children, the poor, and potential addicts. All are thought to fall within the category of "the vulnerable," that is, people for whom gambling is likely to be abnormally dangerous or harmful.

It is taken for granted throughout the United States, and virtually everywhere else as well, that even though it may be desirable that adults be able to consume commercial gambling services, it is certainly not desirable that children be able to do so. Why this should be so is not at all obvious, as indeed is the case with much other legislation that denies children freedoms that are accorded to all other citizens.[3]

The general assumption is that there are desirable activities that many people will want to engage in, but certain activities are likely to be dangerous to people who lack certain personal qualities and capacities. Children are assumed to lack these qualities and capacities generically. In earlier times, children were regarded as lacking in the capacity to reason. Nowadays we are perhaps more likely to talk about the lack of emotional as well as intellectual maturity that typically (and by definition) characterizes children. In either case, the result is that children are in all sorts of ways judged incapable of determining their own best interests, and consequently it is thought justifiable to subject children to "paternalist" or "parentalist" government in which they are denied the fundamental liberal freedom of deciding for themselves how they shall live and are instead compelled to live in accordance with what adults think is best for them. Thus children are not allowed to vote, to enter into contracts, to sell their labor in a free market, to marry or have sex with each other or with older people.

This is, of course, largely unobjectionable. It is true that at least preadolescent children can't look after themselves, and therefore someone else has to look after them. Normally that will be parents, but to protect children from inadequate parental supervision, the law stipulates that, for example, children must go to school and may not be sent out to work. It also stipulates that they may not participate in specified pleasures that are deemed, either on account of their morally corrupting nature or on account of their danger or both, to be permissible only to adults. Gambling is one of these, along with smoking, drinking, and participating in many forms of sexual activity ranging from viewing sexually explicit material in magazines and movies to engaging in sexual activity with others.

It is a more open question than is widely assumed whether gambling really does belong here with the other activities. Gambling does not, after all, damage physical health in the way that smoking does. It also differs in significant ways from drinking alcohol. Also, you can't get pregnant or contract venereal disease from reckless gambling. On the other hand, it is arguably a much less risky activity to adolescents and others than permitting people to drive cars at the age of sixteen. Recognition of this comes from the fact that many European jurisdictions impose no age limit on who may buy lottery tickets (without suffering epidemics of juvenile problem gambling that are measurably worse than elsewhere). In the proposed new legislation, in the U.K. children will continue to be allowed to gamble on machines. Those who are horrified by this should note that there is no evidence that the U.K. has significantly higher numbers of child problem gamblers than other countries, and more particularly there is no evidence that the U.K. winds up with more adult problem gamblers.

It seems, however, to be true that as with all other potentially risky behaviors—including taking drugs and having unprotected sex with a variety of partners—young people are more likely to take the risks and indulge excessively than are older people (though this tendency may well be characteristic of fourteen- to thirty-year-olds rather than under eighteens).[4] On the other hand, there is a danger that by concentrating on the dangers of gambling addiction to young people, authorities may fail to consider adequately whether the addiction is not rather to playing games with or on machines regardless of whether betting takes place.[5]

Another consideration that tells against prohibiting minors from gambling is the fact that if an activity is defined as adults-only, this will add to its attractiveness to many young people. It is quite possible that if marijuana cigarettes were freely available in cafés and similar venues, young people would be less, rather than more, disposed to smoke them—given their unpleasant taste and dismal effect on intelligent conversation. At any rate, the lure of forbidden fruits that are alluring because they are forbidden should not be overlooked. Nor should we think that because we have formally banned something to young people, we have effectively protected them from its dangers.

As with much to do with gambling behavior generally and problem gambling in particular, there is a great deal of relevant empirical information that we simply do not have. For this reason, if for no other, it is probably sensible to lay down that commercial gambling is a form of adult entertainment, most comparable from this point of view to viewing sexually explicit movies. It should only take place, therefore, at locations from which minors can be effectively excluded. An exception to this prohibition on letting young people gamble might be made in the case of purchasing tickets for big-prize electronic lottery games held once or twice a week. The argument here would be that this is an inherently safe form of gambling that is also socially benign because it helps good causes. It would also constitute an exception to the general rule that gambling should not take place in venues where the principal activity is not gambling, that is, where the gambling is "ambient." However, in both cases, the justification for the exception only makes sense if the sale of scratch cards and other gambling products often offered by lotteries is excluded from what may be available to minors at convenience stores and other nongambling venues.

The reality is that the problem of excluding minors does not seriously arise with preadolescent children except perhaps as part of a wider problem of child neglect. With those who are close to adulthood, the problem is where to draw the line and this is largely a matter of "feel." Perhaps sixteen feels too low and twenty-one too high for gambling. So perhaps it's eighteen. But there is no inescapable reason for preferring one number rather than another as the cutoff point.

A final point about adults-only venues may be worth making. It is quite possible that with casinos and bookmakers' outlets, as with bars, adults do not actually want a lot of under eighteens around while they are indulging in their grown-up pleasures—particularly, perhaps, their own children. It may be that this sense unconsciously plays a part in or feelings about adolescent gambling quite apart from our concern about the well-being of the young. As always, of course, we must be wary of regulators telling us that something needs to be regulated when all this really means is that they would like something else to regulate. And officious interfering with the pleasures and liberties of the young has always provided an area in which interfering officialdom can justify its existence relatively easily on the grounds that it obviously knows better than the young themselves what is in their best interests.

How regulation can effectively protect the vulnerable will depend on how the vulnerable are identified and in what their vulnerability is thought to consist. In general, people will be vulnerable to damaging their lives seriously through gambling either because, in some important way, they don't understand how gambling works or because they can't control their appetite for the pleasure that gambling offers. Children may be thought to be for the most part more vulnerable than adults on both scores. Just as they don't know what is good for them from a nutritional point of view and, left to their own devices, would overindulge in unhealthy eating, so it is plausible to argue that they can't really be expected to understand how odds work and, left to their own devices, would overindulge in making losing bets of various sorts. Also, they typically don't have much money of their own and therefore are likely, on the one hand, to be inordinately attracted to gambling as a means of getting rich quickly and, on the other, to be tempted to raise money for gambling in all sorts of undesirable ways ranging from getting into debt to stealing.

How much of this type of reasoning applies to identifiable classes of adults? It used to be thought that there was a strong case for preventing the poor from gambling. Particularly if the poor are also thought of as undereducated and unsophisticated, they may be thought of as being in the same position as children. They will be excessively tempted by gambling and easily gulled into losing much more than they can afford.

It is undoubtedly true that gambling appeals powerfully to the poor. For a certain kind of rich person, gambling provides the gratifications of engaging in conspicuous consumption that depends not on winning but on the awe they inspire, at least in themselves, by the sums that they are willing to lose, in other words, waste. Most gambling in the modern world, however, is indulged in by comparatively low-income people for whom medium-sized wins constitute significant, if transitory, wealth. Indeed, left-wing critics of the gambling industry deplore precisely the fact that most of the winnings of gambling operations come from poor people who can least afford their losses.

It would, of course, be easy to regulate the gambling industry to exclude the poor simply by requiring would-be gamblers to furnish proof of income at a specified level or to prove creditworthiness in a specified amount. To some extent, devices such as dress codes or entrance fees work to discourage at least the very poor from entering casinos. More interestingly, perhaps, some jurisdictions, such as Monte Carlo, that have developed gambling specifically as a means of attracting rich foreign tourists have made it illegal for their own nationals to gamble. Australia, which has decided its own nationals have more than enough gambling opportunities, has considered preventing its own citizens from gambling on Australian-licensed Internet sites.

There are two fundamental problems with regulating to keep the poor away from gambling. The first is practical. As we saw in the previous chapter, one major reason why governments legalize gambling or other popular activities deemed to be morally undesirable or dangerous is the excessive costs and extreme difficulty of try to enforce prohibition. Similarly, measures designed to make it illegal for the poor to gamble are likely to spawn a lucrative illegal industry in betting, numbers games, and backroom casinos.

The more fundamental difficulty in trying to prevent the poor from gambling is a moral one, for it amounts to saying that poor people lack the intelligence and self-control to be able to decide for themselves how to spend their own time and money (even the little of it they have). Worse, it presupposes that poor people may legitimately be subject to paternalist government that takes away their fundamental dignity as autonomous moral agents entitled to chose for themselves how to live even if they—no less than richer people—will often make bad choices. In places such as South Africa and parts of the United States where a majority of the poor also belong to identifiable ethnic groups, this will come perilously close to saying that some people, because of their race, should be assumed to be permanent infants and treated accordingly. Even where this is not so, it is clearly unacceptable in a democratic society, where rich and poor are supposed to have equal rights, to discriminate against the poor by having laws or regulations that are designed to curtail their freedom to pursue pleasure in whatever (otherwise legal) way they choose.

The issue of regulating to stop minors from gambling is relatively uncontroversial. There is political consensus that this should be done, and it is fairly easy to enforce. The issue of regulating to stop only the poor from gambling is also relatively uncontroversial. There is political consensus that this should not be done, and those who wish to protect the poor from the evils of gambling agree that restrictions or prohibitions should apply to everyone equally. This leaves the question of regulating to protect those deemed to be peculiarly vulnerable to developing an addiction-like problem with gambling.

I will discuss in detail what can and should be done by governments to limit the amount of excessive gambling that occurs and the damage that it causes to gamblers and others when I discuss the whole topic of "problem gambling" in chapter 6. In general, the best government can do is to ensure that would-be gamblers are as fully informed as possible about the nature of gambling and the attendant risks, and that the most effective kind of help is readily available to people who do develop problems with their gambling. Otherwise the problem is comparable to that of preventing potential alcoholics from patronizing bars or liquor stores, though I will argue that governments could learn a good deal about what to do about alcoholism from studying the best practices of governments around the world in dealing with problem gambling. The problem, of course, is that, on the one hand, anyone can become a problem gambler, and therefore potential problem gamblers are virtually unidentifiable before they start to gamble. On the other hand, though full-blown gambling addicts are relatively easy to recognize and can in principle be banned from gambling, this might prove formidably difficult to enforce in practice both because of the problems associated with certifying people as mentally incompetent in any respect and because of the ease with which determined addicts would be able to find gambling opportunities where these are otherwise legally abundant. Moreover, many therapists would argue that criminalizing the behavior of gambling addicts may militate against the most effective therapeutic interventions.

REGULATING VENUES

Regulations concerning where gambling may take place concern four main issues:

- Number
- Size
- Location
- Type as defined by permitted activities

One potent reason for regulating the number and size of venues licensed to supply especially casino gambling services is to limit the number of casinos in a jurisdiction and thereby create monopoly or oligopoly profits because suppliers being protected from competition can charge higher prices. These abnormal profits can then be captured by government in the form of taxes of one kind or another. There is nothing intrinsically immoral about this. If people have moral objections to the government capturing what are technically known as "economic rents" from gambling—effectively, profits from the sale of oligopoly or monopoly gambling licenses—their objection is to the securing of benefits for government (i.e., for taxpayers) from an activity they deem to be immoral in itself, or they have principled objections to discriminating against gamblers by making them pay more than the natural market price. We shall explore this issue in the next chapter and consider what can be said for and against the policy of artificially restricting supply as a way of raising funds for government-approved projects. Apart from this aspect of economic policy there are three main reasons why governments seek to regulate the premises on which gambling may take place:

- For ease of regulation
- From considerations relating to problem gambling
- To give expression to the wishes of local communities

Where the regulation of gambling activities requires a substantial measure of on-the-spot monitoring by human inspectors, it is clear that the more premises there are needing to be inspected, the more resource-intensive the inspection process will be. At some point, the expense involved will be intolerable either to the state or to the industry as regulatory costs erode profits.[6] This is sometimes cited as an argument for limiting the number especially of small gambling operations, such as clubs or small arcades or rooms attached to bars or restaurants, that offer gambling facilities such as a couple of dozen gaming machines. The same argument is also sometimes used to support the general undesirability of "ambient" gambling, that is, gambling that takes place at a venue where the primary purpose is to offer services other than gambling—supermarkets and corner shops, laundromats and gas stations, airports and railway stations, et cetera.

Obviously the force of this argument depends on what the regulations needing to be physically enforced are. It is plausible to say that the objective of keeping out minors means limiting numbers and types of outlet, but then presumably all premises licensed to sell liquor could also be licensed to offer gambling machines. Also, it is unclear why preventing minors from gambling on machines requires that they be physically excluded from the premises where these are housed instead of, as with cigarettes, pornography, and scratch cards, requiring vendors to enforce the prohibition against underage customers.

Another argument for more stringent limits on numbers based on the difficulty of regulating large numbers of gambling outlets would be that in the interests of protecting customers—and perhaps taxpayers—the games themselves need to be physically inspected. Perhaps this is thought necessary to check that the measures to prevent cheating are being properly implemented. Perhaps there are rules about whether and where alcohol can be served or smoking engaged in, about what signage and leaflets must be available informing people about problem gambling, about the supervision of minors in nongambling areas, and so on. The difficulty with this argument is that in gambling venues of all sorts, the most effective form of monitoring to prevent cheating is electronic, and most of the other considerations are applicable to many other kinds of retail outlet where the costs of inspection are not unduly burdensome or expensive, partly because they can fairly easily be performed as part of normal policing.

The requirement that the number of places offering betting, selling lottery tickets or providing machine gambling needs to be limited because of difficulties of regulation is not persuasive. What can be said is that when a community is, for whatever reason, somewhat hesitant about introducing legal gambling and wishes to be sure that such gambling as it does allow is closely supervised, then the best way of providing reassurance to the general public may be to have a limited number of relatively large operations dedicated to the supply of gambling services, which can both be, and be seen to be, subject to a high level of personal inspection by regulators, even if this level of supervision is unnecessarily high and unnecessarily highly visible.

There is another consideration relating to ease of regulation and number of legal gambling venues that tells decisively in favor of starting with a limited number of gambling outlets rather than simply leaving it to market forces to determine how many there should be in any particular area. This is that it is always easier to expand the number of licensed premises than to contract it. This has been the experience of jurisdictions as varied as Moscow and Namibia. In both cases, easy access to a license for venues to offer casino-type gambling resulted in what was eventually agreed by almost everyone to be an excessive number of small slot machine casinos. However, so entrenched were the legitimate economic interests of the licensees that it was formidably difficult for government to take away licenses once they had been granted.

Another set of arguments for regulating the premises on which gambling may take place relates to strategies for reducing the risks of problem gambling. There are three arguments of this type that are of especial importance. These relate respectively to regulating

- The location of gambling premises
- The activities that may take place within gambling premises
- The specific anti-problem-gambling measures that must be in place on premises where gambling takes place

The first argument is used against ambient gambling generally and slot routes in particular. (Slot routes are collections of gambling machines operated by one company by arranging to place machines in a variety of sites other than casinos ranging from bars and bookmakers' offices to gas stations and convenience stores. The operator pays the owner a rental, or more commonly, a percentage of the gross gambling revenues—money staked less money paid out in winnings or total player losses.)

The argument asserts that slot routes and ambient gambling foster problem gambling and that, from a problem gambling point of view, it is desirable to have casino gambling only available at some substantial traveling distance from urban population centers. There is a plausible psychological reason for thinking this may be so, which runs as follows. At least some problem gambling is reasonably characterized as an "impulse disorder,"—a function of the fact that people are unable to control their impulses or, to use older-fashioned concepts, that they have a propensity for giving into temptation. When this is so, it seems obvious that the more temptation that is placed in people's way, the more likely they are to succumb. Put more scientifically, it seems reasonable to believe that the more decisions people have to make before they can start gambling and, once started, before they can continue, the less likely they are to succumb to impulsive behavior that offers instant gratification but is overall self-damaging. Put colloquially: force people to stop and think about what they are doing, and the more likely they are to avoid behaving foolishly.

These considerations make resort casinos, located out of town at a fairly substantial distance from an urban gambler's home or work, seem likely to prove a relatively safe venue compared with an urban casino located much nearer to where potential gamblers live and work. The same arguments apply to prohibiting off-course bookmaking and restricting betting on horse races to bets made at the racetrack. To get to a resort casino or racetrack usually involves considerable planning as well as travel time and is most likely something that you will reserve for more or less special occasions. Going to an urban casino or an off-course bookmaker is easier because these venues will be located nearby and can easily be visited whenever you feel like spending an afternoon or an evening gambling. Going to any kind of dedicated gambling venue, however, requires making a conscious decision to go gambling well in advance of actually gambling. If, by contrast, one is simply out shopping or going out for a meal and one is confronted with a gambling machine, offered a scratch card, or given the opportunity to place a bet, then no prior decision is needed, and one is much more likely to gamble impulsively.

The hypothesis that ambient gambling and especially slot routes dramatically increase the opportunities and therefore the temptation to gamble unthinkingly and thereby increase the incidence of problem gambling has some commonsense appeal but has not yet been scientifically confirmed.[7]

The same hypothesis supports the second argument about the regulation of premises to mitigate the incidence of problem gambling. This is the view that regulators should determine both what gambling and what nongambling activities may be engaged within licensed gambling premises. For instance, in the U.K., live entertainment of any sort was until 2002 prohibited in casinos, and alcohol could not be served where betting takes place. Bets may still not be made in bars or pubs. However, although both bookmakers and bars/pubs may have gambling machines, the number is limited as is the size of the maximum stake and prize. This practice of having more restrictive rules governing the size of stakes and prizes for gambling machines outside of casinos than for those located in casinos is almost universal. The thought is that low-payout machines are "safer" from a problem gambling point of view and should therefore be the only type of machine permitted in venues where machine gambling is "ambient," that is, not the principal activity for which the venue is intended. Jurisdictions also often restrict the availability of cash-dispensing machines and the use of credit cards on the assumption that if gamblers have, for example, to leave the premises or at least the gaming floor to get more cash, this will make them less likely to give into an impulse to gamble more than they originally intended.

The third type of regulation that, in the interests of curbing problem gambling, is often imposed on premises where gambling may legally take place concerns the services that must be made available specifically for this purpose on the premises. At the least there is likely to be a requirement that brochures and pamphlets be available warning customers of the dangers of problem gambling and indicating where those with problems can get help. There may also be a requirement that warning signs be displayed on gambling machines or in the areas where gambling takes place. This is similar to the health warnings that governments require be printed on cigarette packets. In some jurisdictions, casino companies even provide a resident counselor or clinical psychologist with an office on the premises who is available to treat people with gambling problems.

As we shall see, when we come to consider the question of problem gambling more comprehensively, it is regrettable that little is presently known about what causes excessive gambling and consequently about what measures are effective in preventing people from engaging in excessive gambling. It seems likely that much regulation in this area is driven by a concern to be seen to be doing something even if there is no great confidence that the regulations imposed will actually reduce the number of problem gamblers. In the absence of better scientific knowledge, a "scattershot" approach to problem gambling, which tries a variety of different measures in the hope that some of them will hit their target, may be the most politically sensible. There is a danger, however, that problem gambling concerns are used illegitimately both by those who are simply antigambling and by commercial gambling operations who are seeking protection from competition.

I suspect that regulations about the number, type, and location of venues where gambling may take place, though often ostensibly about questions of ease of regulation and problem gambling, are really motivated by considerations of giving expression to the wishes of the community. By this I mean that the real reason we don't want gambling machines to be located everywhere that there might be a market for them is that, for some rather undefined reason, we just don't. We don't think it desirable or appropriate that people should be confronted with gambling machines in the same profusion as they are found in Nevada. In Reno or Las Vegas, visitors encounter gambling machines in the concourse of the airport and thereafter at practically every other venue, including shops of all sorts, where conceivably they might fancy playing a few coins. We recognize that this may be appropriate in Reno and Las Vegas because these are places where people go to gamble, and gambling is the principal industry of these cities. However, we as citizens of "normal" towns and cities are disposed to think that so much gambling is just excessive. We don't want gambling machines everywhere, and we probably also want only a limited number of urban casinos and other gambling operations in our city. Our reasons may well be intuitive and, as such, much less tangible than pointing to apparent concrete issues such as regulatory practicality and problem gambling. For example, we may well feel that to have as much gambling as the market will bear will lower the quality of life in our town, or we have aesthetic objections to having gam-

bling houses on every corner. These considerations are not as strong as thinking that all gambling is immoral or dangerous, so the less of it we have the better. They do not support prohibition but rather a view that says, "Let us have
legal gambling in moderation." This is, however, a position that, though eminently sensible, politicians may find it in practice uncomfortable to espouse. For
one thing, it is hard to differentiate it from paternalism. For another, it requires
interference with the operation of free markets and more generally confronts
politicians with the unpalatable and usually unnoticed fact that the requirements of democracy sometimes clash irreconcilably with the demands of individual liberty. For yet another, it is difficult to judge what a majority of people
would agree is the right number and kind of gambling outlets in any particular
community.

For these reasons, politicians find it easier to appeal to other less nebulous arguments when legislating to restrict the number and type of venues in their jurisdiction where gambling may take place. Nevertheless, the argument for
regulating the number and type of gambling premises in a given area in accordance with the wishes of the (majority of) the inhabitants of that area is a strong
one based on the right of communities to democratic self-determination. It is a
much stronger argument in relation to relatively small communities such as a
county than to relatively large ones such as a whole country. The reason for
this is that if a minority of the inhabitants object to the absence of gambling facilities (or of liquor stores or of sex shops) in their county, they can fairly easily move or at least travel to a nearby jurisdiction where these amenities are
legally available. Where a prohibition applies to an entire country, this is not so.
In other words, the democratic case for allowing a majority to restrict the freedom of individuals on moral or aesthetic grounds becomes less objectionable on
libertarian grounds if those individuals can easily exercise the relevant freedom
elsewhere. In many jurisdictions, from California to Switzerland, effect to this
principle is given through the device of referenda that have determined not
only whether gambling shall be legal but where, how much, and what kind of
commercial gambling should be legalized.

It may usually be impractical to subject the minutiae of gambling policy with
respect to gambling venues to referenda. There is, however, another reason, derived from the most compelling of political considerations, why governments
should err on the side of over-restricting the availability of gambling venues of
all sorts. This is that it is much easier to expand the availability of gambling opportunities than to contract them. This is important because often, perhaps
usually, at the point where gambling is about to be legalized or gambling law
liberalized, the general public will not have strong feelings for or against the introduction of new casinos and other commercial gambling operations. A couple
of years or so after changes in the law, especially if this has resulted in what is
perceived as an excessive proliferation of commercial gambling outlets, there
may well be a backlash in public opinion. The typical view will now be not that
we should have stayed with prohibition or with other highly restrictive policies

but that we should not have gone as far as we have. A consensus may emerge that we now have too much gambling. This sort of view prompted the Clinton administration to set up the Federal Review of Gambling. The view is currently also widespread in political circles in Australia and South Africa, where, illogically, it has prompted politicians to seek to ban the supply of Internet gambling services to their own citizens by their own licensed gambling companies while still not making it illegal for citizens to gamble on far less rigorously regulated foreign sites. The reason these governments are behaving in this illogical way is that what they would really like to do is to reduce the number of land-based gambling opportunities available to their citizens, but because of the vested interests that are now entrenched, they cannot do this. They are consequently forced to do something whose effect is purely symbolic.

The conclusion to which all these considerations lead is that it is both necessary and morally desirable that governments should seek to furnish their citizens with neither more nor less commercial gambling opportunities than they or a majority of them want. This justifies government, even more potently than considerations of ease of regulation and the desire to mitigate problem gambling, in regulating the number, size, location, and type of venues at which gambling may take place. In attempting to assess public opinion, governments should not only try to ascertain the current state of public opinion but also try to anticipate how it may change. To the extent that they are uncertain about the long-term state of public opinion and are faced with a choice, they should opt for policies that are likely to leave the public wanting more liberalization rather than less.

REGULATING MARKETING

To the extent that commercial gambling is regarded as simply another sector of the entertainment business, the same rules should presumably apply to the marketing of its products as apply to other "normal" entertainment offerings. In particular, whatever is permissible when advertising a restaurant or a theme park should apply to advertising a casino, and whatever is permissible in advertising chocolate should be permissible in advertising betting services or lottery tickets.

As we have seen, nobody regards the gambling industry as entirely like the restaurant or chocolate industries.[8] For one thing, gambling is thought to be a form of recreation suitable only for adults. This means, perhaps, that there should be constraints on how gambling is marketed, so that children are not targeted and their exposure to gambling advertisements is restricted. Some products can be advertised only in "adult" time on television, and the trailers for R-rated movies have to exclude the scenes for which the R rating was awarded. Also, gambling is deemed to be potentially risky to the mental health, to say nothing of the material well-being, even of adults. Perhaps, therefore, gambling should carry the equivalent of the health warnings that have to be printed on tobacco products as well as being featured in all cigarette advertisements.

But should regulation of the marketing of gambling products go further than this? In the United Kingdom after 1968, a legal doctrine was developed that provided a strong affirmative answer to this question. This was the doctrine that legal gambling should only cater to "unstimulated demand." The result was that demand could not be stimulated by any form of advertising or other marketing strategy. This doctrine was underpinned by, and gave expression to, the view that gambling should reluctantly be tolerated by government, given that some of its citizens seemed determined to gamble whether gambling was legal or not. However, gambling was essentially an undesirable activity, and nothing should be permitted that might encourage people to take up gambling who otherwise would not have done so.

In the United States, answers to the question of whether there should be special restrictions on the marketing of gambling tend toward the negative because of the strong commitment in American political culture to rights generally and the right of free speech in particular. The First Amendment to the U.S. Constitution, which protects freedom of speech, is usually considered to give at least some protection to so-called commercial freedom of speech, that is, the right to say what you like to further your commercial interests. The consequence is that attempts to regulate advertising have to be wary of constitutional challenge, which in practice means that short of being obscene, treasonable, libelous, fraudulent, likely to lead to a breach of the peace, or in some other way contrary to statutory or common law, the general rule in America is that if a commercial activity is legal, it is legal to advertise it. Notwithstanding this, the advertising of gambling has been subject to quite exceptional constraints in the United States.

For a long time, legal gambling in the United States was the only industry in the United States that was not generally allowed to advertise.[9] This situation resulted from the Federal Communications Commission's decision that advertising or indeed information about lotteries may not be communicated by mail or over the airwaves together with the further ruling that all gambling games are lotteries including card games played in casinos. This situation has been subsequently amended. What remains interesting is that opposition to amending federal law so as to permit the advertising of casino gambling came from congressmen who still wished to use the law to inhibit people's freedom to spend their own time and their own money in pursuit of legal pleasures of their own choosing. They wished to inhibit this freedom of choice because they judged gambling to be evil. What this shows is the frailty of the commitment of even American politicians, for whom the right to life, liberty, and the pursuit of happiness are supposed to be self-evidently sacrosanct, to according to people the right to live their lives as seems best to them even if this results in their living lives in ways which others judge to be sinful or contrary to their real best interests.

A more subtle question about marketing gambling products relates to the question of how ordinary codes of conduct governing honesty in advertising work out in practice when applied to gambling. For example, what should happen when people place advertisements offering to teach people how to win at gambling on slot machines or to sell them systems for winning at roulette?

Given that it is impossible, in the long run, to win on these games, presumably the offers must be fraudulent. But should the law rely on the principle of caveat emptor that requires buyers to take suitable precautions against buying fake goods, or should such schemes be outlawed in the way that pyramid selling schemes are outlawed? And what if the recommended technique for winning consists in learning to practice a particular form of prayer or meditation or even developing expertise in such psychic arts as telepathy and telekinesis?

There are no simple and self-evident answers to these questions. However, given the sensitivity of the public to the issues of problem gambling, on the one hand, and of defrauding gambling customers, on the other, gambling regulators—and indeed the gambling industry—have a powerful interest in acting to outlaw the marketing of schemes of this sort.

More controversial is the question of when the advertising of gambling should be banned on the grounds that it is misleading. For example, should it be permissible for lottery and casino advertising to stress how many people have become millionaires through gambling? Arguably, this misleads through suppressing the truth about the probably larger number of people who ruin themselves through gambling and the certainly vastly greater number of people who overall lose money by gambling. Also, what about advertisements that suggest that being a gambler is a highly sophisticated thing to be and one that will improve your attractiveness to potential sexual partners?

The fact is that many advertisements of nongambling products are misleading in similar ways. Logically impossible claims are made for detergents to the effect that they wash not only whiter than other detergents but whiter than white itself—and this thanks to their magic blue ingredient. Sophistication and sexiness are used (or abused) to sell everything from cars to wines to cell phones. And in general, all advertising exaggerates the benefits and minimizes the disadvantages of buying the goods and services being advertised.

The vulnerability of the gambling industry to negative public perceptions means that it may well be prudent for regulators to apply stricter standards against misleadingness in the advertising of gambling than are imposed for other products. In particular, there is a strong case for outlawing any advertising of gambling that creates the impression that the odds on winning are better than they are. Since the odds in any gambling activity constitute its price, perhaps advertisements should be required to include information about what the odds are: this might be rather more effective than a health warning. Be that as it may, as we shall see when we address the question of problem gambling more thoroughly, achieving the desired result of protecting the vulnerable is not so much a matter of prohibiting certain kinds of advertising content; it is rather a matter of having a positive campaign of public information that ensures that people understand what the difficult concepts of random numbers and very long odds mean in practice when applied to betting.

It is worth noting that what matters most to the gambling industry about advertising is not the need to advertise gambling as, for example, an easy way to solve money problems—"Find yourself in debt? Why not borrow some more and stake it all on red at our friendly roulette game? You've got an almost fifty-fifty chance of winning, and if you lose, you'll still only have debts which you can't pay, which is what you've got now. So what have you got to lose?"

What the industry needs—and is in many jurisdictions denied—is the opportunity to make the public aware of the availability of the products and services they offer in a perfectly truthful way. The other thing the industry requires and often does not get is a level playing field that ensures that, for example, if state lotteries can be advertised in one way, then casinos can advertise in the same way.

This also applies to the other main area where regulators often seek to restrict the marketing of gambling services, namely, their attempts to outlaw so-called predatory marketing. Predatory marketing, as the name suggests, seeks to exploit human weakness by making it abnormally difficult for consumers to refuse to buy the goods and services on offer. It invariably involves the creation of a false impression without, however, making any claims that are not literally untrue.

Many complicated hire-purchase schemes have all over the world been used to give especially the poor the impression that they can afford to buy consumer durables when they cannot. The object of the campaign is secure large nonrefundable initial payments and then to repossess (and resell) the item in question after the purchaser has wholly predictably defaulted on two or three monthly payments. Marketing expensive brands of clothes to children on the basis that they will lose face among their peers if they do not wear the branded item may fall into this category. The marketing campaign itself creates the prestige for the branded article among young peers, and the idea is to get children to put pressure on parents that they will find it hard to resist. Cold-calling people and telling them they have won either a luxury car or a foreign holiday on a South Seas island is often another example of predatory marketing. It typically turns out that "winners" have to spend an afternoon or evening being subjected to the marketing of time-share holiday schemes, that they have only won a chance to participate in a draw for a luxury car, and the foreign holiday they have won in the South Seas does not include the huge costs of getting there.

In the area of gambling, marketing to children, even if it is not expressly prohibited, is usually pointless because children are not allowed to gamble anyway. There are, however, two other aspects of the marketing of gambling that are often prohibited or restricted by regulation on the grounds that they are predatory. These are the issuing of credit and the supplying of complimentary goods and services, for example through loyalty programs. In both cases, the worry is that the issuing of credit and the practice of "comping" will form part of a predatory marketing strategy that will lead vulnerable people to gamble more than they can afford.

It is not clear that this worry is well founded. Gambling companies do not normally have an interest in giving people more credit than they can afford. Unlike, say jewelers, there is not even an object that gambling companies can repossess in the event of nonpayment. Moreover, for the vast majority of gamblers, how much credit they can obtain is determined by their banks or credit card companies. It is only in the rarefied world of very high and usually foreign high rollers that gambling companies feel somewhat reluctantly obliged to take the risks involved in extending credit.

Similarly, with offering complimentary drinks, meals, hotel nights, airfares, or whatever to regular customers, typically through the device of a loyalty card, gambling companies are really doing no more than supermarkets or airlines do with their loyalty programs. They have a strong incentive not to do too much of this because the costs of these programs come off their profits. There is an exception in the case of supplying free drinks in gambling venues, but here the obvious worry is that free alcohol will be used as a device for undermining normal prudence and inducing gamblers to bet recklessly. Otherwise, while it is possible that some people gamble more—just as it is possible that some people shop more—because they are "saving up" for some product or service that they can buy with loyalty points, this doesn't seem to be a good reason for prohibiting such programs or lifting them out of the competitive marketplace.

In both cases, it is the special political sensitivity of the gambling industry that makes people think that it should be treated differently from others in respect to marketing, and regulators may for this reason be wise to pay special attention to how the marketing of gambling services is generally perceived. But in general, it seems that the evils of predatory marketing to the extent that they can be defined and clearly identified are more prevalent in industries other than gambling. In other words, with the regulation of marketing gambling products, the case for abnormally restrictive regulation derives, as it does with all other aspects of abnormal regulation in the gambling industry, less from the need to avert objective dangers than from the need to accommodate public perceptions of danger.

NOTES

1. A particularly good example is Nicholas Pileggi's 1996 novel *Casino* (Corgi Books), from which Martin Scorsese made a successful film.

2. It is interesting that the U.K. Gambling Review Report (the "Budd" Report) followed the evidence submitted to it by the Gaming Board of Great Britain in stipulating

that the three objectives I have listed are the only three that justify interfering with the normal operations of market forces in the gambling industry. Subsequently, in discussing the report, Sir Alan Budd himself has added that a fourth legitimate consideration is concern for the social environment.

3. *Journal of Gambling Studies* 16, no. 3 (fall 2002), guest-edited by Rina Gupta and Jeffrey Derevensky, is devoted to the subject of youth gambling and brings together much recent work in the area of measuring adolescent gambling behavior.

4. See R. Stinchfield, "Gambling and Correlates of Gambling among Minnesota Public School Students," *Journal of Gambling Studies* 16, nos. 2–3 (2000).

5. See the discussion in M. Abbot, B. Palmisano, and M. Dickerson, "Video Game Playing, Dependency, and Delinquency: A Question of Methodology," *Journal of Gambling Studies* 9, no. 3 (1995): 247–63.

6. On the whole, the cost of regulation is not much more than irksome to the gambling industry. What is of much greater concern is regulations that affect their profitability such as a ban on smoking in gambling venues, as partially imposed in South Africa. For a study of this kind of regulatory impact in Atlantic City, see M. Nichols, "The Impact of Deregulation on Casino Win in Atlantic City," *Review of Industrial Organisation* 13, no. 6 (1998): 713–26. All aspects of South African gambling law and regulations are set out and discussed in Hendrik Brand, *Gambling Laws of South Africa* (South Africa: Juta, 2002).

7. There is, however, good evidence for the closely related hypothesis that a high degree of general impulsiveness is associated with excessive gambling. See H. R. Lesieur and R. J. Rosenthal, "Pathological Gambling: A Review of the Literature," *Journal of Gambling Studies* 7, no. 1 (1991): 5–39. See also A. Blaszczynski, Z. Steel, and N. McConaghy, "Impulsivity in Pathological Gambling: The Anti-social Impulse," *Addiction* 92, no. 1 (1997): 75–87.

8. For a general discussion, see J. Stearns and S. Borna, "The Ethics of Lottery Advertising: Issues and Evidence," *Journal of Business Ethics* 50 (1995).

9. For a fine account of the legal bizarreries involved in this situation, see I. Nelson Rose, *Gambling and the Law* (Hollywood, Calif.: Gambling Times, 1986), chap. 5.

Chapter 5

The Economics of Gambling

Advocates and opponents of legalizing gambling or of liberalizing gambling law appeal respectively to the economic benefits and the economic costs that will allegedly flow from making commercial gambling more readily available. For this reason, it is vital for policy makers to have an accurate understanding of how the economics of the gambling industry work. We have already discussed (in chapter 3) some of the difficulties in trying to translate a decision about whether to legalize gambling into an objective calculation of the relative costs and benefits of adopting this policy rather than any alternative. We have also seen (in chapter 4) that a vital decision that governments must make in relation to any policy, including gambling policy, is the question of which groups of people they wish to advantage and disadvantage. Notoriously, all policies adopted by governments are likely to have unintended consequences, and part of good policy analysis consists of trying to foresee as accurately as possible what the consequences of different courses of action will actually be. Economics can contribute to good policy making to the extent that it enables us to make explicit the consequences of different possible choices in areas where there are material gains to be made and losses to be suffered.

In this chapter, therefore, we will explore some key economic concepts and insights and apply them to the analysis of different public policy options available to government in relation to commercial gambling. This use of economics will not in itself enable us to prescribe what is the best course of action for governments to pursue, since that will depend on the overarching normative goals and values that governments set themselves and the priority they accord to different goals and values when these conflict. What it will do is to make it easier for governments to avoid making decisions thinking they will have one result when, in fact, they are much more likely to have another.

In this chapter, I will mainly be seeking to explain how some fundamental economic principles apply to the workings of the gambling industry and its regulation. But I will also be advancing a thesis, namely, that under most circumstances introducing or extending the availability of commercial gambling services has relatively small impacts, either for good or for ill, on the overall economic well-being of society. Gambling is rarely a significant engine of economic growth. The main economic benefit accrues to the consumers and suppliers of gambling services, and as we shall see in the next chapter, the main costs consist of comparatively small possible increases in the misfortunes associated with problem gambling. However, a well-regulated gambling industry can play a role of some significance in relation to economic redistribution and as such contribute, albeit modestly, to government objectives in reducing poverty. This occurs if abnormally high gambling taxes are used directly to benefit the least advantaged in society. It also occurs if gambling is so regulated that the economic activity it brings is focused on a particularly needy rural or urban area. It is consequently crucial for policy makers to be able to follow the money involved in the gambling business—where it comes from and where it goes.[1]

The key economic phenomena we will explore in relation to the legalization and regulation of commercial gambling are

- Competition
- Taxation
- Displacement

COMPETITION AND SURPLUSES

The essence of commerce or trade consists in the efforts of people to make themselves better off by exchanging what they presently have for things that others presently have. What people presently have may be material objects, or it may be the time, energy, and talents that enable them to produce various sorts of goods and services for themselves and for others. Exchange is possible only because people value things differently. Since I am rich, I value $100 less than you do who are poor. Consequently, I believe I can make myself better off giving you $100 to cook me a meal or in exchange for a jacket you are wearing. But I will only be able to do this because you believe you will make yourself better off by accepting the $100 and parting with your jacket or giving up your time in order to deploy your culinary talents cooking for me. For us to value the objects of our exchange sufficiently differently that we can strike a deal, it is not necessary that one of us be richer than the other. I might especially like your jacket, whereas you have grown tired of it; and I may hate cooking, while you get a great deal of satisfaction from it. What is necessary is that we both reckon that we gain from the exchange, and this would be impossible if we both valued what we are exchanging identically.

Money is the medium through which we express the value we put on different goods and services, and the price in money at which an exchange takes place
indicates a point at which both buyer and seller think they are making themselves better off. But this point or price is likely to be only one of a range of
points and prices at which a mutually profitable exchange is possible. Typically,
the price could be somewhat higher or somewhat lower, and still both parties
would think that overall they were benefiting from the exchange.

Commerce, then, essentially consists in people trying to buy and sell goods
and services at the price most favorable to themselves, buyers seeking the lowest price and sellers the highest. There is always a highest price at which buyers are willing to buy and beyond which they will simply keep their money for
other purposes, and a lowest price at which sellers are willing to sell below
which they will adjudge it better to hang on to their goods or withhold their
services. Buyers and sellers are both aware of their "opportunity costs," that is,
in the case of buyers, other goods and services on which they could be spending
their money; and in the case of sellers, the other uses to which they could be
putting their capital and labor. The actual price will be along the continuum between the lowest price at which sellers are willing to sell and the highest price
at which buyers are willing to buy.

In a free market where government does not interfere with the bargains that
willing buyers and sellers strike among themselves, what this actual price is
will be determined by how much competition there is among buyers and sellers. Now, clearly, if a commodity is in short supply, there are likely to be many
buyers and few sellers. In this case, the sellers will be able to sell at a higher
price. Conversely, if the product is readily available, there are likely to be many
sellers and few buyers. In this case, the sellers will have to lower prices. Competition among sellers drives the price down toward the lowest price at which
sellers are willing to sell, and absence of competition among sellers drives the
price up toward the highest price at which buyers are willing to buy.

Obviously individual buyers and sellers will have their own maximum and
minimum prices. If the price rises above a certain level, some buyers, but not
others, will drop out of the market and use their money for other purposes. If
the price falls below a certain level, some suppliers, but not others, will devote
their time, talents, and energies to other lines of business or perhaps to leisure
pursuits. This means that there is an optimal price from the sellers' point of
view, which results in the best possible combination of large numbers of people
and high prices so as to ensure that the total amount of money being spent on
the sellers' products is as great as possible. This optimal price is what sellers
would charge if they did not have to compete for business.

From the buyers' point of view, the advantage of having many sellers competing with one another is that their purchases cost less. Conversely, with many
buyers and few sellers, the price goes up, and so do profits to sellers. In the absence of competition—when, for example, the price is set by government—the
price may be set too low because government wants to be popular with con-

sumers. The market will then be undersupplied either in terms of the quantity of the goods and services available or in terms of their quality. (Californians will not be able to get electricity, for example.) When the government sets the price too high, typically because it is beholden to the owners or workers in particular businesses, consumers pay high prices for low-quality goods and services.

Clearly the total amount of money that would be spent by consumers paying the highest price that they will reluctantly pay for a commodity (if their only alternative is to do without it) will be larger than the total amount that will actually be spent if competition drives down the price of a commodity to the lowest point at which suppliers are still willing to supply it. The difference between the maximum and minimum total amount of expenditure is called the surplus.

If competition or any other economic force drives the price down below the highest price they are willing to buy at, this means that consumers have money left over (a surplus), which they can now spend on other things. If absence of competition drives the price up beyond the lowest price at which sellers are willing to sell, what would have been a consumer surplus now becomes abnormal profits for the suppliers—known as "monopoly profits" if competition is so restricted that there is only one supplier, or "oligopoly profits" if competition is restricted so that there are only a few suppliers.

How big this difference is with respect to any product depends on how sensitive that product is to variations in price. If the price of a particular vegetable or soda goes up sharply, it is probable that consumers will settle for a cheaper alternative vegetable or drink, so there is not much room for pushing the price up by taxation or by cornering the market on cabbages or Coca-Cola. On the other hand, people will probably continue to buy gas or alcoholic drinks in nearly the same quantities even of the price does go up considerably. This is technically known as the "price inelasticity of demand." A product is said to be "price elastic" if changes in price result in significant changes in demand and "price inelastic" if demand tends to stay constant whatever the price. It is a crucial fact about the gambling business that its products, like the products of the liquor industry, are price inelastic, meaning that people will continue to play at poor odds (pay a high price for the pleasure of gambling) if those are the only odds available. Consequently, the potential surplus with respect to gambling products is very large, and it is possible to levy exceptionally high rates of taxes on gambling products and make exceptionally large profits from a monopoly.

This is a fact of vital importance to the gambling business because it means that profitability is likely to be crucially determined by how far above the minimum price for gambling products, which would be set by free-market competition, suppliers can set the actual price. In other words, profitability is crucially related to the degree to which suppliers are protected from competition.

When a product becomes more readily available for whatever reason—technological innovation, lowering of tariffs on imports, decriminalization or deregulation, increased supplier enthusiasm, et cetera—the surplus increases: buyers are presumably willing to pay the same maximum price as they were before, but sellers are willing to sell at a lower price, so the gap widens.

The question of what happens to surpluses, that is, to the money that is the difference between the maximum amount of money that consumers are willing to pay and the minimum amount of money that sellers are willing to accept, is a crucial question for economic policy generally and for economic policy in regard to gambling especially. There are three potential beneficiaries from increases in the surplus:

- Suppliers, who may succeed in securing a monopoly (or oligopoly) and use this power to retain the new surplus in the form of increased profits
- Consumers, who may capture the surplus in the form of lower prices
- Government, and through government the general public, which may capture the surplus in the form of taxes

Normally, in free-market economies, governments legislate to prevent the development of monopolies or oligopoly cartels. They do this to ensure, on the one hand, that consumers benefit from the greater choice, better products, and cheaper prices that competition generates and, on the other, that people who would like to enter the market as suppliers are not unfairly prevented or inhibited from doing so. However, even in societies committed to free markets, there are some economic activities where supply is necessarily restricted by the nature of the product. This is true of public utilities and of exploitation of the airwaves. Here government typically seeks to preserve the benefits of competition by regulating prices to consumers and by issuing licenses to a limited number of suppliers through a competitive tendering process.

To the extent that governments seek to capture a part of the surplus for the public, they normally do so by imposing value-added or general sales taxes that are neutral between different types of goods and services and do not discriminate, for whatever reason, against one form of business as opposed to another. Sometimes, however, governments decide to tax some goods at abnormally high rates either because they wish to discourage consumption or because they think the higher prices that these abnormal taxes will generate will not be unduly unpopular. The obvious cases of this are taxes on tobacco, alcohol, and gambling.

Where a commercial activity is illegal, however, it is likely to avoid paying taxes and will not be vulnerable to normal antimonopoly laws. Moreover, it is likely to be supplied by criminals who are relatively uninhibited about using force to further their commercial interests. It is likely, therefore, that criminal monopolies and cartels will be established and that the surplus will largely accrue to suppliers in the form of monopoly profits.

COMPETITION, SURPLUSES, AND THE LEGALIZATION OF GAMBLING

Let us now consider how the general economic principles regarding competition apply to the legalization or deregulation of commercial gambling.

In the commercial gambling business, what is traded is the pleasure of playing games for money. The price at which the trading takes place is mainly set by the odds against winning that the players accept. Worse odds for players are higher prices. If a gambling machine has a hold of 10 percent, this means that the odds against winning are 10:9. If it takes ten minutes to play $100 in a machine without recycling the winnings, then on average, at the end of ten minutes, you will have $90 left, and it will have cost you $10 for the pleasure of ten minutes' playing time. Perhaps you would still play the machine even if the hold were 30 percent and ten minutes of play cost you $30. Perhaps the operators of the machine would still find it worthwhile to supply you even if the hold were only 2 percent and your ten minutes of gambling pleasure cost only $2.

The surplus in the commercial gambling business, as in any other, is the difference between the total amount of money that can be extracted from players in conditions of perfect monopoly and the total amount that will in fact be extracted from them if perfect competition drives the price down to lowest point at which suppliers remain willing to supply.

If a government decides that it will make commercial gambling more readily available—by licensing lotteries or casinos, for example, or by extending the number of events on which bets may be taken or of venues where gambling machines may be located—this is likely to have two consequences with respect to the surplus.

First, the previously prohibited gambling activities will cease to be only available from illegal suppliers who pay no taxes and are not subject to antimonopoly laws. This means that the surplus in the existing business is now more likely to be captured either by consumers in the form of better prices or by government in the form of taxes.

However, legalization also eliminates the costs, both material and psychological, to consumers and suppliers alike, of acting illegally. Suppliers shed the costs of evading law enforcement and can therefore supply at cheaper prices. Also, mainstream businesspeople who are unwilling to be involved in illegal activities will now enter the market. Competition and lower costs will drive down the price of gambling to consumers who will also not have to overcome their unwillingness to break the law. This means that the size of the total gambling market will be likely to grow substantially.

Those who are opposed to gambling on principle and believe that governments should do whatever they can to reduce the amount of gambling that takes place in society are thus right to oppose legalization and deregulation. The result of these measures is indeed very likely to be an increase in the amount of gambling that takes place, and it will not simply be a case of those who were previously forced to gamble illegally now doing so in a controlled and legal environment.

Be that as it may, what is principally relevant for our concerns here is that as the gambling industry expands, so does the surplus. There is now more money overall that can potentially be extracted from gamblers by charging monopoly prices rather than the prices that perfect competition would result in. What happens to this new enlarged surplus under conditions of legalization?

If governments decide to treat gambling as simply another part of the pleasure business and treat selling lottery tickets and operating a casino as no different from selling chocolate or running a theater, then they will leave the supply of gambling to the operation of normal, competitive market forces, charging only the normal consumption taxes that they charge on (almost) everything else. Under these circumstances, the bulk of the surplus would be returned to the consumer in the form of better prices and cheaper gambling.

But governments hardly ever do treat gambling as simply another part of the entertainment or pleasure business.[2] As we have seen, they typically restrict the number and type of businesses that can supply gambling services because they foresee unmanageable problems with effective regulation or because they are seeking to reduce the incidence of excessive gambling or because they intuit that the public want a limited but not an unlimited number of gambling outlets. They also typically realize quickly that gambling is an exceptionally attractive industry from the point of view of generating tax revenues. This is for three reasons. First, abnormally high taxes can be imposed without affecting the profits of suppliers so adversely that the business ceases to attract investors. Second, the consumers to whom the taxes are passed on in the form of higher prices or worse odds either don't realize that this is happening or, if they do notice, don't mind.[3] Third, nongamblers and even gamblers probably prefer to pay high taxes on a luxury leisure activity that feels inessential than, for example, on gasoline expenditure, which feels like a necessity even when it isn't.

When these two kinds of considerations come together—the opportunity to be simultaneously socially responsible and fiscally popular—the case for government to secure abnormal tax revenues becomes resistible only where there is strong principled opposition to gambling or where government views the potential contribution to tax revenues as trivial.

We must now consider, therefore, in more detail the various ways in which government may capture an abnormally large share of the surplus from the gambling industry for the benefit of the general public.

TAXATION: GENERAL PRINCIPLES

Taxation is the device whereby members of a community contribute to the funding of goods and services that benefit them collectively.[4] Taxation makes sense only to the extent that it is more effective and efficient to provide and pay for these services on a communal basis administered by government than to allow or require individual members of the community to make their own arrangements to secure these benefits. Government thus raises taxes to protect us from foreign aggression, and we all wind up being better protected because this service is communally provided than if we each had to protect ourselves from foreign aggressors. The same is true of the protection that governments afford us with respect to our basic rights (however identified) and in preventing others from using force and fraud against us to further their interests at the expense of ours.[5] Probably, the same is true with respect to protecting the environment. Perhaps it is true of ensuring that adequate health care and educational services and a minimum standard of living are available to all regardless of wealth or ability to earn.

To avoid the injustice that would arise if some members of a community contributed to these common goods while others did not—the problem of "free riders"—taxation has to be compulsory. Everyone is subject to taxation, and how much individuals contribute is determined by governments. In theory, governments set taxes on the basis of what will be fair and efficient. In practice, at least in democracies, they are influenced by considerations of how their taxation policy will affect their popularity and, therefore, their chances of reelection.

Despite this, it is not surprising that citizens do not typically like paying taxes, and in a democracy, if they feel strongly enough that they are not getting good value for the taxes they are paying, they can do something to remedy the situation without defying the law or resorting to revolution. Indeed, it is one of the great moral advantages of democracy over other forms of government that the people collectively have the ability to vote governments out of office if they think they are being overtaxed or poorly serviced and think they would get better value for their tax dollars from a new set of rulers.

Democracy is a system of government that by its very nature forces politicians to constantly confront the problem of how to acquire and retain enough electoral popularity to get elected and reelected. Now, political popularity depends on giving people—or at least causing people to think they are getting—what they most want; and what people most want is extensive and high-quality public services combined with low taxes. People, in seeking this combination, are behaving as rational consumers of political products. Nevertheless, combining high-quality public services with low taxes confronts all democratic governments with a delicate balancing act. In these circumstances, any strategy for raising funds for the public purse that is minimally resented by, or is even popular with, the general public will be highly attractive to government. Raising money from gambling constitutes precisely such a strategy.

TAXATION AND MONOPOLY LOTTERIES

State and national lotteries furnish the clearest and most widespread examples of how this works. Commonly in the United States and elsewhere, lotteries have been illegal. Often they were made illegal because unscrupulous operators defrauded the public by absconding with the proceeds. Otherwise, they were outlawed on the grounds that they are a form of gambling and as such immoral. In recent times, many governments—thirty-nine state governments in the United States, including the District of Columbia—have reintroduced them as a way of raising money for public interest projects. Historically lotteries were introduced to fund special, one-off projects such as the construction of canals, bridges, and other items of transport infrastructure or of additional facilities for schools and colleges.[6] More recently, lotteries have been used effectively to supplement the general operating budgets of governments by having the proceeds earmarked for services that the government would otherwise have to provide out of general taxation, such as the running costs of education or health or police or fire services. We will return to the implications of these different ways in which governments spend lottery profits. First we need to look carefully at how these profits are generated. From the point of view of governments, the principal purpose of licensing lotteries is to produce contributions to public expenditure that will be less unpopular than raising ordinary taxes. Government is therefore not concerned to make itself popular with lottery players by ensuring that the surplus that legalizing lotteries creates is returned to consumers. Rather, they wish to appropriate this surplus for the public purse. Consequently they wish to ensure that the lottery generates monopoly profits that can then be captured by government in the form of either direct or hypothecated (i.e., earmarked) taxes. Governments consequently protect their lotteries from competition as far as possible and typically permit only one substantial lottery to be operated in their jurisdiction.

A particularly clear and successful example of how this works in practice can be seen by looking at the national lottery in the United Kingdom that was introduced in 1994 and benefits from having been able to learn the lessons of best practice from older lotteries around the world in North America, Europe, and Australasia. The U.K. lottery is now one of the largest in the world, played regularly by over 70 percent of the population and with a turnover of about £5.5 billion ($7.75 billion) per annum, of which well over 80 percent comes from the National Lotto game, the rest from scratch cards.[7]

This lottery is a monopoly as was recommended by the Rothschild Commission,[8] which proposed its creation in 1978. No other lottery organization is allowed by law to offer prizes of over £100,000 ($150,000), and in practice no other organization competes significantly with the national lottery with respect to offering huge prizes for very small stakes. When it was introduced, the national lottery all but wiped out the football pools industry, whose share of this market fell from nearly 100 percent to around 10 percent. The national lottery also has about 95 percent of the scratch card market.

What happens to all this money? The answer is that for every £1 ($1.50) spent on the U.K. lottery, the distribution is as follows:

- Fifty percent is returned to the punter in the form of prizes.

- Twenty-eight percent goes to a government-regulated fund for "good causes," most of which goes to projects that government might otherwise be expected to fund in the areas of health, education, the environment, the arts, sport, heritage, and public works; the rest goes to private charities.

- Twelve percent goes to government in the form of straight taxation.

- Five percent goes to the 25,000-odd Lotto retailers and the 10,000-odd instants-only retailers.

- One percent goes to investors in the form of profits.

- The remaining 4 percent goes to operating costs, including the costs of competitive salary packages for employees.

In practice, the contribution to good causes averages a little higher than 28 percent, mainly because uncollected winnings are also added to this fund. Leaving this aside, the key numbers show that the odds against winning are 2:1, which means that the equivalent of the house advantage or "hold" is a massive 50 percent as compared to the less than 10 percent typical of gambling machines in casinos. On the other hand, what the suppliers are actually taking is not 50 percent of turnover but only 10 percent. This means that under circumstances of untrammeled competition, the price of play as determined by the odds against winning would be driven down to at least 10:9, and 90 percent of the price of all lottery tickets would be returned as prizes. What these numbers show is that the surplus in lottery products—the difference between the highest price punters will pay and the lowest price sellers will sell at—is at least 40 percent or, on a turnover of £5 billion, £2 billion. This is the money that government captures to promote the public interest by combining a straightforward 12 percent tax with a quasi-tax in the form of compulsory contributions of at least 28 percent to good causes overseen by government.[9] Put another way, the U.K. lottery is effectively taxed at 80 percent of gross gambling revenues, that is, money wagered less money paid out in prizes.

The U.K. government could in theory extract even more for itself if, like state and provincial lotteries in North America and many other parts of the world, it owned and administered the lottery itself. However, the U.K. government took the plausible view that operating gambling businesses, including a large lottery, is best left to professionals rather than civil servants. Consequently, it devised a competitive tendering process to select an operator.

It is particularly interesting to see how this has all worked out from the point of view of securing the interests of politicians, which, as we have seen, consists in raising taxes and quasi-taxes in a manner that is minimally resented (not vote losing) if not indeed positively popular (vote winning). The success of the U.K. lottery in capturing the surplus from a well-patronized lottery business has been huge. Because it is a monopoly, the U.K. national lottery, like other national or state lotteries, has been able to charge monopoly prices in terms of the odds it offers. Consequently it has generated monopoly profits that have been spent by government and its agencies. There is no question that the U.K. lottery has been successful as a revenue generator.

The U.K. lottery has, however, come in for public criticism in three areas. First, the salaries and bonuses of its senior management, though in accord with initial contracts and in line with other remuneration packages for top executives, have come in for especially sharp criticism. This is undoubtedly because there is a feeling that a lottery that is intended to be funding good causes assumes something of the character of a charity. This means that the public think it wrong for lottery managers to be paid the high fees that are commanded by other captains of industry, since the money is coming from what would otherwise be available for good causes. It may be in general that in the U.K., and a fortiori in the United States, senior executives of publicly listed companies are overpaid. But there is no objective reason to think that lottery executives are unusually overpaid given their levels of responsibility. This public perception, however, even if it is thoroughly unwarranted, may be a good reason for having a lottery entirely run by public officials—as is the norm in the United States and most other parts of the world.

Second, the U.K. lottery has been criticized for misspending the money that has accrued to good causes. The most notorious example of this has been the funding of the Millennium Dome in London, which has caused the government acute embarrassment, given that almost immediately after opening, the Dome proved economically unsustainable as an entertainment complex. More generally, there is a feeling that lotteries fund extravagant projects that would not get past the normal competition within government for public funds. A particular complaint that is often leveled against lotteries is that they constitute a regressive and therefore unfair form of taxation, since most of the money comes from the poor, and at least a disproportionately large amount of it gets spent on projects that mainly benefit the middle classes such as college scholarships and subsidized opera.

Finally, the U.K. lottery has come in for a lot of criticism for the way it has awarded the monopoly license to its operator. In particular, allegations of dishonesty and incompetence were leveled against the competing bidding companies, and charges of political skulduggery as well as incompetence were leveled against both the license-awarding body and the U.K. government itself.

What these criticisms show is that where monopoly lotteries are used as an exceptionally effective way of raising money for governments, governments need to be especially sensitive to negative public perceptions. The point of introducing these lotteries was, after all, to make government look good by funding public interest projects in a relatively painless manner. If, however, governments bungle the way the funds are expended or the way the monopoly license is awarded and operated, they will find that they make themselves politically unpopular. In addition to all this, governments, especially in the United States, face strong criticism from the antigambling lobby, which believes that it is wrong for the state to be benefiting from, let alone becoming dependent on, revenues from gambling.

TAXATION: CONVENIENCE GAMBLING

Governments do not, however, need to go the monopoly route to capture a substantial share of the surplus from the gambling business.[10] The most radical alternative is to permit unlimited and competing gambling outlets and tax them all at an optimally high rate. This is what happens with convenience gambling, which seeks to ensure that whenever someone might feel like gambling, the opportunity to do so is always conveniently located nearby. Convenience gambling also covers all forms of "ambient" gambling—gambling at venues where the principal activity is something else like drinking or shopping—and includes scratch cards sold in shopping malls and bets offered in bars. However, the most extensive form of convenience gambling is provided by slot routes, that is, gambling machines outside of casinos—in bars, taverns, restaurants, grocery stores, gas stations, and the like. This is called the "slot route" industry because a number of gambling machines in different venues are owned and operated by a single company and may, indeed, be linked for purposes of generating jackpots. From the point of view of a government considering only tax revenue maximization, gambling machines located outside of casinos represent a highly attractive means of capturing the surplus from the public's appetite for machine gambling. This is because the cost of supplying machine gambling outside of casinos is very low. A few machines in a bar or at a filling station require very little space, maintenance, and human supervision. Otherwise, the costs to the suppliers are the cost of the machine and the rental of the site where the machine is housed. In theory, such machines can offer an identical product in terms of games and odds to what is offered in casinos (though without the glamour and glitz). This means that if a government can tax gambling machines in casinos at a rate 20 percent higher than "normal" businesses, then maybe it can tax gambling machines outside casinos at an additional 50 percent without making the price of play less attractive to consumers than it is in casinos or less profitable for suppliers.

Perhaps then, as we noted in the previous chapter, we should have a free market in the supply of gambling machines, except that we would tax them at an exceptionally high rate. This would have the advantages that people would on the whole prefer that their governments raise revenues through gambling taxes rather than through increases in income taxes, property taxes, or taxes on other consumer products such as gasoline. It would also ensure that the market for machine gambling was saturated, since machines would appear wherever there was a market for them. Consequently, government would be getting the maximum possible tax by capturing the whole of the surplus in the largest possible market.

Governments usually reject this. Indeed, the case of slot routes shows that, and explains why, hardly any policy makers anywhere in the world are pure free-marketeers with respect to the gambling industry. Given that, other things being equal, gamblers prefer to play their game of choice at the venue that is geographically closest to them, a free market would result in gambling machines proliferating in whatever number and offering whatever combination of stakes and prizes at every venue where there might be a market. Typically, there would be some restriction on venues because of the need to keep out minors, but most venues could fairly easily cordon off an area of their premises for machine gambling to which minors were prohibited access. This would make machine gambling approximately as easily accessible as buying cigarettes or liquor or erotic magazines.

Why don't governments pursue this policy—especially governments that are otherwise committed to free markets—and treat gambling generally as a part of the pleasure industry, which it is quite reasonable to tax at abnormally high rates? The real answer is that public opinion wouldn't stand for it. Whether because they feel that gambling generally (and machine gambling in particular) is unhealthy or merely unattractive, majorities of electorates probably feel that though they welcome some commercial gambling outlets, they do not want too many of them; they don't want gambling to be "everywhere." Also, some substantial and vocal minorities want as little gambling as possible and will vote for any party that promises to reduce gambling opportunities. On the other hand, very few voters think failure to provide more gambling facilities a good reason for voting against a government. This means that governments have little reason to fear providing too few gambling opportunities and much reason to fear providing too many. Governments do, after all, get thrown out by electorates for permitting the emergence of what the public decides is too much gambling. Such prudent political caution is reinforced by the consideration that it is always easy to expand gambling opportunities if it turns out that that would be popular, but it is very difficult to reduce them if, as commonly happens, a popular backlash against gambling sets in after legitimate commercial interests have become established.

Governments, then, seldom permit the development of machine gambling, in particular, in response to market forces alone, and the reasons they give for not pursuing market policies in this area include the following:

- It would risk exacerbating problem gambling.
- It would be impossible to regulate properly.
- It would run counter to the wishes of the electorate.
- It would be difficult to reverse if that became desirable.

A further and often decisive reason that influences government is that a slot route industry is likely to cut into the revenues from other forms of gambling and therefore undermine the share of revenues that government secures for itself. This latter point does not matter to government from a pure revenue generation point of view. If the contributions of lotteries or casinos or bookmakers to the exchequer fall because of slot routes, this can be more than compensated for by the taxes that the routes themselves generate.

However, if the revenues are earmarked in some way, and especially if they are bound up with labor-intensive infrastructural projects designed to benefit the community as a whole, then it may be economically and politically disastrous to allow slot routes to undermine other gambling revenues. This is at least part of what went wrong in New Orleans, where the casino revenues were to some extent undermined by video lottery terminals. The consequence was that for this and other reasons, the casino simply could not generate the gaming revenues necessary to fund all the developmental and cash contributions to the state government that it had promised to secure the monopoly license.

Governments, then, need to remember what some call the fundamental lesson of economics: you can't have everything.[11] As a general rule, they are happy to limit the availability of convenience gambling and accept that this will probably reduce their overall tax revenues from gambling. They do this for reasons of political acceptability and indeed would probably like to outlaw all convenience gambling if they could. The only really decisive pragmatic argument in favor of having a slot route industry is in circumstances where the alternative would be to have a vigorous illegal industry.

CASINOS

Trying to discover and design the best policy for a jurisdiction to adopt in relation to the introduction of casino gambling constitutes the subtlest and most demanding challenge with which the regulation of the gambling industry confronts governments. There are at least four reasons for this.

First, casinos can be treated by governments with respect to taxation at any point on the continuum between monopoly lotteries and unrestricted slot routes. In other words, casinos can be given a monopoly in a particular area, and governments can then seek to capture the monopoly profits; or casinos can be allowed to proliferate in response to unfettered demand, and government can impose uniformly high taxes.

Second, casinos are often intended to offer a range of amenities other than gambling with a view to attracting nongamblers within the jurisdiction and both gamblers and nongamblers from outside of it. This means that casinos can be both local entertainment centers and tourist attractions. This is likely to excite both hopes and fears among local citizens both about the nature of a substantial new amenity and about the prospect of attracting a lot of tourists.

Third, casinos are usually large buildings that are likely to be highly visible within a community as well as attracting visibly large crowds of customers. Their impact, therefore, on the public consciousness is likely to be dramatic whether for good or ill. Unlike either lottery outlets or slot route venues, which are likely to be very small and integrated with other retail outlets, casinos are usually freestanding and imposing structures that tend to act as a focus for all the public's thinking about gambling generally.

Fourth, and most important of all, casinos offer economic benefits to governments other than those that accrue from gambling taxes. In particular they may offer jobs of all sorts, especially during the construction of the casino. Government may, in addition, extract from the casino companies a commitment to building additional structures, sometimes called "add-ons," which are not related to gambling but thought to be of general benefit to the community. These additional structures may include conference centers, hotels, theme parks and rides, and even upgrades of transport infrastructure or the construction of canals or monorails.

With casino policy, then, more than with any other form of gambling, government has to be clear about what it wants its policy to achieve and whom it wants to benefit. It must also realize that there will have to be trade-offs between different public policy objectives and different interest groups. Moreover, because there are different alternative policies that serve different interests and promote different objectives, there is no one best policy for any particular jurisdiction. Communities have to make up their own minds about what, if anything, they want from casino gambling in their area and must express those wishes through ordinary democratic processes. Only after governments have worked out what they want to achieve on behalf of their electorates will they be able to address the question of what policies and regulations will be the most effective in securing their chosen objectives.

It is necessary to begin a discussion of these alternatives with some definitions and discriminations. This is, perhaps, surprising, since it might be thought obvious what people are talking about when they talk of casinos. However, unless there is clarity on the issue of definition policy makers are liable to succumb to confusion, and laws to end up full of loopholes and inconsistencies.

The core definition of a casino is that it is a place of business where the primary business is selling the opportunity to play games for money. This, however, covers everything from small gambling houses with a bar and a dozen or so slot machines in them as found in Namibia, through the luxury high-roller gambling clubs of London, to the massive hotel-casino complexes of Las Vegas. Casinos emerged in the United States from the gambling clubs and other exclusive and expensive venues of eighteenth- and nineteenth-century Europe, where the dominant activity was cards and dice and later roulette. In fact, casinos, as they are now found in the United States and in the rest of the world that has followed the American example, are large structures, catering to mass markets, in which many forms of gambling are offered, usually including table games, but where the dominant activity is the playing of large numbers of—at least a few hundred—gambling machines. Casinos also very often offer other forms of entertainment and invariably offer food and beverages. Commonly, there is a hotel attached to them. This is what people understand by the word "casino" throughout North America, in Europe with the peculiar exception of the U.K., in Australasia, and in those parts of Asia and Africa where casinos of any sort exist. Rarely, however, is a casino defined in law by minimum size or by the types of activity that may or must be offered in it.

Casinos could, therefore, be places where the only gambling activity was machine gambling and the size of the venue very small—housing, say, a couple of dozen machines. This means that casino-style gambling could mainly take place in venues that are no more than arcades with gambling machines in them. This is what happens, for example, in Spain, where gambling machines in bars and arcades generate about ten times the revenues of the casinos. This is important because the smaller the venue in which machine gambling is permitted, the closer it approximates to convenience gambling and the more, consequently, any benefit that accrues to the state will come in the form of straight taxation rather than in the form of job creation or additional buildings and facilities. The point at which a casino industry ends and a slot route industry begins is not self-evident, and legislators and regulators need to make a decision about this.

The other main misunderstanding that needs to be cleared up in relation to what casinos are arises because, thanks to film and television, casino gambling is closely associated in the popular imagination with Las Vegas. A common illusion among governments and electorates is that by legalizing casino gambling in their area, they are paving the way for Las Vegas–type economic activity and prosperity. In particular, they think that if they allow the building of Las Vegas–style casinos with exotic themes, enormous gaming floors, vast hotels, and live entertainment ranging from musical extravaganzas to boxing matches, they will attract leisure and business tourism from all round the world.[12]

This does not happen for clear economic reasons. The principle that people normally gamble, playing their preferred casino games, at the venue that is closest to them means that the catchment area for a casino grows larger in proportion as casino gambling is not available in its environs. If casino gambling is unavailable throughout most of a continent because it is illegal everywhere else, the result will be that the casinos where gambling is legal will have a huge, continent-wide catchment area from which to attract customers. This is, of course, precisely what happened in Nevada, and especially in Las Vegas, after World War II. It also happened in Monte Carlo and to a lesser extent in resorts such as Baden Baden in the nineteenth century that were the only places in Europe to have legal casinos. In this way, Las Vegas became a gambling destination, a place that people visited to gamble because they could not gamble nearer to home. The result was that Las Vegas, like its European predecessors, had a huge customer base and huge gambling revenues. As a result, gambling companies could afford to invest in expensive capital developments as well as keeping many other prices artificially low, such as accommodations, food, and travel. In this way, they could entice people to take gambling holidays rather than other kinds. Nevada government policy was naturally to encourage the development of Las Vegas as the world's premier gambling destination resort. They encouraged fierce competition within Nevada because this was the best way of ensuring that out-of-state customers got the best possible value for money and would there-fore be maximally disposed to spend their leisure dollars in Nevada. Moreover, politicians found that they could pay for most of the public services their elec-torate demanded by imposing only modest taxes on the casino business. They also found it prudent to subject their operators to stringent probity checks so that the public would be reassured that they were not being cheated.

Nevada is a stunning success story, and it is not surprising that other juris-dictions would like to emulate it. However, despite the fact that Las Vegas looks like a monument to the power of free markets, competition, and capitalism, the truth is that what was done in Nevada was only possible because Nevada se-cured for itself an effective monopoly by being the first, and for a long time the only, state in the United States where casino gambling was legal. What will happen to Nevada now that it faces competition from casinos operated by In-dian tribes in California remains to be seen. Perhaps Nevada will be able to reinvent itself as a general holiday destination whose profitability depends only to a small degree on gambling. Clearly this is the strategy the state is pursuing, and it may well prove a sufficiently strong brand to make the transition effec-tively. What is certain in Nevada is that unless Las Vegas and Reno succeed in generating substantial nongambling sources of income, the state's prosperity will decline dramatically as Californian gamblers find they can visit a casino much closer to home than the four-hour drive from Los Angeles and San Fran-cisco to Las Vegas and Reno respectively.

Las Vegas is the world's most sensational example of a gambling destination resort, but it is not the only one. After Nevada, New Jersey sought to capture major economic benefits for itself by licensing casinos in Atlantic City. The thinking relating to New Jersey was significantly different to that which drove the development of casinos in Nevada. In Nevada the idea was to create a fun capital for the whole of America, and indeed for much of the rest of the world as well. In New Jersey the idea was to harness gambling to the economic re-generation of an area that had suffered a decline in the prosperity it formerly derived from local tourism. Again, however, the key to success was having a large population nearby where casino gambling was illegal, most notably the population of New York. To what extent these economic objectives were real-ized is disputed.[13] In particular, it is disputed whether enough of the profits re-ally went to benefit the local population as opposed to being captured by the out-of-town casino companies and their shareholders. In the United States there seems to be a stronger consensus that the licensing of casino gambling in Biloxi, Mississippi, has been highly successful in cross-subsidizing the develop-ment of an expanded and revitalized tourist industry.[14]

In both cases, it is unclear to what extent the casino industry would be able to withstand competition in their principal catchment areas. In Atlantic City some competition already comes from Indian casinos of the sort that have been developed in Connecticut at Foxwoods and the Mohegan Sun. In the South, government seems to be quite concerned to protect Biloxi's success on the grounds that the whole region benefits. The New Orleans casino, by contrast, expected significant revenues from out-of-state tourists, but these did not materialize, and the bulk of the casino's gambling earnings comes from locals.

The general lesson from gambling destination casinos is that people don't travel to them to gamble unless they have no choice. This is confirmed by the experience of two other gambling destination resorts outside of the United States. Macao has been a highly successful gambling destination, even though it has had a murky reputation and its casinos have hitherto exhibited the poor standards of quality characteristic of businesses that are effective monopolies. Its success has owed much to the fact that in neighboring Hong Kong and elsewhere in the region, casinos are illegal. The example of Sun City in South Africa also confirms the point. Initially, it had a monopoly in providing casinos to the Johannesburg market. Subsequently that monopoly was destroyed when casinos became legal throughout South Africa. The result was that Sun City had to reinvent itself as a general tourist destination rather than as a gambling destination. It has been able to do this partly because its initial monopoly revenues from gambling enabled it to sustain huge investments in tourism infrastructure.

It is obvious that if a government is hoping to develop a gambling industry effectively as an export business in which most casino customers come from other jurisdictions, it will pursue very different policies to those that will be appropriate if it anticipates that the bulk of its casino's clientele will be local people. In the vast majority of jurisdictions around the world, and increasingly in the United States, the casino business depends on the demand for casino gambling among local people. Once it is recognized that legalizing casinos is not going to attract large numbers of people who will come into the jurisdiction to gamble, then the public policy decisions in relation to casinos are likely to be more restrictive. Government will want to satisfy the market for gambling at least to the extent that it provides a more attractive alternative to illegal gambling but will not necessarily favor the saturation of the market that a free market in casinos would ensure. Government will want to be able to defend itself from charges of negligence with respect to minors and problem gamblers and for this reason may want to limit the number of casinos it licenses. Government will also want to ensure that public perceptions of casino gambling remain positive, and government will be sensitive to the considerations that make it better to have too few casinos for public taste than too many.

Crucially, however, government will also realize that to the extent that the money from gambling is coming from its own citizens, the introduction of casino gambling is not going to bring new money into its jurisdiction; it will merely be recycling existing money. This means that economic benefits to the region will consist only of the following:

- Private benefits to consumers and suppliers
- Savings in public costs for policing, et cetera, by not having to enforce the law against illegal gambling operations

- Benefits from not having either to raise taxes in more unpopular ways or to forgo the government's ability to fund additional public interest projects

- Benefits from nongambling amenities and other infrastructure paid for by the casino

- Benefits from redistributing from richer to poorer rather than from poorer to richer, to the extent that that is considered in the public interest

I will return to these issues when I discuss displacement. Meanwhile what we need to consider are the choices that confront government about securing its share of the surplus from the introduction of casino gambling into its jurisdiction. Essentially there are five policy options in relation to tax:

- Have abnormally low taxes for casinos

- Treat casinos like any other segment of the leisure or pleasure industry, subjecting them only to normal planning regulations and normal taxes: allow casinos to proliferate like restaurants in response to supplier skill in satisfying consumer demand

- Treat casinos like any other segment of the leisure industry as above, but subject them all to abnormally high taxes: treat gambling like liquor and allow casinos like bars to spring up in response to market forces

- Treat casinos like state or national lotteries and create monopolies with a view to capturing the monopoly profits for the state

- Pursue a policy that combines elements of two or more of the above

The first or second options, as we have seen, are entirely appropriate when a jurisdiction is hoping to develop casino gambling as an export or tourism business in which the objective is to make casinos as attractive as possible to potential customers. This is because competition without the additional costs of abnormally high taxation—and indeed perhaps, as in Las Vegas, with artificially reduced costs through abnormally low taxation—is the best way of ensuring that customers get the most attractive range of products possible. The undoubted beneficiaries of free competition, in this area as in all others, are consumers. Where the state benefits from having more consumers because more consumers mean more foreign earnings, a policy of maximizing the number of (honest) suppliers will also maximize the benefits that accrue to the community as a whole.

A jurisdiction might also decide to have a pure free market in casinos on principle. It might take the view that free markets are the only morally defensible form of trade because they minimally restrict the liberty of consumers and suppliers. In this view, any non-neutral tax, which discriminates against a particular product or service, constitutes an unjustifiable attempt by government to direct consumer conduct. Alternatively, government might take the view that it should be consistent in its regulation of commercial activity and that there are no cogent reasons for treating casinos differently from hairdressing salons. In fact, political reality rarely yields to the consistent application of clear principles, and politicians, when developing a policy for casinos that are going to be overwhelmingly patronized by their own citizens, rarely forgo the opportunity to raise some relatively unresented tax.

Historically, the high, "sumptuary" tax options have been justified in relation to activities deemed to be "sinful," or if not sinful, at least sufficiently bad for those who engage in them that it is legitimate for government to use taxation to discourage consumption that it cannot or does not wish to outlaw. It has seemed natural to governments to discourage people from engaging in activities it deems undesirable by imposing high taxes and thereby making indulgence very expensive. This might be all right if, say, all the taxes raised from smokers were earmarked for projects designed to prevent or treat smoking-related diseases. The trouble is that governments rarely do this. Instead they use the revenues from smoking to fund general health care, education, and poverty relief programs. It then becomes very difficult for governments to pursue antismoking policies with the single-mindedness and clarity necessary to make them effective when they know that success will cause their revenues from tobacco taxes to shrink or disappear. This argument also applies to gambling. Fear of losing large tax revenues from gambling that supplement the general operating budget would be likely to vitiate any policies government might have for containing or reducing the amount of money that people, or some of them, spend on gambling.

If governments want to discourage gambling, then they should do so. If they want to raise money for the public purse, then they should do that. What they should not do is to fool themselves that by doing the latter, they are also doing the former. Probably, as we shall see, they are not because of the addictive nature of problem gambling, and they may make matters worse by creating the illusion of addressing the problem while in practice avoiding the measures that would, perhaps, be effective but would also lower tax revenues.

Once government has decided that it wishes to take advantage of the opportunity to raise additional and relatively unresented taxes from casino gamblers, the first decision it must make concerns how much of the surplus, over the period of time for which the casino license is given, it wishes to capture for itself, and how much, if any, it wishes to see returned to consumers in the form of cheaper prices. In doing this, the government needs to judge accurately the ideal proportion of the gross gaming revenues (player losses) it can tax away so as to maximize its revenues in dollar terms. It must not set the tax rate so high that it reduces total spending by so much that its net revenues are reduced.[15]

When government has reached a view on this question, it must then choose between alternative methods of doing this. There are advantages and disadvantages associated with each of the two main alternatives: unrestricted supply and restricted supply.

Unrestricted supply means that anyone with a project and the capital to back it can get a license to proceed, provided only that the new operator can meet the jurisdiction's qualifying requirements in terms of probity, et cetera. New casino projects will not be vetoed on the grounds that they would do damage to existing casinos or on the grounds that they would be unlikely to succeed given the

existing provision of casino gambling. Instead, if a would-be new operator believed that it could secure an adequate return on investment by growing the
market or by taking business away from current suppliers, government would
do nothing to prevent the new operator from trying.

The main advantages of this competitive option are the following:

- Competition will grow the casino market till it approximates to saturation, with the
  result that the earnings of casinos available for taxation will be maximized.

- Competition will ensure a better quality and variety of product is available to customers at a better price than would be the case if casinos did not have to compete for
  customers.

The main arguments that may tell in favor of limiting the number of casinos are:

- The greater the degree of exclusivity a casino license confers, the more the state can
  extract in terms of cash or investment in physical infrastructure from which the general public, rather than gamblers, will benefit.

- A limited rather than an unlimited number of casinos may accord better with what a
  particular community believes to be socially desirable.

Broadly, with respect to casinos, the majority of whose customers are going
to be local people as opposed to tourists, economic arguments favor a strategy
of competition in a free market, and political considerations favor a policy of restricting the number of casinos. Moreover, economic arguments favor general
taxes, but political arguments favor hypothecated or earmarked taxes.

The danger with hypothecated taxes is that they are both uncertain and in-
flexible: government cannot know from year to year how much people are
going to spend on the community lottery or at the casinos. It is sometimes consequently argued, especially within government, that all hypothecated taxes
are inefficient, and that this is especially clear when gambling is used to fund
public services. The problem is that income to government from lotteries and
other forms of gambling is uncertain, vulnerable to fluctuations in the popularity of particular gambling activities and in general levels of prosperity. This
means that government is likely to be getting either too much revenue for the
public service in question or too little. Suppose, for example, that casino revenues are used to fund the public library service. It is easy to imagine that a
highly successful casino will mean a library service so well resourced that it
cannot spend all the money that is earmarked for it. At the same time, public
schools and hospitals may be palpably underfunded. (In fact, these services are
always and necessarily underfunded to the extent that there is no limit to the
improvements that could in principle be made with increased funding.) Hypothecation ties government's hands and prevents it from transferring budget
from the library service to the schools and hospitals.

On the other hand, suppose that the money from lotteries or casinos is used
to fund some part of the running costs of the education or health services. Is

government supposed to fire teachers or nurses because a decline in the popularity of gambling or simply in the money people have available to spend on
gambling means that the hypothecated revenues also decline?

The truth is that hypothecated taxes do not make good economic sense. They
do, however, make excellent political sense, at least in some cases, of which
gambling is certainly one. The general political case for hypothecation is that it
reassures the public that the government officials are not squandering the taxpayers' money, in particular by spending it on themselves. Of course, if public
officials spent all tax revenues with the wisdom and altruism of Plato's philosopher rulers, then public suspicion would be groundless. Unfortunately public
officials are fallible, and the perception is plausible that if revenues from whatever source are not earmarked, much of the money will be wasted feeding the
insatiably gluttonous maw of the government's general operating budget. If
this happens, gambling will not be seen as providing any palpable public benefits. This will be particularly important when, as commonly happens, there is a
backlash against gambling a few years after the results of legalization or liberalization have become apparent.[16] This backlash, which focuses on the perceived
negative social and perhaps aesthetic impacts of casinos, is typically as unreasonable and ill founded in hard evidence, as were many of the public perceptions about the benefits in terms of economic salvation that casinos would bring
when legalization and liberalization was first being discussed.

Nevertheless, politics is about perceptions. What happens in politics is determined not by actual realities but by what people believe to be realities. It is
therefore important that when people start accusing government of having em-
barked on a policy of licensing too much casino gambling, government be able
to point to popular public interest projects—fully equipped sports complexes at
local high schools in deprived areas, or grants for research into, say, the causes
and treatment of addiction. In practice, in democracies, when political and economic considerations come into conflict, politics trumps economics. In the case
of the provision of casinos, the economic downside is small. If a city has a monopoly casino as opposed to as many as the market will bear, the vast majority
of potential gamblers will still go to the monopoly casino. Perhaps a free market would grow the local market, by providing a better casino gambling product at more convenient locations, by at most 20 percent. The additional tax that
could be extracted from this 20 percent (allowing for displacement, as described
in the next section) is likely to be negligible as a proportion of the total tax income of the licensing government. On the other hand, if the only contribution
to the public purse that casino developers have to make is a tax on earnings,
then they will only invest in buildings and facilities that they believe will increase their share of the gambling market and so their bottom-line profits. In
practice, this means they will keep their capital expenditure to a minimum and
build sheds full of gambling machines with perhaps a few table games as well,
where such accessories as there are—adequate car parking, some food and beverages—will be designed to meet the needs of gamblers as cheaply as possible.

Moreover, because the casinos are serving local people, casino companies will seek to place casino gambling facilities as close to where their customers live as possible. This will tend to favor a proliferation of casinos of the smallest size compatible with satisfying the taste of gamblers. How big that would be will depend on what the critical mass of gambling machines is for giving people enough "buzz" at their local casinos not to wish to travel to a bigger casino farther away. For casino gamblers there is a trade-off between convenience and proximity, on the one hand, and glamour and glitz, on the other. It is not unreasonable to speculate that in an average urban jurisdiction with a free market in casinos but with no slot routes, most machine gambling would take place in large number of casinos with two hundred or fewer machines.

As I have indicated, most jurisdictions reject this scenario on the rather nebulous, usually unarticulated, but nevertheless quite profound grounds that it would result in more casinos of a not very attractive sort than the public would be happy with. More positively, most jurisdictions regard restricting the number of casinos as a way of increasing the value of those licenses. Clearly, casino developers will make more money from their casino in proportion to the degree of exclusivity that the casino enjoys in its area, because they can charge higher prices. If government restricts the number of casinos in its area, it creates a degree of exclusivity for the casinos it does license, and it can consequently expect the casinos to pay for this exclusivity. Economists call this capturing the "economic rents." What this amounts to is government selling a degree of exclusivity or protection from competition to would-be operators over a specified period of time. Obviously the greater the exclusivity, the more valuable the license, and the more government can charge for it.[17]

This is the mechanism that enables governments to use the introduction of casino gambling as an opportunity to secure economic benefits for their community as a whole. In the simplest case, governments follow the Australian model, which is to have a single monopoly casino license per city and to sell this license by auction to the highest bidder. The price paid is the proportion of the anticipated revenues over the period of the license that the bidding company believes they can forgo and still make a satisfactory return on investment.

However, governments may choose to try to capture the equivalent of this sum in kind rather than in cash up front. If so, they will typically require casino developers to fund capital projects that further the public interest rather than only the interests of punters. Such projects range from building conference centers through restoring old buildings to installing or rehabilitating transport infrastructure. It is important for governments to understand that the natural economic benefits from introducing casinos—more business for restaurants, cabbies, pawnbrokers, et cetera—will mainly accrue in the area in and around the casinos themselves. Outlying areas may actually experience a decrease in economic activity. However, government may very well and wisely stipulate that the casino must fund specific projects in other parts of the jurisdiction. In Cape Town, South Africa, the casino undertook to fund, in terms of its successful bid, the construction of a canal and a conference center in the center of the town some ten miles away from the casino. In another South African jurisdiction, the casino proposed to finance a wildlife sanctuary in a totally different part of the region from where the casino was to be located. Both these projects were expected to enhance their respective regions' earnings from nongambling tourism. Because the money for these projects is coming overwhelmingly from local gamblers, governments try to harness casino projects to bringing economic benefits to areas perceived to be especially in need. This means that governments try to ensure that the net effect of introducing casinos is to benefit the poor by using funds spent by relatively affluent gamblers—they must be relatively affluent, or they wouldn't be able to afford to gamble at the casino—to make the poor better off. Most commonly they try to harness the introduction of casino gambling to projects of resort rehabilitation, urban renewal, and regional development.

The single most important lesson that all these considerations have for government is this: before they commit themselves to any policy in relation to limiting or not limiting the number and size of casinos, or to capturing, in advance or on an ongoing basis, some share of the surplus in cash or in kind, the first thing they need to do is to answer the question "What is it that we want the introduction of casino gambling to accomplish for our community?"[18] Cogent answers will range from using market forces to eliminate or prevent the emergence of an illegal gambling industry, to raising additional taxes, to securing funding for tourism infrastructure. Some of these objectives may be to some extent combined, and they will usually all need to be linked to strategies for minimizing the negative social impacts of casino gambling. If, however, government is adequately clear about what it is trying to accomplish by permitting the emergence or extension of casino gambling, then the best ways of securing its objectives are likely to seem fairly obvious. By contrast, when governments fail to sort out their priorities with respect to introducing casino gambling, the result is typically confusion and disappointment.

There is a difficulty about trying to capture monopoly or oligopoly profits by awarding the licenses to the best projects rather than to the highest bidders in an auction. If there are relatively few casino licenses being offered, there will typically be competition for them, and some form of tendering process will be needed to adjudicate between competing bidders. The advantage of an auction is that it is easy to set down the minimum conditions that every bidder must meet and then to adjudicate between qualifying companies on the basis of which one is prepared to contribute the largest amount of cash to government coffers. Under this system there is no uncertainty about which company has made the best offer, and the price is by definition the highest that any suitable candidate company is willing to pay. Neither of these things is so if a government prefers to say, "We shall award a specified maximum number of licenses to the companies whose projects, all things considered, promise the greatest overall benefits to the citizens of our area." In this case, it will be less clear, and therefore more controversial, why some bids are judged to be better than others. It may also be uncertain that the government has extracted the maximum value from the license-awarding process. As against these disadvantages, the "best project" approach has the substantial advantage over the "highest bidder" approach that it harnesses the creativity of the private sector in determining how to make the introduction of casino gambling maximally attractive to the widest possible section of the population.

Moreover, the difficulties of awarding the license equitably and intelligently can be to some extent mitigated if the authorities are adequately clear about the kind of public benefits they are seeking and the criteria they are using for adjudication. To demonstrate the fairness of their processes and avoid allegations of corruption or incompetence, they will also need to operate with a high degree of transparency, making public the consultation process they will adopt, the scoring or other evaluation system they will employ, and the content of their deliberations. Where licenses are awarded intelligently and honestly on the best project principle, it is probable that this is system that best secures the overall interest of the community, and it should not be more difficult to implement than any other competitive tendering process.

It should finally be noted that both objectively and from the point of view of satisfying the largest number of departments within government, it may be best to combine the ways in which the government captures the share of the surplus that is created by restricting the number of casinos. Thus some of the benefits to government and, through government, to the public might be taken in straightforward sales taxes; others might be secured through charging a substantial license fee either up front or annually, which may be earmarked as a contribution to good causes in one form or another; finally government might plan to collect the remainder in the form of developmental "add-ons" to the casino project itself.

To the extent that government decides to take some of its share of the earnings from gambling in the form of add-ons, it is important for government to calculate accurately what any proposed add-on is actually worth to the public. An add-on to a casino project is any item of capital expenditure that is not essential to the sale of gambling products. The core items of capital expenditure in a casino are the part of the building used to house gambling operations—the gaming floor and "back-of-house" offices and surveillance rooms—and the equipment used for gambling. Capital expenditure on anything else is an add-on. In the normal course of events, the developers of a casino would invest in add-ons that they believed would increase the volume and therefore the profitability of their gambling business. They would invest in parking if they thought that the cost of making parking available would be less than what they would forgo if they did not have parking facilities. They will typically offer basic food and beverage on this principle, not primarily concerned whether this part of the business is profitable or not in itself but rather with the gambling business they might lose if gamblers were deterred from visiting the casino because they couldn't get food and drink there. They might also invest in other activities if they thought these might be profitable in their own right without detracting from their earnings from gambling. They might supply cinemas and theaters and high-class restaurants on this basis. Ideally, from the casino's point of view, add-ons will serve both functions. A theme park with rides, for example, might be a profitable attraction in its own right, as well as serving to encourage gamblers to come and play at the casino while the nongambling members of their family go to the park. To the extent that any of these add-ons are subsidized from the earnings from gambling, they should be accounted part of the company's spending on marketing.

If by contrast, to secure a license, a casino company offers to spend $50 million on the construction of a conference center at a location far removed from where the casino is or on the upgrading of facilities at the local airport, then the casino company will benefit from this expenditure no more and perhaps less than other businesses in the jurisdiction. In this case, the project should be accounted a developmental (rather than a marketing) add-on and should be treated as a contribution to the public purse equivalent to paying $50 million in taxes or license fees.

It is not always easy to make the necessary discriminations in this area. For example, if a casino company commits to building a Ferris wheel on its property and to subsiding this to the tune of $1 million per annum, this will no doubt constitute a desirable addition to the available entertainment in the jurisdiction. However, it will also serve to encourage gamblers to spend more time and money gambling at the casino. Probably, most of the value of this investment is going to the casino and only a small part of it to the general public. Suppose now, by way of contrast, that the casino company offers to build the biggest Ferris wheel in the world, not necessarily located on the casino premises, and to subsidize this to the tune of $1 million per year. In this case, it may well be that people will come from far and wide to visit the jurisdiction with the world's biggest Ferris wheel. In this case, the value of the wheel is going mostly to general public and may do nothing for the casino's revenues from gambling. Under these circumstances, the subsidy may well be accounted a contribution to the public purse.

These accounting considerations are vital in competitive tendering process where a license is to be awarded to whichever project is deemed, all things considered, to secure the maximum benefits for the public as a whole. It should be noted that what is crucial here is to assess the value to the public, not just the cost to the casino. Bidding companies, in exercising their creativity, may after all have bad ideas as well as good ones. In particular, they may propose expensive projects that yield little value to the community as a whole.

These complexities sometimes incline jurisdictions to have a cash auction, which has the advantage of being unambiguously objective, or else to claim that its judgments have to be purely subjective, like preferring one architectural design to another. The truth is that measuring the value of add-ons in a manner that is fair confronts licensing authorities with difficulties, but they are not insuperable. And, indeed, from the licensing authority's point of view, it is well worth their while to master these difficulties, since it is by the add-ons that casino projects are overwhelmingly judged by the general voting public.

It should be noted in conclusion that it makes no difference to the casino companies how public authorities collect their share of the revenue. They are concerned only with the amount of cash they have to pay out of their potential earnings either to public authorities in terms of taxes, license fees, and developmental add-ons or to customers in terms of more competitive prices. Obviously they would prefer to capture some of the monopoly profits for themselves, and they may be expected to use all the arguments they can think of to persuade public authorities to enable them to do so. Provided, however, they can get an adequate return on their investment while paying themselves adequate salaries and fees, where "adequate" means better than they can get by deploying their capital and labor elsewhere, they will continue to do business.

The situation as a whole can be summarized diagrammatically as shown in figure 5.1.

The steps in the economic process that this diagram illustrates are as follows:

- Whether gambling is legal or not, players need to lose enough to cover the capital costs of supplying gambling, including paying a sufficient return in the form of interest or dividends to investors to ensure that they don't deploy their capital elsewhere.

- Whether gambling is legal or not, player losses also need to cover the operating costs, including paying employees enough so they won't take their labor elsewhere.

- Legalization brings down the cost of supplying gambling products (sometimes, as in the case of large casinos, from prohibitively high to affordable) and thereby creates or increases the surplus.

- Since government action creates this surplus, government decision will determine what happens to it.

- Government may decide that it should go to monopoly suppliers. A corrupt government may give gambling monopolies to its friends. More commonly, government may decide that the monopoly supplier should be itself. This is what normally happens with state lotteries and in, for example, Canada and Holland, with casinos.

- Government may decide to return the surplus to consumers. In command economies, they would try to regulate the odds, and therefore the price, so as to ensure this. By far the most effective way of ensuring that the consumers capture the surplus is for government to ensure that there is a fully competitive market.

- Finally government may decide to capture the surplus for itself in kind or in cash.

Figure 5.2 illustrates the options available to government in spending whatever share of the surplus it allocates to itself.

Quite often when governments are contemplating what to do about gambling, they begin to understand the logic of capturing the surplus from gambling and using it to fund economic development and provide an additional source of revenue for their exchequer. This in turn suggests to them the exciting prospect of major economic gains secured very easily. Excitement is likely to be intensified if they go on a fact-finding mission to Las Vegas and conclude

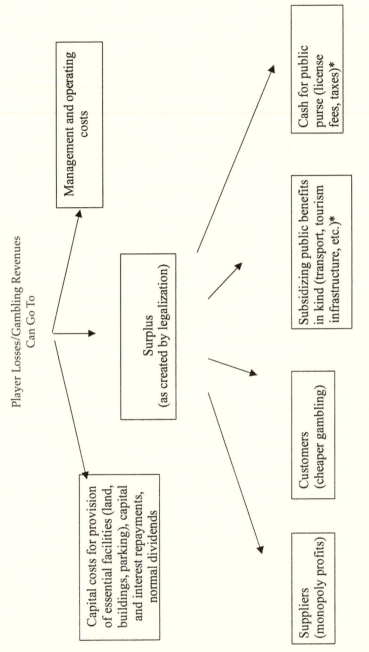

Player Losses/Gambling Revenues
Can Go To

Management and operating costs

Capital costs for provision of essential facilities (land, buildings, parking), capital and interest repayments, normal dividends

Surplus (as created by legalization)

Suppliers (monopoly profits)

Customers (cheaper gambling)

Subsidizing public benefits in kind (transport, tourism infrastructure, etc.)*

Cash for public purse (license fees, taxes)*

Figure 5.1 Destinations of Player Losses/Gambling Revenues
*=Benefits public

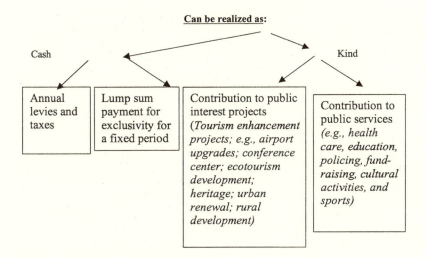

Figure 5.2 Feeding the Public Purse
Percentage (up to 100 percent) of the anticipated abnormal profits that public authority requires in return for restricting competition.

that introducing casino gambling is a surefire way to create, revitalize, or expand a tourism industry. Unfortunately, they neglect to ask the fundamental question that determines what kinds of economic benefits for the public the legalization of gambling might make available. This question is "Where is the money coming from? In particular, what is the money that is now being spent on gambling no longer being spent on?" What governments need to understand here is what economic activities new expenditure on gambling is likely to displace. To these questions we now turn.

DISPLACEMENT

It is convenient to identify four broad areas of spending from which the money that people spend on gambling might come. These can be represented diagrammatically, as shown in figure 5.3.

If the money that is being spent (i.e., lost) on gambling services after the legalization of new forms of gambling is money that would otherwise have been spent on existing forms of gambling, then that may be unfortunate for the existing suppliers who previously had their businesses protected from the new form of competition. Obviously, if new forms of gambling are introduced into a community, their success is likely to depend to some extent on their ability to compete with older forms of gambling. This will not necessarily be damaging to the old forms, since one of the things that often happens when new forms of gambling are legalized is that the overall market for gambling grows, so that

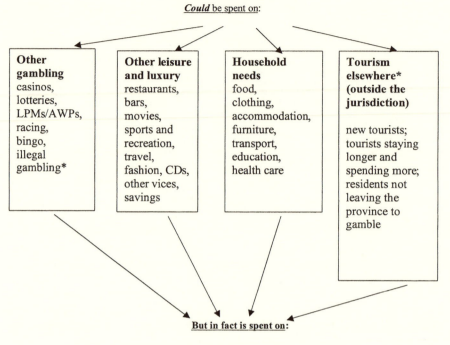

Figure 5.3 Sources of Income
*=Clearly benefits jurisdiction where gambling is allowed.

there are more gambling dollars to be shared among all sectors of the gambling industry.

However, some new forms of gambling will prove to be more attractive substitutes for older forms of gambling, and the older forms will consequently decline.[19] Lotteries with very large prizes of the sort that state lotteries are able to provide will typically displace smaller lotteries and other forms of pool betting. Off-track betting may mean less on-track betting, and the more ready availability of machine gambling frequently results in a decline in betting on horse races. However, government has no particular incentive—beyond that of winning favor with the threatened industries—in protecting one form of gambling from competition from another form of gambling. Indeed, considerations of satisfying gamblers' preferences and perhaps consequently of having a larger amount of gambling expenditure to tax will incline government toward encouraging competition. Certainly, to the extent that government is committed to free markets in principle, it will not regard it as appropriate to steer consumer choice as between competing gambling products.

The area where the case for protection is lobbied most strongly is horse racing.[20] It is argued, quite correctly, that if people stop betting on races and instead spend their money betting on gambling machines, the racing industry will suffer, and many jobs may be lost. Lobbyists for the racing industry often argue as if the fact that jobs will be lost, particularly perhaps jobs for people not easily employable elsewhere, automatically entails the conclusion that government ought to protect the racing industry. One way government could do this is by banning casinos and slot routes in areas where there are substantial numbers of people who currently bet on horses. The difficulty with this argument is that not only will government be interfering with consumer choice and discriminating against casino and slot route entrepreneurs; it will also be adopting a principle that would require government to ban all forms of technology, automation, and techniques for lowering prices that put low-paid people out of work.

An alternative suggestion is that government should accord racetracks special treatment with respect to being allowed to offer machine gambling. If government adopts a free-market attitude toward machine gambling generally or toward at least casinos, then racetracks will acquire licenses to offer machine gambling on the same terms as anyone else. This, however, is not likely to satisfy them because under a free-market dispensation, machine gamblers are likely to have equally attractive facilities located much more conveniently. If, on the other hand, it is suggested that racetracks should have an automatic claim in a situation where the number of licenses is restricted to maximize economic benefits to the region, then the question arises of why what, as we have seen, is effectively a hypothecated tax, should be deployed to benefit employees of the racing industry rather than being used to fund some other deserving cause. If there is a case to be made for using public funds to subsidize the racing industry, it is the same kind of case that needs to be made with respect to subsidizing any other business. And if there is a case for restricting the availability of machine gambling on social grounds (e.g., to reduce the risks of problem gambling), that case must be judged on its merits and without reference to its impact on the economic interests of other suppliers of gambling services, including the owners of racetracks.

There is, of course, nothing inherently wrong in a decision by government to legalize machine gambling for the specific purpose, inter alia, of preserving racetracks and the jobs associated with the racing industry. If government does this, however, it must be alive to the opportunity costs as well as to the more specific question of whether its policy will actually achieve the intended result. In particular, there is a risk, that if racetracks merely become local casinos, then the racing activities and the jobs associated with them are likely to decline anyway.[21]

The most plausible argument that can be made for according racing special treatment in competing with other forms of gambling derives from the fact that the costs of supplying betting opportunities on horse races are much higher than the costs of supplying betting opportunities on machines. This explains why the inability of racing to compete for the gambling dollar with machines is not due to the incompetence of the racing industry and therefore in some sense deserved. By itself this does not amount to a case for special treatment, since many deserving business fail in the face of competition with other businesses that can supply substitute products at a cheaper price. However, if government has a strong desire, based on the requirement of distributive justice, to promote the interests of the least-advantaged society, this may justify a policy of trying to protect employment for the rural poor. In this case a possible strategy would be to level the playing fields in terms of costs by imposing appropriately high taxes on machine gambling. In the event that the racing industry still failed to survive the competition, at least government would have tax revenues that it could redistribute to the rural poor.

Another interesting case of government intervening in gambling markets to secure the interests of one group of suppliers against another is the decision to grant special opportunities in the gambling business to Indian tribes in the United States.[22] This depended on exploiting a loophole in the law that allows tribes, as self-governing nations, to engage in any activities that are legal in the state where their reservation is located. The loophole lay in the fact that while states could make gambling activities legal or illegal throughout their territory, including the Indian reservations within it, they could not regulate how the games were played on Indian reservations. This meant, for example, that once California had in 1976 legalized charity bingo with a maximum jackpot of $250, the Seminole whose tribal land is located within California could offer bingo games with a jackpot of $50,000. Obviously Indian bingo competed with charity bingo games, to the detriment of the latter. This was done because of the perceived need to make reparation to Indian communities in the United States for past injustice. The law also allowed the development of commercial poker clubs by Indian tribes and eventually and most lucratively of casinos in areas such as Connecticut, where otherwise casino developments are not permitted. The result has been casinos such as Foxwoods and Mohegan Sun, which have made large fortunes for members of the resident Indian tribes, as well as for their non-Indian operating companies.[23] Permission for Indian tribes to offer casino gambling in California was finally granted in 2000 after a referendum in which huge sums of money were unsuccessfully spent by Nevada interests seeking to protect themselves from competition. How much damage will be done to casinos in Las Vegas and Reno by the introduction of Indian casinos in California remains to be seen.

In general, the decision by U.S. government agencies to allow Indian tribes to benefit from unique opportunities to offer various forms of gambling, which are not otherwise available in the states where the reservations are located, constitutes a rare and intriguing example of deliberately creating monopoly profits and allowing the supplier to enjoy them. This is a unique case. The only other circumstance where government deliberately ensures that the suppliers benefit from monopoly or oligopoly profits is where governments corruptly issue a limited number of gambling licenses to relatives and cronies of government members.

In the case of allowing Indian tribes to offer gambling opportunities unavailable elsewhere the idea is to capture much of the surplus in a restricted gambling industry as a way of promoting what Robert Nozick calls justice in rectification.[24] In particular, it enables federal and state governments to make restitution to the descendants of people whose forebears were collectively wronged by earlier American governments. The economic effect of the law favoring Indian tribes is to recirculate gambling dollars that would otherwise be spent elsewhere in the state (or, more attractively from the state government's point of view, in other states) to members of identifiable ethnic minorities. It also has the effect not only of recirculating existing gambling dollars but also of creating new or better choices for consumers between gambling and other forms of leisure or other discretionary expenditure. To this extent, Indian casinos may not only hurt lottery businesses and other casinos catering to the same general market; they also may hurt restaurants, theaters, CD retailers, fashion boutiques, and other businesses within the casino's catchment area.[25]

This brings us to the second main category of business that new gambling expenditure may displace, namely, other leisure and luxury expenditure. One reason why the construction of casinos is often opposed is because local businesses fear that their businesses will be damaged. Conversely, one of the claims almost invariably made by would-be casino developers is that the casino will be good for local businesses by bringing more people into the area who will spend with the local businesses as well as with the casino. One of the complaints commonly made about Atlantic City is precisely that although the casinos brought much new money into Atlantic City, almost all of it went into businesses located within the casinos and not to restaurants and retailers outside the casino campuses. Be that as it may, governments need to understand that the money that is going to be spent on new gambling opportunities is money that is not going to be spent on other things. In this sense, whether displacement occurs is not a matter that requires empirical investigation, since it is a necessary truth. What requires empirical investigation is what economic activities new expenditure on various forms of gambling actually displaces under particular circumstances.

As a matter of fact, for reasons partly to do with levels of economic development and partly to do with cultural tradition, the countries where the laws relating to gambling are the most permissive are also countries that in general are committed to free-market economic policies. It remains true that even in countries like the United States and the U.K., many people (including many politicians) in practice find it difficult to resist the urge to interfere in the free commercial and lifestyle choices of their fellow citizens. Nevertheless the general principled commitment to free markets puts governments under strong pressure to be neutral with respect to whether their citizens choose to spend their own time and money gambling rather than going to concerts or supporting local sports teams. Individual politicians may regret that people have such poor taste in entertainment that they prefer to play slot machines rather than going to performances of Mozart operas, but they probably recognize that it is not for them to dictate in such matters.

Using the law to protect existing businesses is protectionism. There are no doubt circumstances in which politicians will judge protectionism to be right or at least expedient or at least politically unavoidable. (The United States and Europe are both much more protectionist in relation to domestic industry and foreign competition than their official policy pronouncements warrant and despite the damage this does to poor countries.) There may be similar reasons of political expediency in why regional governments choose to protect local businesses from competition with gambling businesses. This is ultimately something for electorates to decide. However, it is important to be clear that if commercial gambling opportunities are being restricted to prevent displacement from existing businesses, this is in fact what the reason is. What typically happens, of course, is that existing businesses—for thoroughly sound political reasons—argue not that liberalization would be bad for us but that it would be bad for the community on general moral or social grounds. Clarity is important here, not least because otherwise the whole issue of problem gambling becomes muddied, as we shall see in the next chapter. Meanwhile it is worth noting that gambling companies themselves are frequently guilty of concealing their protectionist agenda beneath the rhetoric of social responsibility. It is rare for a sector of the gambling industry to wring its hands about the damage that its own business does in terms of producing problem gamblers. It is not at all rare for sectors of the industry to worry loudly and publicly about how bad it would be in terms of problem gambling if their competitor sectors were given greater freedom to offer their products and services to the public. This explains the unholy alliance between the American Gaming Association representing land-based casino interests and antigambling groups who oppose gambling on moral grounds with respect to the legalizing of Internet gambling in the United States—an alliance that has now dissolved as the land-based casinos have recalculated their commercial interests in this matter.

In fact, the question of what commercial activity new gambling expenditure displaces is vital to an understanding of problem gambling, but only in relation to the third category of potential displacement in figure 5.3. If the money that people are spending on gambling is money that they are not now spending on feeding, clothing, and housing themselves and their families—if in other words the money is coming from what should be budgeted for household necessities—then that is one way of defining problem gambling. Such a definition does not imply the presence of any psychological, let alone physiological, disorder and this, as we shall again see in the next chapter, is helpful for getting to grips with the true nature of the problem we are trying to address with respect to problem gambling. What this suggests is that if governments are concerned to measure the extent to which gambling has negative social impacts, not in the economist's technical sense of reducing the aggregate amount of wealth in a community, but in the ordinary sense of making life worse for people than it otherwise would be, the place to look is in the effects on money lending and debt collection businesses.

The last category of answer to the question "Where does the money spent on gambling come from?" identifies what jurisdictions most commonly hope for, namely, that the money will come from nonresidents. Where this happens, the liberalization of gambling law effectively creates new export earnings with the additional advantage that any negative social costs arising from problem gambling get picked up by the governments of the gambler's home state or country.

Unfortunately, the politicians' dream of introducing casino gambling into their jurisdiction as a means of attracting significant new tourist expenditure proves unrealizable in the overwhelming majority of cases. The illusion that gambling leads to sustainable booms in tourism is nourished by the highly visible examples of Nevada, especially in Las Vegas, and, to a lesser extent, of New Jersey in Atlantic City. These examples of successful casino resorts are almost entirely misleading. The success of Las Vegas and its junior sibling, Reno, is founded on the fact for years they have been able to attract large numbers of gambling enthusiasts to their casinos from parts of the United States and indeed parts of the world where casino gambling is illegal. This has enabled them to plow the profits from gambling into the development of many sorts of ancillary attractions ranging from cheap (subsidized) hotel rooms and meals to spectacular rides and first-rate conference facilities. In other words, Las Vegas and Reno were able to develop as highly successful resorts offering many facilities other than gambling and attracting the bulk of their business from non-Nevadans because Nevada in its heyday had a monopoly, and still retains a high degree of exclusivity, within the United States on casino gambling. In particular, because casino gambling has been illegal in neighboring California, Las Vegas and Reno have been able to attract substantial business from Californians, located in the Los Angeles and San Francisco areas respectively.

How this will change with the advent of Indian casinos in California is uncertain, but both Las Vegas and Reno are rightly fearful and are seeking to decrease their reliance on gambling as opposed to other tourist attractions. Significantly, also, with the legalization during the 1990s of casinos in many other parts of America, the share of its earnings that Las Vegas derives from gambling has been reduced from about 80 percent to less than 50 percent.

The same is true of Atlantic City. The casinos in Atlantic City were able to flourish because they could draw on a vast constituency of clients from neighboring New York State and Massachusetts where casinos are illegal. Nor is this phenomenon confined to the United States. Wherever we find a successful gambling resort, that is, a place where people visit from outside the jurisdiction to gamble, we find the same phenomenon. In Macao, casinos have access to the huge Asian market from countries where casinos are prohibited and most particularly from neighboring Hong Kong. At Sun City in South Africa, the casino was able to flourish because gambling was illegal in the rest of metropolitan South Africa and particularly in the adjacent area surrounding Johannesburg. In the nineteenth century, the success of Monte Carlo as a gambling resort was founded on the fact that casino gambling was illegal in most of the rest of Europe, including France, Italy, and Britain.

The general rule of gambling behavior is this: other things being equal, people will gamble at the nearest venue to where they live which offers their preferred form of gambling. Moreover, the other things that need to be equal—amenities, price, safety, et cetera—are usually in fact made equal by competition. This rule is predicated on the assumption that customers for the core business of casinos, namely, regular casino gamblers, go to casinos for the gambling experience, not for the view or the food or the rides or the shows. If these other attractions are offered, it will be because they are profitable in their own right or because they may, for example, attract families with nongambling members, thus securing the custom of the family members who do gamble or because they attract people who are likely to gamble incidentally in the course of their visit or because they encourage gamblers to stay longer by furnishing them with enjoyable things to do other than gambling. However, casinos that offer all such amenities and more at fifty—let alone five hundred—miles from where their gambling customers live will not be able to compete for the gambling business with casinos offering the same gambling opportunities five miles away.

It is therefore crucial for governments, in considering the introduction of casinos or any other form of commercial gambling, to ascertain what proportion of the anticipated customers will be local people, and what proportion will be visitors from outside the jurisdiction. In all but a handful of cases, the answer will be that the casinos and other gambling outlets will be primarily servicing the demand for gambling from locals. And in the handful of cases where the customers will come from outside the jurisdiction, this will be because in neighboring jurisdictions it is illegal to supply the relevant gambling services or, at least, illegal to supply them on comparably attractive terms.

However, there is one other and more positive consideration relating to tourism and displacement, which governments need to take into account in considering the legalization of commercial gambling activity or liberalization of the laws and regulations that govern it. This is that if gambling services are unavailable or only available on comparatively unattractive terms in one jurisdiction, gamblers in that jurisdiction will take their business to a neighboring jurisdiction. One good reason for liberalizing gambling law may therefore be to retain the money spent on gambling within the jurisdiction that would other-wise be spent outside it.

This kind of defensive legalization has been a significant feature of the argu-ments in many individual states in the United States.[26] It may well turn out to have a significant role in debates about legalizing the provision of Internet gambling services. If people are going to gamble anyway, it is better that they should do it in their home state so that the revenues and other benefits accrue to their fellow residents rather than spending their gambling money in neigh-boring states, where it only benefits "foreigners."

The logic of this argument, however, is that all states will permit everything that all other states permit, and almost all gambling will be conducted under the auspices of people's home jurisdiction. This, indeed, has been the logic be-hind much of the extension of legal gambling between the United States.[27]

This reinforces the view that genuine gambling resorts, that is, places to which people travel from outside the jurisdiction to gamble, are likely to be-come even rarer than they are at the moment. They depend on exploiting a his-torical moment when gambling is still largely prohibited but the demand for it is substantial and is not being adequately met by an illegal industry.

CONCLUSION

All these economic considerations are so fundamental to good public policy in the area of gambling that, even at the risk of repetitiveness, it will be helpful to conclude by summarizing our findings and spelling out their implications for policy.

From the point of view of promoting the economic interests of the general public, there are only two situations in which the legalization of gambling un-ambiguously provides such benefits. These are when an illegal industry is re-placed by a legal one, and when legalization enables a jurisdiction to attract substantial gambling revenues from outside or retain substantial gambling rev-enues that would otherwise go "abroad."

In the case of using legalization to eliminate illegal gambling, law enforce-ment costs are hugely reduced. This is not only because the direct costs of en-forcing the law against gamblers and their suppliers are immediately eliminated. There are two additional considerations. The first is that tight regulation, and the concomitant passing of the management of gambling businesses into the hands of respectable executives in public companies, means that criminal activity that was formerly linked to gambling such as prostitution, drug dealing, money laundering, and loan-sharking will be all but eradicated from the gambling business. The second is that gambling venues, especially casinos, will have such a strong incentive to ensure that their patrons feel safe that they will them-selves hire the necessary additional security.

The other main benefit to the public from eliminating illegal gambling is that a portion of the surplus now accrues to the public in the form of taxes of various sorts.

In the case where gambling is legalized to promote tourism earnings, the benefits to the public, to the extent that the endeavor is successful, are the substantial ones associated with developing any new export business. These benefits accrue mainly to all those in the community who are involved in supplying gambling services (direct employment) and then all those who benefit commercially from the new prosperity of these new suppliers (indirect employment).

Where gambling is successfully developed as an export business, the result is an economic boom. Where this export business can be sustained over a long period as in Las Vegas, the result is a spectacular boom that provides the foundation for lasting prosperity. Unfortunately, this prospect is so attractive to legislators that they do not pause to consider how peculiar and largely unrepeatable have been the circumstances that enabled Las Vegas to achieve this spectacular success. In particular, they overlook the fact that Nevada had a long and virtual monopoly on casino gambling that enabled it to establish itself as *the* international gambling destination. Now that this monopoly looks as if it is being fatally eroded, the future even of the Nevada casino business is in doubt.

The truth, therefore, is that legislators would be wise to assume, whatever the would-be casino operators tell them, that *all* gambling revenues will be coming from their own locals and not from outsiders. If this is so, there will probably be no net benefit in terms of jobs because the money residents spend on casinos will be money they are not spending with other local businesses which also employ people. There may be a net gain in local jobs if the casino displaces expenditure that would otherwise go to businesses—like movie theaters—that employ fewer local people. But there may also be a net loss if the displacement is from businesses like restaurants that are more labor intensive.

The myth that legalizing casinos is good for job creation is nourished because a new casino will employ a large number of people in one place. If the casino draws from a reasonably large catchment area, even as little as a half hour's drive time, the displacement effect will be dispersed and to that extent rendered less noticeable. As a general rule, the economic benefits of introducing a casino will mainly accrue in the area where the casino is located. The economic costs will be dispersed throughout the area from which casino gamblers come. Overall, the costs and benefits will roughly cancel each other out.

This conclusion will not be popular with those who make the argument that gambling generally, and casinos in particular, can be an engine of economic development. For the most part, as with lotteries, gambling merely recirculates existing money within a community rather than bringing in new money. In the particular case of casinos, it draws money from a relatively large area and focuses it in a relatively small one, and it probably does the same with jobs. This has the result that the benefits in the vicinity of the casino are typically visible and measurable, whereas the costs are typically diffused over a sufficiently large area that they escape both notice and measurement.

What this really means is that governments looking for the economic benefits of legalizing gambling, when the effect of gambling will be to recirculate the discretionary spending money of its own citizens, should not be looking to what gambling can do in terms of economic growth, Instead they should look to what it can do in terms of benign redistribution by generating tax revenues in cash and or their equivalent in kind.

Now, contrary to what some opponents of gambling take for granted, it is not self-evidently a bad thing for government to be using people's desire to gamble as a way of funding good causes. Everything depends on where the money comes from and how government spends it. In theory, all money raised in taxation is spent on good causes that benefit the community as a whole. So if the use of gambling as a vehicle for raising taxes means that there is more money available for good causes, then that, in the most natural sense of the expression, is a public benefit. Alternatively, if the funds raised from gambling enable government to tax us less in other ways, that too benefits the general public. This, of course, does not mean that all taxation is equally good. On the contrary, taxation strategies vary greatly in relation their efficiency in actually securing the public benefits which they are designed to pay for. They also differ greatly in the extent to which they are judged to be fair.

As we saw, the particular political case for hypothecation that applies to gambling is that it furnishes government with an answer to those who criticize its tolerance of commercial gambling and point to the perceived or actual negative social impacts. To the extent that criticism of gambling policy is based on moral or aesthetic distaste for various forms for gambling—and widespread distaste, as we have seen, commonly follows as a backlash a year or two after liberalization of the law—government has an effective counter if it can point to the hospital wards and the new computer centers in schools that gambling has paid for, or perhaps to the new conference or cultural center that has been built, or the historic buildings that have been restored with the profits from gambling.

In particular, government will be in a strong position to deal with the backlash if it can point to the nongambling tourist infrastructure that gambling profits have cross-subsidized and are now attracting tourists—and creating jobs—who would not otherwise be coming. This can, of course, go wrong. If government legalizes casinos on the promise that they will pay for tourist facilities that will create new wealth and employment, and two years later the hotels are empty, the conference center unbooked, and the theme park patronized only by locals, then government's problems will be compounded, and it may even cost them reelection.

Taxes, then, including gambling taxes, need to be, and to be seen to be, efficiently raised and, above all, efficiently spent. They also need to be, and to be seen to be, fair. This is problematic to the extent that people have different no-tions of fairness—often reflecting, as Marx has taught us, competing material interests. In particular, people disagree about how the principle that people should be treated equally should be interpreted so as to accord with the requirements of justice. Fortunately, though there is widespread disagreement about what—if anything—governments should do to promote equality, there is widespread agreement that it is desirable for government to pursue policies aimed at the reduction of poverty.

It is therefore crucial to understand the impact of gambling taxes on poverty. Since all tax is redistributive in the sense that it takes money from some people and transfers it to others, to understand taxes' impact on the poor, we need to understand where the money comes from and where it goes. In the event alluded to earlier that government is able to use the tax it generates from gambling on constructing tourism infrastructure, this may bring new business and leisure tourists into the jurisdiction and thereby provide jobs for poor people. It is to be noted that this is quite a different strategy from relying on the gambling facilities themselves to attract tourists. As we have seen, this only happens when the target tourists cannot legally gamble in the jurisdiction where they reside. What a government may, however, succeed in doing is to capture the share of the surplus from the expenditure on gambling by local people and then invest this money in nongambling capital projects that enhance the effectiveness of the area as a tourist destination. This is what happened, for example, in Deadwood, South Dakota, and in Cape Town, South Africa.

From the point of view of poverty alleviation, this is probably the best of all strategies where it is workable because it essentially creates sustainable employment rather than simply fattening the welfare budget. Otherwise, of course, the use of gambling to alleviate poverty will only be effective to the extent that the money from gambling is coming from the better-off and going to the worse-off.

Critics of gambling claim that this is precisely what does not happen. They claim that gambling extracts money from the poor and transfers much of it to the comparatively wealthy, who not only benefit disproportionately from the kinds of things that gambling revenues are often used to fund, such as college tuition fees and opera performances, but are also the principal beneficiaries as managers or shareholders in the gambling businesses.

This argument is quite complicated to evaluate. It is certainly true that relatively poor people are disproportionately represented among the gambling population. This is especially so among lottery players, which is unsurprising given that lotteries provide a cheap form of gambling and offer the poor, in many cases, the only chance they will ever have of becoming fabulously rich.

To the extent that gambling is viewed as just another pleasure for which people pay with their losses, it does seem unfair to tax a form of entertainment that is particularly popular with the poor at an abnormally high rate. This injustice is compounded if the proceeds are used to subsidize the pleasures of the rich, as they are when lottery proceeds are used to subsidize "high culture." On the other hand, the whole point of taxing gambling at an abnormally high rate is that such taxes are paid comparatively willingly by everyone, including the poor.

The same argument, of course, applies to taxes on cigarettes and beer. The truth seems to be that governments originally impose taxes on these activities because they think it is a way of discouraging what they cannot prohibit. Then when they decide either that there is nothing wrong with these activities or that even if there is, it is not appropriate to use high taxes to try to stop people indulging in them, governments nevertheless find it acceptable to continue to impose high taxes because the revenues they generate would have to be compensated for in some other and politically less acceptable way if these "sin" taxes were reduced to the standard rate.

The surest way to meet the charge that gambling is a form of regressive taxation is to ensure that the benefits really do accrue to the poorest sections of society. This may be achieved when a casino, even though it is relying on local gambling revenues, is situated in a very poor area with high unemployment and protected from competition with casinos in more salubrious areas where they might be more popular with punters. This result cannot be easily achieved by simply taxing the casino wherever it is situated and using the proceeds for equivalent urban renewal, regional development, or resort rehabilitation. The reason is that what makes for economic regeneration of the kind desired is sustainable work, and a casino-based entertainment complex with regional exclusivity can provide this in a way that few other government-promoted job creation schemes can achieve.

Another way of meeting the charge that gambling is a regressive tax on the poor would be to ensure that the proceeds from lotteries really were spent on sound poverty alleviation schemes and not as a way for governments to fund nice-to-have public interest projects that, however, are not thought to be sufficiently important to justify the expenditure of normal taxes.

What all this shows is that taxation policy with respect to gambling, like all other taxation, is fundamentally and quite rightly driven by political considerations rather than economic ones. Politics is about the management of the myriad perceived interests in society that are sometimes congruent, or can be made so, but just as often cut across one another and need to be brought into rough harmony if they are not to conflict intolerably. In this process, the role of economics is to expose the limits that reality imposes on what is possible and to draw out the consequences of adopting one policy rather than another: in other words, to make sure that when politicians make their political choices, they are not under illusions about what they are doing.

What economics tells us with respect to gambling is that except in the rare cases where jurisdictions have a predominantly foreign customer base for their gambling businesses, the best that government can extract for the general public from the judicious use of its licensing powers is a modest but not insignificant contribution to the alleviation of poverty. Otherwise the benefits of legalizing gambling or liberalizing gambling law are all to be found in the benefits—both material and moral—that accrue to consumers and suppliers when they are allowed to exercise commercial freedom of choice.

NOTES

1. For good general discussions of the economics of gambling, see Eugene Martin Christiansen, "Gambling and the American Economy," *Annals of the American Academy of Political and Social Science* 556 (March 1998): 36–52; William R. Eadington, "The Economics of Casino Gambling," *Journal of Economic Perspectives* 13, no. 3 (summer 1999): 173–92; and Douglas M. Walker and John D. Jackson, "New Goods and Economic Growth: Evidence from Legalized Gambling," *Review of Regional Studies* 28, no. 2 (fall 1998): 47–69.

2. The exception or apparent exception is Las Vegas, which, as we shall see, was really applying the same economic principles of competition and monopolies to what was initially and for a long time a unique situation. Even in Las Vegas, public authorities indignantly drew the line at putting slot machines in nursing homes. See Jerome H. Skolnick, *House of Cards: The Legalization and Control of Casino Gambling* (Boston: Little, Brown, 1978), 333–34.

3. Critics of gambling often point to this as evidence that gambling taxes are unfair. See Mary O. Borg, Paul M. Mason, and Stephen L. Shapiro, "The Incidence of Taxes on Casino Gambling: Exploiting the Tired and the Poor," *American Journal of Economics and Sociology* 50, no. 3 (July 1991): 323–32. More generally, gambling is often described as a tax on the stupid.

4. For a general discussion, see, for example, Charles Adams, *For Good or Evil: The Impact of Taxes on the Course of Civilization* (New York: Madison Books, 1994).

5. A classic exposition and discussion of the political philosophy of taxation is to be found in Robert Nozick, *Anarchy, State, and Utopia* (Oxford: Oxford University Press, 1974). Nozick also discusses the essentially redistributive nature of taxation and famously wonders whether taxation actually *is* forced labor or is only like forced labor.

6. See, for example, Richard A. McGowan, *Government and the Transformation of the Gaming Industry* (Northampton, Mass.: Edward Elgar, 2001), chap. 1.

7. For a full discussion of the U.K. lottery see I. Walker, "The Economic Analysis of Lotteries," *Economic Policy* 27 (1998).

8. Royal Commission on Gambling, Final Report, vol. 1, chap. 13, pp. 213–39.

9. Conceptually, it might be claimed that lotteries fall between taxation and charitable giving. They are typically used in the first instance to fund projects that would otherwise have to be privately subscribed. It is usually not long before governments use lottery proceeds to fund projects and activities that would otherwise have to be funded out of normal taxation. See A. Szakmary and C. M. Szakmary, "State Lotteries as a Source of State Revenue: A Re-examination," *Southern Atlantic Journal* 61, no. 4 (1995): 1161–81.

10. For an overview of taxes in the United States, see the National Gambling Impact Study Commission's report, (*National Gambling Impact Study Commission Final Report,* 1999. www.ngisc.gov). See also Ranjana G. Madhusudhan, "What Do We Know about Casino Taxation in the United States?" in *Proceedings of the Ninety-First Annual Conference on Taxation* (Washington, D.C.: National Tax Association, 1999), 85–95. For other English-speaking countries, see Francois Vaillancourt, "Government Gambling Revenues, 1985–1995/6: Evidence from Canada, Great Britain, and Australia," in *Proceedings of the Ninety-First Annual Conference on Taxation* (Washington, D.C.: National Tax Association, 1999), 96–103.

11. The best discussion of these options is William R. Eadington, "Contributions of Casino-Style Gambling to Local Economies," *Annals of the American Academy of Political and Social Science* 556 (March 1998): 53–65.

12. For a discussion, see Michael Przybylski, "Does Gambling Complement the Tourist Industry? Some Empirical Evidence of Import Substitution and Demand Displacement," *Tourism Economics* 4, no. 3 (September 1998): 213–31.

13. Contrasting views that apply to the gambling industry in general and to Atlantic City in particular are found in K. Marshall, "A Sure Bet Industry," *Perspectives on Labour and Income* 8, no. 3 (1996): 33–41; and T. O'Brien, *Bad Bet: The Inside Story of the Glamour, Glitz, and Danger of America's Gambling Industry* (New York: Random House, 1998). See also M. N. Browne and N. K. Kubasek, "Should We Encourage Expansion of Casino Gambling?" *Review of Business* 18, no. 3 (1997): 9–13.

14. M. Olivier, "Casino Gambling on the Mississippi Gulf Coast," *Economic Development Review* 13, no. 4 (1995): 34–39. In relation to Mississippi as well as to Colorado and Idaho, see M. D. Larsen, "Gaming Industry Development: A Comparison of Three States," *Economic Development Review* 13, no. 4 (1995): 4–8.

15. See I. Walker, "The Economic Analysis of Lotteries." It is also important to understand the potentially competitive relationship between casinos and lotteries as sources of public revenues. See J. Dense, "State Lotteries, Commercial Casinos, and Public Finance: An Uneasy Relationship," *Gaming Law Review* 3, nos. 5–6 (1999): 317–28.

16. The backlash in the United States and also in Canada and Holland is well described in Robert Goodman, *The Luck Business* (New York: Free Press Paperbacks, 1995), 80–85.

17. Where governments create a monopoly but fail to capture the monopoly profits efficiently, government is likely to be getting the worst of both worlds. See Ricardo Gazel, "The Economic Impacts of Casino Gambling at the State and Local Levels," *Annals of the American Academy of Political and Social Science* 556 (March 1998): 66–84.

18. For a characteristically lucid discussion see William R. Eadington, "The Legalization of Casinos: Policy Objectives, Regulatory Alternatives, and Cost/Benefit Considerations," *Journal of Travel Research* 34 (1996): 3–8.

19. This general issue is discussed in Charles Lieven and Donald Phares, "Casino Gaming in Missouri: The Spending Displacement Effect and Net Economic Impact," in *Proceedings of the Ninetieth Annual Conference on Taxation* (Washington, D.C.: National Tax Association, 1998), 431–38.

20. There is a good discussion of the ways in which U.S. state governments have responded to the threat to horse racing from machine gambling in McGowan, *Government and the Transformation of the Gaming Industry,* 61–72.

21. A qualified case, which still, however, fails to address the fundamental question of why machine gambling revenues should be used to benefit employees and owners of racetracks rather than anyone else, is found in W. Thompson, *"Racinos* and the Public Interest," *Gaming Law Review* 3, nos. 5–6 (1999): 283–86.

22. The political and historical origins of Indian gaming are described and discussed in William R. Eadington, ed., *Indian Gaming and the Law* (Reno, Nev.: Institute for the Study of Gambling and Commercial Gaming, 1990). Many of the enduring as well as the early issues of public policy are discussed here, including the gambling version of the old political-theory conundrum of whether self-regulation is more important than good regulation. A more recent discussion is G. Anders, "The Indian Gaming Regulatory Act and Native American Development," *International Policy Review* 6 (1997): 84–90. See also S. Cornell, J. Kalt, M. Krepps, and J. Taylor, "American Indian Gaming and Its Impacts: A Report to the National Gambling Impact Study Commission" (Cambridge, Mass., 1998). See also Daniel L. Vinje, "Native American Economic Development on Selected Reservations: A Comparative Analysis," *American Journal of Economics and Sociology* 55, no. 4 (1996): 427–42.

23. The most successful casino in the world is Foxwoods in Connecticut, owned by the Mashantucket Pequots. Like Nevada, however, Foxwoods had a peculiar set of advantages favoring its success, which are not readily repeatable. See Anne-Marie d'Hautesterre, "Foxwoods Casino Report: An Unusual Experiment in Economic Development," *Economic Geography,* extra issue (1998): 112–21.

24. Robert Nozick, *Anarchy, State, and Utopia,* (Oxford: Basil Blackwell, 1974, pp. 129–32).

25. This question is discussed in D. N. Steinnes, "Have Native American Casinos Diminished Other Gambling in Minnesota? An Economic Answer Based on Accessibility," *Journal of Regional Analysis and Policy* 28, no. 1 (1998) 18–32. The conclusion reached is that if a negative impact on the lottery and on charitable gambling could be detected, it was very small.

26. See Glen Atkinson, Mark Nichols, and Ted Oleson, "The Menace of Competition and Gambling Deregulation," *Journal of Economic Issues* 34, no. 3 (September 2000): 621–34.

27. See Goodman, *The Luck Business,* 87–101. Chapter 5 is titled "Chaser Governments."

Chapter 6

Problem Gambling

Such benefits as are generated from making legal gambling more readily available accrue either to gamblers in the form of enhanced enjoyment or to employees and shareholders in the gambling and allied industries or to the general public to the extent that the gambling industry is harnessed to the furthering of the general policy objectives of promoting prosperity, funding public interest projects, or reducing poverty. But clearly these benefits may be outweighed by the costs that accrue either to gamblers and nongamblers whose lives are adversely affected by the expansion of legal gambling or to the general public. It is therefore vital for policy makers to form an accurate view about what these costs will be.

As we have seen, there will be costs to existing businesses that may now have to compete with new gambling businesses. There may also be costs in the form of distress to people who really hate the idea of gambling being legally available at venues in their community, just as they might hate the idea of there being legal brothels, even though they would never themselves be tempted to visit or work in such places. There may also be costs in terms of people's well-being in an afterlife, whether this is understood in the form of future punishment for present wrongdoing or of the working out of bad karma. There may also be costs in that an expanded gambling industry somehow contributes to the dumbing down of society as a whole and therefore diminishes the capacity of its members to enjoy richer, more profound, and more abiding kinds of pleasure.

In fact, however, it is very difficult for policy makers in liberal democracies committed to free markets to base policy on any of these kinds of consideration. In these societies, competition is assumed to be desirable; tolerance of others with respect to their private choices is taken to be a corollary of protecting fundamental human rights; public policy may not be based on any particular reli-

gious belief; and the principle of equality requires that every person's preference count for one and no one's for more than one regardless of whether people prefer watching soap operas or listening to Beethoven symphonies. For this
reason, almost all the arguments that are deployed against the liberalization of
gambling law focus on something that it is indisputably the business of liberal
democratic government to address: the costs in terms of undeserved harm
caused by excessive gambling, that is, the issue of problem gambling.

Moderate gambling is, by definition, harmless in terms of the damage that
gamblers do to themselves and others. Excessive gambling, however, may
clearly harm not only gamblers and those close to them but also society in general. This happens whenever dealing with an increase in family poverty and
crime generates welfare, medical, and law enforcement costs that society
chooses to fund from the public purse. Moreover, even if gamblers harm only
themselves through excessive gambling, this is something that government
would be justified in legislating to prevent if excessive gambling is a function of
something like a disease, which means that gamblers are not really exercising
free choice with respect to their gambling behavior but are instead in the grip
of some form of compulsion.

Governments, then, rightly feel obliged to address the question "What
should be done about problem gambling?" Governments would like to be able
to answer this question by identifying policies that will minimize the extent to
which people become problem gamblers and the harm that those who do gamble excessively inflict on themselves and others. Unfortunately, this requires
much greater knowledge about problem gambling than anyone presently pos-
sesses. Consequently, the question for public policy needs to be qualified to
read: "What should governments do about problem gambling, given how little
is known about this subject?"

In this chapter I will try to do two things:

- Identify the nature, extent, and sources of our ignorance and make some suggestions
  about how this ignorance might be lessened
- Propose what I take to be some sensible public policy prescriptions, pending a far
  greater understanding than we presently have of the nature, causes, consequences,
  and best methods of treating problem gambling

I begin by elaborating on the context of the debate about problem gambling.

People who believe either that gambling should be prohibited, or that the availability of legal gambling opportunities should be drastically restricted, overwhelmingly rely on the claims that legal gambling greatly increases the incidence
of problem gambling and that government has an important responsibility in
minimizing the harm caused by problem gambling. In other words, they claim
that legalizing gambling results in significant and avoidable harm being done to
innocent third parties by those who profit by trading in gambling services. In this
respect, they argue, the gambling industry is like the narcotics business.

Against this, people who believe that gambling should be treated as simply a normal part of the entertainment business argue that problem gambling is a very small problem, which in any case is not best addressed by banning or limiting the availability of commercial gambling opportunities. They argue that the gambling business is most properly compared to the liquor trade.

Consequently, wherever and whenever the legalization and regulation of gambling is controversial—and that is virtually everywhere—the issue that is most likely to dominate the discussion is problem gambling. This in turn means that government has to form a view about how much otherwise avoidable harm will be unleashed by making legal gambling more easily available in its jurisdiction. Will liberalization result in a great deal of unnecessary unhappiness that is not compensated for by the pleasure that nonproblem gamblers derive from gambling, the earnings of employees and shareholders in gambling companies, and the benefits that flow from gambling taxes? Or is problem gambling a relatively small problem in terms of the harm it does; which affects only a very small proportion even of the gambling population; which would not be greatly reduced by prohibition or other legalized discouragements; which in many cases is a function of other disordered and self-damaging conditions, so that even in the absence of the ability to gamble, problem gamblers would cause unhappiness to themselves and those close to them, for example through other addictive behavior; whose incidence can be minimized by effective preventative measures; and which, as a behavioral disorder, can be effectively treated?

Enormous effort is expended by regulators and policy makers in their attempts to understand what to do about problem gambling. Governments commission major reports that address the issue as thoroughly as possible. They hold extensive public hearings and receive input from all relevant experts. Discussions of gambling matters in academic literature are quite disproportionately focused on problem gambling, as are presentations made at academic conferences that deal with the study of gambling. Gambling companies themselves fund independent research and go to lengths unprecedented in comparable businesses, such as the fast-food business, to persuade regulators and the general public that they take all reasonable steps to deal responsibly with the problem of excessive consumption of their products.

And yet, at the end of the day, not only is there astonishingly little known about problem gambling; there is also astonishingly little agreement on the most elementary aspects of what we need to do to remedy this lack of knowledge. Thus, there is no agreement about

- How to define problem gambling
- How to measure the incidence of problem gambling
- How to identify problem gamblers
- How to identify those at risk of becoming problem gamblers

- How to measure the costs of problem gambling to gamblers, to those close to them, and to society in general
- How to prevent people from becoming problem gamblers
- How best to counsel and treat them and their families when they become problem gamblers
- Who should be responsible for trying to minimize the incidence of, and harm caused by, problem gambling

Some of the reasons for this ignorance are legitimately related to the difficulty of the subject matter and the fact that scientists and scholars have only fairly recently begun to study problem gambling with the same seriousness as is accorded to other maladaptive behaviors.

It is noteworthy, in this connection, that there is a similar lack of agreement about the answer to the equivalents of the questions listed earlier with respect to alcoholism.[1] However, for better or worse, there seems to be much less official anxiety about problem drinking than about problem gambling, and at least since the disastrous experience of prohibition in the United States between 1920 and 1931, it is rarely suggested that we should limit the number of bars we license to combat alcoholism, that we should ban home delivery by liquor stores, that we should require venues selling liquor to display leaflets warning of the dangers of drinking too much and indicating where help for drinking problems can be found, or to require the liquor industry to fund treatment for excessive drinkers. This official anxiety about problem gambling is not necessarily misplaced. For one thing, there are real differences between the dangers of liquor and the dangers of gambling. For another, a strong case can be made for thinking that legislators and regulators should be doing much more to combat alcoholism, including adopting many of the measures that are used to combat problem gambling.

However, because the issue of problem gambling generates such powerful passions and because the potential for official action in this area will have the effect of helping or harming a whole range of financial interests, there are other, less honorable reasons for lack of agreement about basic problem gambling issues. These flow from deceptions and self-deceptions generated by ideological and economic self-interest. To the extent that this is so, discussions of problem gambling are bedeviled by many sorts of self-serving intellectual dishonesty that it is important to identify at the outset.

First, as already suggested, there are people who disapprove of gambling on other grounds and really want gambling limited or reduced on these other grounds but regard it as likely to be politically more effective to base their opposition and their demands on claims about the unacceptable consequences in terms of gambling addiction that the liberalization of gambling laws would allegedly have. This is often quite clearly the case with people who disapprove of gambling on religious grounds but find that in modern liberal democracies it is extremely difficult, because of the democratic commitments of such societies, to get laws enacted and enforced by legislatures and constitutional courts, which compel people to conform to the ethical teachings of a particular religion. It is also extremely difficult, because of the liberal commitments of such societies, to get laws enacted and enforced that prevent people from pursuing pleasure in whatever way is most attractive to them on the grounds that they are running the risk of harming themselves but no one else. (This is incidentally why drug laws in Western societies are so incoherent and why laws against sexual activities engaged in by consenting adults in private have almost completely disappeared from statute books.)

It should be noted, however, that it is not only those who object to gambling on religious grounds who are prone to rely on the alleged dangers of problem gambling in order to buttress antigambling arguments that are really founded on quite different considerations. Many people object to the presence of commercial gambling venues, especially in large numbers or in very large premises, on the grounds that this will detract from the quality of life in their community. Sometimes this argument is straightforwardly aesthetic: people think that casinos, in particular, are just vulgar, brash, and unattractive. They will spoil the character of the neighborhood, especially if the neighborhood takes pride in being respectable or classy. Sometimes this argument appeals to some such concept as cultural degradation, which, though somewhat nebulous, is not on that account to be lightly dismissed. Large numbers of commercial gambling outlets would, on this view, not only lower the tone of the neighborhood; they would undermine its cultural vitality perhaps by threatening more civilized entertainments such as going to theaters and concerts or eating at good restaurants or perhaps simply by being there as both a monument to, and an enticement to indulge in, what is seen as an essentially cretinizing activity. Those who find such arguments persuasive may nevertheless be reluctant to adopt them forthrightly because although they do not appeal to any puritanical religious considerations that may well not be widely shared, they may seem to be vulnerable to charges of elitism. They do indeed have elitist components and may be none the worse for that, although there is also an entirely respectable democratic argument, which need not be elitist at all, for claiming that communities should be able to decide for themselves how much commercial gambling and of what kind they want, if indeed they want any. This democratic argument allows for the issues of both immorality and cultural degradation to be given political influence proportionate to their importance in the minds of individual voters. This is why referenda often precede the introduction of legalized gambling of various sorts in many jurisdictions. Nevertheless it remains easier to win the political argument against commercial gambling by claiming that it is dangerous than by claiming that it is morally objectionable or simply distasteful. Those arguing against gambling in local contexts consequently have a tendency to try to bolster a case that rests primarily on other considerations by playing up the problem-gambling argument and stressing, as poignantly as possible, the damage that problem gambling causes to innocent family members.

Intellectual honesty about problem gambling is compromised in the foregoing cases by ideological commitment. It also tends to be compromised by people
who abuse, inflate, or otherwise distort problem gambling arguments because
they have a financial vested interest in the issue. Everyone is familiar with the
position that used to be taken by gambling industry executives worldwide but is
now mercifully being replaced by a more farsighted and responsible view. The
old view used to be: "There is no such thing as problem gambling. And if there
is, it's a very small problem, which moreover is caused by sectors of the gambling industry other than my own. And if there is a problem among customers
of my sector, it's their problem, not mine." As we shall see, this position has now
been largely abandoned by the industry for compelling prudential reasons as
well as for moral ones. On the other hand, it is not uncommon for sectors of the
gambling industry to use arguments about the dangers of problem gambling that
coincidentally—and to put it charitably—strengthen their case that *competitor*
sectors should not be permitted to operate. Following the Gambling Review Report of the U.K. government chaired by Sir Alan Budd, machine manufacturers,
threatened by competition from American, Australian, and other foreign manufacturers, began to argue that the proposed reforms would seriously increase the
incidence of problem gambling. In South Africa, casino operators who had not
previously opposed the introduction of a slot route industry, began to do so
when their profit margins turned out be less satisfactory than they had anticipated. Above all, the original hostility of American casino operators to the legalizing of Internet gambling on the basis of the terrible social consequences this
would have happened to fit conveniently with the view that legalized Internet
gambling would negatively affect the profitability of land-based operations.

It is of course a professional duty of gambling company executives to find the
most telling arguments for persuading politicians not to do things that will adversely affect their shareholders' interests; and arguing that legalizing competition will damage one's profitability is not normally the most telling of such
arguments. It is perhaps more disconcerting to note that those who research,
those who treat, and those who regulate problem gambling also often have a financial interest—as well quite often as an ideological interest—in making immoderate claims about how widespread and harmful problem gambling is.
Researchers, after all, are dependent on attracting research grants, therapists
need patients/clients, and regulators need to justify their existence and their
salaries by identifying things that need regulation. Also, all these professionals
are in competition for status and esteem among their peers, and this is enhanced if they are seen to be engaged in understanding and containing a major
source of human suffering.

There exists, then, a complex concatenation of interests that attach to discovering the facts about problem gambling and setting appropriate policy. This in
part explains the extreme thinness and unreliability of the evidence base on
which judgments about problem gambling have to be made. Howard Shaffer,

perhaps America's foremost and most scientifically scrupulous medical researcher in the area of problem gambling, describes the state of the research as "chaotic,"[2] and the U.K. report chaired by Sir Alan Budd deplores how little is known about problem gambling on which policy makers can rely.[3] Under these circumstances, policy must be made on the basis that there is a great deal we do not know about problem gambling, although part of that policy is likely to include implementing strategies for finding out a great deal more about gambling generally and problem gambling in particular. This is, indeed, the approach which the U.K. Gambling Review Report recommends.

Before addressing the question of what policy should be given the current state of our ignorance, I wish to try to propose ways in which that ignorance might be lessened.

DEFINING AND MEASURING PROBLEM GAMBLING: THE CURRENT SITUATION

Ideally, governments addressing the question of what to do about problem gambling would be able to refer to a well-established body of scientific knowledge, which would tell them how much harm and to whom proposed changes in gambling laws would cause (or prevent). This would require at least an accurate estimate of

- The number of people who presently have a gambling problem
- The number of additional people who would develop a gambling problem if the law were changed
- The increase in material and human costs to gamblers and others which would result

To get accurate estimates on the first of these, we would need agreement about what problem gambling is, how to treat it, and how severe a problem it needs to be to warrant governmental or therapeutic intervention. To get agreement about the second, we would need know what causes people to become problem gamblers and what can be done to prevent this condition from occurring or to reverse it when it does occur. We would also need to know how reliable are our actual attempts to measure problem gambling and how effective are the prevention and treatment strategies that are presently available. To get agreement about the third, we would need to agree on how to quantify the harm that problem gamblers do to themselves and others as well as on the essentially moral question of which forms of harm it is appropriate for government to try to prevent by deploying the force of law.

If knowledge of this sort were available, we can imagine that legislators, considering the liberalization of gambling law, might reason in any of the following ways:

- The evidence strongly suggests that liberalizing gambling law will result in the number of people who are addicted to gambling growing from less than .5 percent of the population at present to over 10 percent. Since gambling addicts on average cause serious harm to five other people, this means that more than 50 percent of the population will be adversely affected by gambling addiction. There are no reliable ways of preventing this increase in gambling addiction. The increase in gambling addiction will result, given the social principles on which our government is based, in an increase of law enforcement costs of not less than x, of medical costs of not less than y, and of welfare costs of not less than z. There will also be a substantial increase in the total volume of human unhappiness. These costs clearly outweigh the benefits to nonproblem gamblers, to those who would otherwise have worse jobs or no jobs, to investors who would get less good returns, and to the beneficiaries of gambling taxes. Therefore we will not liberalize.

- Gambling addiction is rare. It presently affects less that one person in ten thousand. This number is more or less constant across different the populations of different jurisdictions that have very different regulatory dispensations ranging from complete prohibition to a free market. Gambling addicts, moreover, have a well-defined medical condition, such that they will find a way to gamble regardless of how much legal gambling is or is not available and of what kind. If anything, in jurisdictions where legal gambling is widely available, it is easier to identify and treat gambling addicts than in jurisdictions where gambling addicts are by definition criminals. Consequently, the amount of harm to gamblers and others that restricting the availability of legal gambling would prevent is very small and, in any case, is not the kind of harm that justifies the violation by governments of the freedom of individuals to pursue happiness as seems best to them. Therefore there are no adequate grounds for seeking to limit the amount of available commercial gambling based on the harm caused by problem gambling. Consequently we shall ignore the issue of problem gambling in formulating public policy in this area.

- At present, about 2 percent of regular gamblers are problem gamblers in a population where 35 percent of the population gamble regularly. The lives of this 2 percent are intimately bound up with an average on three other people whose welfare is seriously affected and whom it is appropriate for government to try to protect. The proposed liberalization would double the number of regular gamblers and expose double the number of people to a significant risk of becoming problem gamblers. This risk can be reduced by a factor of x by employing suitable prevention and treatment strategies. Liberalization will therefore result in some increase in avoidable harm to gamblers and others. The costs to taxpayers of trying to mitigate this harm will be y. On the other hand, in comparison with many other forms of legal self-indulgence the harm caused and the costs imposed by problem gamblers is small, and there will only be a comparatively small increase in the harm and costs after liberalization. This is not sufficient to justify the substantial erosion of the freedom of the vast majority of purely recreational gamblers that results in the absence of liberal gambling laws. Therefore we will liberalize (cautiously).

Despite the heroic efforts of a fairly large number of scholars in the field of problem gambling research, we seem to be still regrettably far from achieving the kinds of agreement that would support the foregoing kinds of argument. We still have definitions that are ambiguous and contested and measuring instruments that are crude and of limited reliability. We lack relevant economic and other data, and we lack agreement about what economic and other data is or should be relevant. Very conspicuously, we lack clarity about the normative principles that we think ought to be decisive in shaping public policy in this area, and even when our judgments are unsullied by ulterior motives, we perhaps lack courage in facing the fact that the requirements of liberty and the requirements of compassion in public policy may conflict irreconcilably.

Given this, it is obviously sensible for policy makers to make rather few assumptions about what the consequences of any proposed liberalization will be for problem gambling. Equally obviously, however, policy makers need to be familiar with where current discussions in the area of problem gambling research have got to and how they might be expected to make progress.

Problem gambling is most naturally understood as gambling behavior that, in some way and to some extent, is harmful to the gambler and to others. This suggests that gambling problems may range in intensity along a continuum from mild to severe and that the problems may be of various kinds. These two considerations rightly underpin the bulk of scholarly attempts to define and measure problem gambling. They define problem gambling in terms such as "gambling to a degree that compromises, disrupts or damages family, personal or recreational pursuits."[4] They then employ one or more of three main and overlapping instruments for identifying the point on the continuum at which gamblers become problem gamblers and for assessing the prevalence of problem gambling in a population.

The most authoritative definition of problem gambling is authorized by the American Psychiatric Association and set out in *The Diagnostic and Statistical Manual of Mental Disorders* (4th ed., 1994). Here problem gambling is equated with "pathological" gambling, indicating—as is wholly appropriate—that the authors are concerned with a phenomenon that can appropriately be accounted a disease. Pathological gambling is defined as "persistent and recurrent maladaptive (gambling) behavior that disrupts personal, family or vocational pursuits." The *DSM-IV* then goes on to list ten descriptions, which, if any five apply, are sufficient to warrant a diagnosis of pathological gambling.

1. Is preoccupied with gambling (e.g., preoccupied with reliving past gambling experiences, handicapping or planning the next venture, or thinking of ways to get money with which to gamble).

2. Needs to gamble with increasing amounts of money to achieve the desired excitement.

3. Has repeated unsuccessful efforts to control, cut back, or stop gambling.

4. Is listless or irritable when attempting to cut down or stop gambling.

5. Gambles as a way of escaping problems (e.g., feelings of helplessness, guilt, anxiety, or depression).

6. After losing money gambling, often returns another day to get even ("chasing one's losses").

7. Lies to family members, therapist, or others in order to conceal the extent of involvement with gambling.

8. Has committed illegal acts such as forgery, fraud, theft, or embezzlement to finance gambling.

9. Has jeopardized or lost a significant relationship, job, or educational or career opportunity through gambling.

10. Relies on others to provide money to relieve desperate financial situation caused by gambling.

These criteria have been adapted by Dr. Sue Fisher to compose a screen for use in surveys intended to estimate the prevalence of problem gambling.

An earlier version of the manual *(DSM-III)* is closely associated with the questionnaire most widely used in surveys to measure the incidence of problem gambling in populations. This is the South Oaks Gambling Screen (SOGS) developed by Lesieur and Blume.[5] The basic version of this questionnaire asks the following questions:

1. When you gamble, how often do you go back another day to win back money you have lost?

2. Have you ever claimed to be winning money when in fact you lost?

3. Do you spend more time and money gambling than you intended?

4. Have people criticized your gambling?

5. Have you felt guilty about the way you gamble or what happens when you gamble?

6. Have you ever felt you would like to stop but didn't think you could?

7. Have you hidden betting slips, lottery tickets, gambling money, or other signs of gambling from your spouse or partner, your children, or other important people in your life?

8a. Have you argued with people you live with over how you handle money?

8b. If yes, have these arguments centered on your gambling?

9. Have you missed time from work, school, or college due to gambling?

10. Have you borrowed from someone and not paid them back as a result of your gambling?

11. Have you borrowed from household money to finance gambling?

12. Have you borrowed money from you spouse or partner to finance gambling?

13. Have you borrowed money from any other relatives to finance gambling?

14. Have you borrowed money from banks, building societies, loan companies, or credit companies to finance your gambling?

15. Have you made cash withdrawals on credit cards to get money for gambling or to pay gambling debts?

16. Have you received loans from "loan sharks" to get money for gambling or to pay gambling debts?

17. Have you cashed in stocks or bonds or other securities to finance gambling?

18. Have you sold personal or family property to finance gambling?

19. Have you borrowed money from your bank or building society account by writing checks that bounced to get money for gambling or to pay gambling debts?

20. Do you feel you have a problem with betting money or gambling?

These questions can be answered yes or no or by ticking a frequency option. Also, they can be focused on lifetime experience ("Have you ever ... ?") or on more recent experience ("Have you in the last year ... ?"). Significantly, the earlier versions of SOGS identified "problem gamblers" as those with scores of three or four affirmative answers and "probable pathological" gamblers as those with five or more. More recently, for reasons that seem mainly to reflect the fact the lower scores were providing implausibly high numbers, especially in Australia, five affirmative answers is now usually taken to be the cutoff for identifying "problem gamblers."

Finally there are the older twenty questions used by Gamblers' Anonymous (GA) to enable gamblers to determine for themselves whether they are "compulsive" gamblers. These twenty questions, like most of the rest of the work of Gamblers' Anonymous, are derived from the practices of Alcoholics Anonymous (AA). The AA twenty questions were originally developed by the Johns Hopkins Medical School and validated by consensus among recovering alcoholics about some of the main ways in which their drinking behavior differed from that of normal or social drinkers. These questions are adapted by GA as follows:

1. Have you ever lost time from work due to gambling?

2. Has gambling ever made your home life unhappy?

3. Has gambling affected your reputation?

4. Have you ever felt remorse after gambling?

5. Have you ever gambled to get money to pay debts or otherwise solve financial difficulties?

6. Has gambling made you less ambitious or efficient?

7. Have you ever felt you must return as soon as possible, after having lost, to try to win back the money you have lost?

8. After a win, have you ever felt a strong urge to return and win more?

9. Have you ever gambled until your last dollar was gone?

10. Have you ever borrowed money to finance your gambling?

11. Have you ever sold any real estate or personal property to finance your gambling?

12. Have you ever been reluctant to use "gambling money" for normal expenditure or have you ever used money earmarked for household necessities for gambling?

13. Has gambling ever made you careless of the welfare of your family or yourself?

14. Have you ever gambled longer than planned?

15. Have you ever gambled to escape worry or trouble?

16. Have you ever committed or considered an illegal act to finance your gambling?

17. Has gambling caused you difficulty in sleeping?

18. Do arguments, disappointments, or frustrations bring on an urge to gamble?

19. Do you have an urge to celebrate good fortune by a few hours gambling?

20. Have you ever considered self-destruction as a result of gambling?

The cutoff point for identifying problem gamblers is seven affirmatives.

Prevalence studies are typically conducted internationally by using one or more of these instruments in a survey and counting the number of people who score above the relevant threshold. This number is then taken to yield, often with astonishing and uncritical confidence, the percentage of the population who are problem gamblers.

Among the weaknesses of this approach, which apply to all instruments, are the facts that:

- The cutoff points are more or less arbitrary and in the case of *DSM-IV* and GA were not intended for use in prevalence studies. Instead they were intended to provide (as they do quite effectively) a rough rule of thumb for helping clinicians to diagnose patients or for helping gamblers to diagnose themselves.

- The instruments do not discriminate between more and less severe symptoms: feeling remorse or guilt in relation to gambling and selling one's home or contemplating suicide because of gambling all count for one and only one.

- It is doubtful how far lists of symptoms compiled as an aid to clinicians when making a diagnosis of a patient who has already recognized and presented himself or herself as being in need of treatment can be used accurately in a survey of the general and generally healthy public.

To the reservations about results that these considerations prompt must be added the reservations that apply to any survey that asks people to tell an interviewer about their personal habits, especially if these may be thought to be shameful.

Among the general problems here are the facts that:

- In surveys, people are often reluctant to tell the truth to strangers about their gambling and drinking habits. (Addictive gamblers in recovery often claim that they would have lied about their gambling had they been surveyed when they were still gambling.)

- People vary greatly in the extent to which their answers are influenced by their attitude to the interviewer. Some answers are distorted by the respondent's desire to please the interviewer, others by resentment of a perceived intrusion into the respondent's privacy.

- People with problems of any kind, including addiction problems, are more likely to avoid being caught in a sample. (They're busy gambling or drinking and so not available to answer the phone or the door.)

- Addicts have a strong tendency to deceive themselves about their behavior and to deny the existence of their problem or its severity.

- Some of the items may identify behavior that is abnormal in some cultures but not in others or much more likely to affect the poor than the rich. Borrowing money to gamble may fall into both these categories.

- Most individual items pick out significantly more people who score below the cutoff point and are therefore not accounted problem gamblers than those who score above the cutoff point.

- All surveys depend on the competence and honesty of the people who administer the questionnaires, which is likely to vary.

For all these reasons, surveys are bound to capture a significant number of both false negatives (people who do have gambling problems that don't show up) and false positives (people who are identified as having a problem but in fact don't). They also make international comparisons especially invidious where the general problems of measuring the incidence of problem gambling in a population are compounded by significant differences in the character of samples. The situation is summed in an appendix to the U.K. Gambling Review Report, which identifies what is perhaps the principal underlying reason for the unsatisfactoriness of most attempts to measure problem gambling: "It is not clear what one has identified unless the purpose for which one is attempting to identify problem gambling is made clear." The report concludes that "the existing tests may serve some purposes, but it is unsafe to place too much reliance on them" (235).

DEFINING AND MEASURING PROBLEM GAMBLING: SOME PROPOSALS

Here are three proposals designed to ameliorate this unsatisfactory situation.

The first concerns generating greater clarity about what we are trying to do when we seek to develop screens or tests for identifying and measuring problem gambling such as the three described in the previous section. This will enable us to make better sense and use of the information that prevalence studies typically collect. I propose that we distinguish clearly the two main purposes that prevalence studies designed to measure the incidence of problem gambling might be, and in fact currently are, expected to serve. First, such research might be useful to those concerned with assisting policy makers to formulate laws and regulations intended to reduce the incidence of, and harm caused by, excessive gambling. In combination with estimates of the average costs to individuals and to society as a whole that each problem gambler generates, knowledge of the incidence of problem gambling in various populations, including their own, would assist policy makers in judging how much harm changes in their gambling laws would be likely to produce. It is clearly important for policy makers to have a realistic estimate of how much problem gambling there presently is in their jurisdiction, and by how much this would be likely to increase if various proposals for liberalization were adopted, or by how much it would decrease if measures to reduce the availability of gambling were put in place. Being able to compare the number of people who gamble problematically in different jurisdictions with different regulatory environments would obviously be useful in estimating the impact on behavior of different policies. For the same reason, it would be valuable to have studies that compared the number of problem gamblers in a community before and after liberalization of gambling. Having identified the problem gamblers in a population, it would also be useful to know what their demographic characteristics are: are they mainly rich or poor; young or old; well or poorly educated; strongly or weakly attached to particular religious traditions; in good or poor mental and physical health; from gambling or from nongambling families? If governments think it right to frame gambling law to "protect the vulnerable," it is important to know who the vulnerable are and how to assess the extent of their vulnerability.[6] Knowing the size of the problem would also be one important element in deciding on the allocation of public resources to address the problem.

The second clear purpose that research into problem gambling might be expected to serve is to help make more effective the work of those charged with preventing problem gambling from occurring, mainly through various forms of education, and with attempting to cure or relieve the condition when it does occur. Here what is needed in the first instance is a list of typical symptoms—almost certainly much fuller and more graduated than those currently in use—which tend to distinguish problem-free gambling from problem gambling. Such a list will not only assist in enabling therapists and gamblers themselves to decide whether they have a problem, and if so how serious it is. It will also be useful in setting goals for prevention and treatment programs by identifying the behaviors they are seeking to prevent or eliminate while, at the same time, not discouraging people who don't need to be discouraged from gambling as a way of enjoying themselves harmlessly.

Both these objectives require inter alia knowledge of the reasons why people gamble excessively and must allow for the probability that there are many different such reasons ranging from mental disorder to simple ignorance of how gambling works. To understand the causes of problem gambling, it is also necessary to understand how and why problematic or excessive gamblers differ from those who gamble moderately and without experiencing or causing problems. This objective also suggests that there should be much more research than is presently available into how former excessive gamblers succeeded in giving up gambling or bringing their gambling behavior under control and how they differ from people who do not so succeed. Finally, it should be recognized that problem gambling is likely to be a matter of degree, and it therefore requires judgment to decide at what point gambling behavior becomes sufficiently problematic to warrant the attention of government, on the one hand, and of the therapeutic community, on the other. To describe this as a matter of judgment, of course, does not imply that the decision is arbitrary and that anyone's judgment is as good as anyone else's.

My second proposal seeks to reduce current confusions about what to call "problem gambling" and what to understand when talking of "gambling addiction." In addition to the expression "problem gambling" itself, epithets that are applied to gambling to indicate that something "problematic" is going on include "pathological," "addictive," "compulsive," "disordered," and "excessive." These expressions all have somewhat different connotations in different contexts with respect both to the kind of problem they imply and to the degree of severity they suggest.

The proposal is that we apply the terms "compulsive," "pathological," and "addictive" interchangeably to gambling when we wish to identify gambling behavior that closely resembles the behavior of alcoholics and other drug addicts. These are occasions when we can plausibly speak of "gambling addiction" and have in mind a condition that is appropriately thought of as an identifiable disease. The expressions "problem gambling," "excessive gambling," and "disordered gambling" should be treated, again interchangeably, as generic terms for any kind of gambling behavior that causes harm to gamblers and to others.

Addictive, pathological, and compulsive gambling would thus count as only one species of the genus "excessive," "disordered," and "problematic" gambling behavior. Many people will gamble too much, either regularly or on occasion, whose problem will not be appropriately accounted an addiction-like problem or indeed any sort of mental health problem. Sometimes, for example, people's gambling problem is part of a more general money management problem. Sometimes, and I think very importantly, people often gamble too much because they are ignorant of how gambling works. Often too, reckless gambling behavior turns out to be part of a more generally "wild" disposition. Sometimes again, though part of a mental health problem, excessive gambling may turn out to be merely one, perhaps rather unimportant, component in a pattern of morbidly self-destructive behaviors. Nor is it necessarily the case that addictive gambling is a more "severe" version of problem gambling. "Severity" is most usefully understood as a measure of the degree of damage that problem gamblers cause to themselves and others. Consequently, the severity of problematic gambling behavior will depend mainly on how much money is lost as a proportion of disposable income, regardless of whether the excessive gambling is a function of addiction. Poor people gambling too much out of ignorance may do more harm to themselves and their dependents than rich addicts who have no dependents.

In this connection, it should be borne in mind that almost any activity that affords people pleasure can become addictive in some sense. An inordinate and, to some extent, uncontrollable passion for playing bridge or golf, for going to church, or for engaging in local politics can result in one (or more) members of a family doing palpable damage to themselves and to others. In that sense we may colloquially and, in part, metaphorically speak of "addictions." We probably don't think of these cases as being cases of real addiction because partly because the harm done is relatively small and partly because we think that the behavior in question is more readily thought of as a product of free choice rather than of compulsion. On the other hand, activities such as eating, shopping, working, and making love are paradigmatic of normal activities that, however, some people engage in a way that is both highly damaging and clearly compulsive. This is why it makes sense to talk here of addiction in a much less metaphorical sense and to use words like "food addict," "shopaholic," "workaholic," and "sex addict" to capture the analogy between the behavior of people who engage in these activities excessively, obsessively, and compulsively and the way in which the behavior differs from that of normal eaters, shoppers, workers, and lovers. Probably the main reasons why uncontrollable and highly damaging use of psychotropic drugs, including alcohol, is taken as paradigmatic for addiction is that they involve a systematic attempt to induce an artificial euphoria by physiological means, which becomes for the addict, but not for the nonaddict, so attractive that he or she becomes indifferent to the harm that excessive indulgence causes.

It is clear from these considerations that gambling can become an addiction in a straightforward, nonmetaphorical sense. In particular, almost all of the differences in behavior that distinguish the alcoholic from the normal or social drinker also distinguish the gambling addict from normal or recreational gambler. For example, gambling addicts are, as nonaddicts are not, obsessed with the object of their addiction and think about it constantly from the moment they wake up—"What am I going to gamble on today? Where will I get the money? Who will I con or lie to or beg, borrow, or steal from?" They also replay past gambling experiences obsessively inside their heads. Again, for addicts but not for nonaddicts, gambling is a way of escaping the pain of reality rather than of enhancing its pleasures. Gamblers will tell you they only feel alive, or normal, or that life is worth living, when they are gambling.

It is also clear, however, that as with other addictions, gambling addiction is a continuum that stretches from mild to severe, depending on the damage caused, on the one hand, and the difficulty of controlling or giving up the activity, on the other. Addicts themselves, including gambling addicts, frequently speak of a "shadow line" in reflecting on their addictive careers. By this expression, they identify what seems to have been a point of no return in their use of their "drug of choice," when the takeover of their lives by their addiction seems to have become irreversible. After this, it seems as if there is nothing that can happen or threaten to happen that will deter them from their addictive behavior. They will sacrifice their ability to work and all their most important personal relationships; they will face bankruptcy, imprisonment, painful and

chronic sickness, and every conceivable kind of humiliation; they will be unde-
terred by the high risk of dying prematurely, disagreeably, ignominiously and
alone; they will live one day or one part of a day at a time, consumed with the
single project of securing their fix and enjoying the temporary relief that it affords; otherwise they live in a state of helplessness and hopelessness. Such a
condition may appropriately, and with deliberate unattractiveness, be called
"full-blown addiction," and it is clearly a condition that a small minority of
people reach through gambling as surely as others do through the use of narcotics.

For good reasons, both governments and therapists are rightly concerned
with addictive behavior when it has reached, or appears to be on the way to
reaching, this stage. In this respect, addictive gambling is indistinguishable
from alcoholism, which causes immense suffering to a small minority of
those who drink and to those close to them. Like alcoholism, addictive gambling is plausibly accounted and treated as a disease, and government rightly
seeks to prevent people from developing this condition and to ensure that
treatment is available for those who do nevertheless succumb to the disease.
However, this is also rightly not the only concern of government. In the case
of gambling, it is especially important that government seek to minimize the
incidence of problem gambling that may result from ignorance or lack of relevant skills. One might wish that government did as much about the evils of
excessive drinking or eating as they do about excessive gambling. After all,
these other activities might be thought both more widespread and more life-
threatening than excessive gambling. However, excessive gambling has one
characteristic in terms of which it is clearly more dangerous than excessive
drinking, eating, taking drugs, or indulging in any other addictive activity.
This is that the substance that excessive gamblers abuse is money, and it is
possible to spend huge amounts of money on gambling in a very short time.
This means that excessive gambling is uniquely dangerous when it comes to
threatening people's financial health. It also means that excessive gambling is
an activity to which poor people are especially vulnerable simply because
they are poor.

My third proposal derives from the first two. It is that we recognize that
whatever instruments we use to identify and measure problem gambling we
set two cutoff points: a lower one to pick out as problem gamblers those who we
think are in special need of being warned and advised about the dangers of excessive gambling, and a higher one to identify people clearly in need of the kind
of help that other addicts need. Clearly, those picked out by the first criterion
may be people who are in the early stages of developing an addiction to gambling. But, importantly, they need not be: their problem may be both different
in character and more amenable to good advice about how to gamble moderately.[7]

It should be recognized that all tests or screens, including the three described earlier, are merely collections of telltale signs or symptoms that, if

present in large enough numbers, probably indicate that gambling behavior is causing significant harm. This means that the most we can hope to get from the use of such instruments is very *rough* numbers about the incidence of problem gambling in a population. But this does not matter. Rough numbers are adequate for the purposes of formulating both good public policy and good educational and therapeutic practice. From this point of view, it matters less than might be thought what instruments are used to measure problem gambling as long as they contain a sufficiently large numbers of items that tend to distinguish problem from nonproblem gamblers for sensible cutoff points to be set.[8]

On the other hand, it would clearly be of great benefit to researchers to have an instrument that was objectively validated so that everyone knew what it was claiming to measure and commanded international agreement. To achieve this, I believe, the present instruments need to be refined, consolidated, and expanded to include a wider range of symptoms, especially probably some of those identified by people who work in casinos and other commercial gambling outlets. The individual items need to be scored differently to reflect their effectiveness as discriminators. For example, anyone who has contemplated suicide because of gambling or embezzled money ought to count as a problem gambler even if he or she has never felt remorse about gambling, so these items should by themselves take respondents to the minimum cutoff point for problem gambling. On the other hand, most people who have felt remorse after gambling are not usefully accounted problem gamblers. This item should therefore take respondents only a small distance toward the cutoff point for problem gambling. Finally, whatever instruments are used should be properly validated against substantial samples of former problem gamblers and nonproblem gamblers rather than against samples of those in especially the early stages of treatment where the relevant diagnosis may be unsafe.

A final point about measuring problem gambling concerns the population to be sampled. If numbers are to be informative, particularly international numbers, we need to be clear about what they are numbers of. To compare, say, the proportion of the population of the United States with the proportion of the population of Russia who are problem gamblers is not likely to serve any useful purpose unless it is linked to other numbers such as the availability of gambling and the number of people who gamble regularly—a notion that also needs, but does not presently have, an agreed definition.

I do not believe it would be particularly difficult to develop a set of test items along these lines. It would also be particularly valuable if tests of this kind could be combined with attempts to ascertain the truth about what people are *not* spending money on so that they have money for gambling. As indicated in the previous chapter, if their gambling funds come out of their budget for leisure and luxuries, this is not a problem, but if it is coming out of their budget for household necessities, then by definition it is a problem, and how big a problem it is will be a function of how much individuals and families are having to forgo to pay for the gambling. It might in due course be possible to develop different sets of questions for people who engage in different types of gambling activity and to discriminate questions revealing problems deriving from ignorance, from poor money management skills, and from personality disorders of various sorts, including other addictive problems. For the moment it would be a giant step forward to get agreement on a single test, which worked across different cultures, and where there was agreement about what the results mean.

RESPONSIBLE GAMBLING PROGRAMS

Given that there is great ignorance about the nature, prevalence, and causes of problem gambling, what should governments do? It is tempting to reply that the obvious policy for government to adopt is one of prohibition pending more and better research. After all, suppose a government were considering whether or not to legalize a cigarette industry in circumstances in which it was unsure what the public health risks are—whether smoking is addictive, how much damage smokers do to themselves, and how much to others. Surely it would be prudent for government to adopt a highly cautious approach, particularly if they are taking their decision in circumstances where there is no demand from potential consumers to have greater freedom to smoke. Surely, indeed, it is much to be regretted that through ignorance governments allowed a massive cigarette industry to develop before discovering that virtually all smoking is addictive in that the main reason for smoking is to avoid the distress of withdrawal, and that smoking is a major contributing cause of a variety of horrible diseases. Had they been more cautious, they would have banned smoking in the absence of research showing that cigarettes can be smoked safely and then made the ban permanent when it became clear that cigarette smoking is as unredeemedly dangerous as we now know it to be. Moreover, this course of action would have been politically possible had it been taken before the emergence of a large population of cigarette addicts and the establishment of a large tobacco industry with huge financial interests.

For reasons I have elaborated in earlier chapters, I think there are strong arguments of a moral sort that tell against prohibiting commercial gambling and clearly in many jurisdictions prohibition is not practical politically. In particular, the diversion of scarce law enforcement resources to prevent people from gambling would be highly unpopular with the result that an illegal industry would flourish. Nevertheless, where refusal to liberalize gambling laws is politically possible, and especially if there are no countervailing public benefits, then our ignorance about how addictive, say, slot machine gambling really is, and how much harm gambling addiction actually does, may be good reasons for a government to refuse to liberalize.

Meanwhile governments that do decide to legalize or liberalize have to decide what, if anything, they are going to do about problem gambling. Because, all over the world, the gambling industry is so vulnerable to the charge that it callously ruins lives in pursuit of profit, and because governments are vulnerable to the charge that they recklessly permit this and themselves profit from it, there has been a movement recently in many jurisdictions that, for whatever reason, have decided to permit a substantial amount of commercial gambling toward the development of "responsible-gambling programs." The development of these programs is often strongly supported by the gambling industry, which recognizes that it has a clear interest in ensuring that everything that can realistically be done to minimize the damage caused by problem gambling is in fact done.[9] What does "doing everything that can realistically be done" mean in practice? I suggest that the answer to this question has three components, which need to be integrated into a coherent program for addressing problem gambling. The three components are understanding, prevention, and treatment.

To increase our understanding of problem gambling, we need to research all aspects of the incidence of problem gambling—how widespread it is, the demographic characteristics of the people most likely to be affected, and how the incidence grows or decreases over time. We also need research into all aspects of the causes and consequences of problem gambling, which will include careful monitoring of whatever regulatory, prophylactic, and therapeutic measures are adopted to combat problem gambling. Finally, I believe, we need research into nonproblem gambling so that we have a much clearer idea than we presently have of the difference between harmless gambling and problem gambling and in particular of the pleasures people derive from gambling and how these can be safely supplied and enhanced.

The main ingredient in a strategy for trying to prevent people from becoming problem gamblers will be educational. The general public need to be made aware of how gambling works, how to gamble sensibly, how to recognize the danger signs for problem gambling, and what to do if they or someone close to them develops a problem.

It seems likely that a fair amount of excessive gambling results from simple ignorance of odds. People do not understand the nature of chance and in particular that if they are betting on outcomes determined by chance from tossing coins, to playing roulette and random-number gambling machines, then past good or bad fortune is no guide either way to future probabilities. No matter how often the coin has come down heads, the roulette wheel has come up red, or how close the gambling machine has come to paying out or for how long it has failed to pay out, the odds on the next result being the same or different are exactly the same as they always are, namely, a function of the ratio of favorable to unfavorable outcomes that are built into the game. People also do not understand the nature of very long odds. They often reason in relation to lotteries that if they buy one ticket, they will have some chance of becoming fabulously rich; that if they buy two tickets they will have twice as much chance; and if they scrape together all the money they can get hold of to buy five hundred lot-tery tickets, then they will have a really, really good chance of winning, whereas in fact they still face odds of several million to five hundred, which is far from being a "really good chance."

Ignorance about odds is often reinforced by superstition. People believe in runs of good and bad luck; that fortune is or is not smiling upon them; that if they engage in particular rituals like rolling their eyes heavenwards, they will win favor with the gods and alter the percentages in their favor. We know rather little about the role of superstition in gambling behavior. It may be sim-ply a harmless way of adding to the fantasy that is part of the pleasure of play. Clearly, however, superstition when it is believed can be very dangerous and needs to be combated, especially if it turns out that there is a correlation be-tween relative lack of education, proneness to superstition, and vulnerability to problem gambling.[10]

Educating people with a view to diminishing the likelihood of their becom-ing problem gamblers should also include teaching them about good money management strategy. People who decide before starting to gamble how much they are prepared to lose in the course of that session as a way of pay-ing for the pleasure of playing, and who then stop when they have lost that amount, will not develop problems. People who additionally decide how much they will be satisfied with winning when they get ahead will not only not de-velop gambling problems; they will also ensure that they are getting good value in terms of playing time for the relatively small amount of money they will lose over the long term. Alternatively, players may simply decide in ad-vance the length of time they are going to play for and then quit when the time is up whether they are winning or losing. This suggests that one option for governments that are especially worried about problem gambling would be to compel players to make and abide by decisions of this sort—though, as with all government regulation of this sort, there is a price to be paid in terms of liberty.

There is perhaps no area where the lack of solid knowledge in relation to problem gambling is more regrettable than in that of treatment. We know very little about what kinds of intervention will be effective in preventing people from developing a full-blown gambling addiction, or of enabling them to re-cover from it once they have developed it. This, however, is a state of affairs that is by no means peculiar to problem gambling and applies not only to the treat-ment of addictions generally but also to the whole field of psychiatric medicine. In relation to addiction, part of the problem seems to be that while there seem to be a number of therapies that work reasonably well for people who are highly motivated to get well, the core of the problem seems to be precisely the absence of appropriate levels of motivation. On the other hand, large numbers of people do recover from addictions and report a wide variety of ways in which recovery comes about from religious conversion through self-help groups and the practicing of a twelve-step program to cognitive therapy, transactional analysis, and other forms of talk therapy. Also, many people seem to recover from addiction, just as they recover from other psychological disorders such as depression, without any specific intervention; it is as if they simply and spontaneously grow out of their condition.

Given these general considerations, it is not surprising that programs for problem gamblers that offer a telephone help line, personal counseling, and individual and group therapy, whether offered by medical professionals or within self-help groups or both, report some measure of success.[11] On the other hand, they all agree that only a small proportion of those who need help actually seek it, and a discouraging number of those who get over their problem for a substantial period subsequently relapse.

Part of the truth may be that at least until we know a great deal more about the physiological bases of psychological phenomena, there is little that can be done for people who suffer from a disease one of whose characteristic features is a conviction on the part of sufferers that there is nothing wrong with them, or alternately that causes them to believe that any "cure" would be worse than the disease. Conversely, it may also be true that if the desire to recover is present, there may be all sorts of different ways of reinforcing that desire and providing practical assistance in realizing it. This would suggest that rather than insisting, as people who treat addictions are sometimes inclined to do, that there is only one right way of helping people with addictive problems, it would be better to list the range of available treatments that are available with a description of how they work and a summary of what is claimed with respect to their strengths and weaknesses. Problem gamblers wishing to recover could then choose among the various treatment options.

In addition to questions of content, it is important to satisfactorily settle the question of how responsible-gambling programs should be funded and supervised. In general, there is a strong case for encouraging the industry to be involved, and to contribute financially on a voluntary basis rather than treating it as an enemy to be subdued or a corporate delinquent to be chastised and compelled to conform. From the government point of view, a relationship of voluntary collaboration is likely to yield a more effective program, which reflects the fact that a highly regulated and taxed gambling industry is in reality always a partnership between private and public sectors, in which there is a common interest in both the profitability of the industry and its good reputation as a responsible corporate citizen. The program will be more effective because industry has a great deal of relevant knowledge about the behavior of its customers and because some of what needs to be done requires willing cooperation from industry employees.

From the industry point of view, the advantages of voluntary cooperation are even clearer. The alternative to voluntary participation is a program that is imposed on them under circumstances that make them appear callous and greedy and where they have no influence over either content or costs and can conse-

quently exercise no restraining influence on the self-interest of both regulators
and the providers of problem gambling services. Such a situation makes poor
sense from a public relations point of view in an industry where public relations are crucial. It also affords the industry scant protection against the kind of
predatory litigation that sooner or later is likely to be brought against the gambling industry in the aftermath of the suits brought against the tobacco industry. In fairness, it should also be said that people who work in the gambling
industry are not more wicked than anybody else and typically wish to think of
themselves and to be thought of as providing entertainment rather than sys-
tematically profiting from the ruination of their customers' lives.

On the other hand, it is imperative that responsible-gambling programs
neither become nor are perceived to have become creatures of the gambling
industry. It is imperative that the relevant research have a high degree of
credibility and that, in general, the combined endeavors of industry and government not be perceived as merely an exercise in whitewashing and to-
kenism. This means that whatever portion of the bill industry pays directly
and voluntarily, the industry should neither appear to nor in fact control the
program. Politicians need to be able to assert credibly that they are exercising
ultimate responsibility for minimizing the damage caused by problem gambling, and they will be particularly sensitive to the charges that their opponents will make that they are in the pocket of the gambling industry in this
matter.

Because both public officials and industry professionals have vested and
competing interests—particularly with respect to how much money should
be spent on problem gambling—it is imperative that there be a strong independent component, drawn from civil society, in the supervision of responsible-
gambling programs, though this should not be drawn from the community of
researchers and treatment professionals who specialize in problem gambling;
they, after all, have their own vested interests. Ideally, perhaps, all decision
making about funding matters would be made by people who are knowl-
edgeable about gambling but independent of the industry, the regulators,
and the service providers. What is certain is that budgeting should be needs
driven; that is, what is spent should have a clear and concrete connection
with the objective of reducing the incidence of, and harm caused by, problem
gambling. The effectiveness, including the cost-effectiveness, of what is
spent should be evaluated with the same rigor as should be expected for
other budgets in the private and public sectors. Finally, there should be candid recognition that how much is spent will always be to some extent a matter of what is deemed reasonable or proportionate. It will always be possible
to make a case for spending more or less on research, on public education,
and on the subsidization of treatment. The objective of supervisory structures should be to ensure that when the necessary judgment is exercised in
determining these matters, that judgment is honest, well-informed, sensitive, and reasonable.

NOTES

1. See the seminal review article by H. J. Shaffer, "The Most Important Unresolved Issue in the Addictions: Conceptual Chaos," *Substance and Misuse* 32, no. 11 (1997): 1573–80.

2. Ibid. See also H. J. Shaffer and M. N. Hall, "Estimating the Prevalence of Adolescent Gambling Disorders: A Quantitative Synthesis and Guide towards Standard Gambling Nomenclature," *Journal of Gambling Studies* 12, no. 2 (1996): 193–214.

3. See U.K. Department of Culture, Media, and Sport, *Gambling Review Report*, 2001. Part of paragraph 17.1. on p. 85 reads, "problem gambling remains an under-researched area and the research that has been undertaken does not produce much in the way of definite conclusions."

4. Used inter alia by K. Sproston, B. Erens, and J. Orford, *Gambling Behaviour in Britain: Results from the British Gambling Prevalence Survey* (London: National Centre for Social Research, 2000).

5. H. R. Lesieur and S. B. Blume, "The South Oaks Gambling Screen (SOGS): A New Instrument for the Identification of Pathological Gamblers," *American Journal of Psychiatry* 144 (1987): 1184–88.

6. A number of studies have investigated the relationship between problem gambling and other psychological conditions, including other addictions and substance abuse. The consensus is that problem gamblers are significantly more likely to have other psychiatric and dependency problems than nonproblem gamblers. See, for example, D. W. Black and T. Moyer, "Clinical Features and Psychiatric Co-morbidity of Subjects with Pathological Gambling Behaviour," *Psychiatric Services* 49, no. 11 (1998): 1434–39; R. M. Cunningham-Williams, L. B. Cottler, W. M. Compton, and E. L. Spitznagel, "Taking Chances: Problem Gamblers and Mental Health Disorders—Results from the St. Louis Epidemiologic Catchment Area Study," *American Journal of Public Health* 88, no. 7 (1998): 1093–96; and B. Spunt, I. Dupont, H. R. Lesieur, H. J. Liberty, and D. Hunt, "Pathological Gambling and Substance Abuse: A Review of the Literature," *Substance Use and Misuse* 33, no. 13 (1998): 2535–60.

7. This proposal is, and is intended to be consonant with, the practice of identifying "level two" and "level three" gamblers as proposed in Shaffer and Hall, "Estimating the Prevalence of Adolescent Gambling Disorders." It would also accommodate the distinction between potential and probable pathological gamblers as discussed in D. Dube, M. H. Freeston, and R. Ladouceur, "Potential and Probable Pathological Gamblers: Where Do the Differences Lie?" *Journal of Gambling Studies* 12, no. 4 (1996): 419–30. However, my suggestion differs in wishing to construct a test that allows us to distinguish the populations we wish to identify as being in need of whatever treatment is suitable for addicts and those we wish to target for preventative education whether or not they are actual or potential pathological gamblers.

8. SOGS and the GA 20 questions seem to correlate quite well in any case. See M. P. Ursua and L. L. Uribelarrea, "Twenty Questions of Gamblers Anonymous: A Psychometric Study with [the] Population of Spain," *Journal of Gambling Studies* 14, no. 1 (1998): 3–15.

9. Nationwide responsible-gambling programs, funded by the industry on a voluntary basis, have been pioneered in South Africa and New Zealand. The U.K. industry, at the urging of government and in response to a specific recommendation in the Gambling Review Report, chap. 32, is also in the process of setting up voluntary structures to address problem gambling.

10. If the role of ignorance and irrationality is substantial in the development of problem gambling behaviors, then it is unsurprising that cognitive approaches to treatment should be at an advantage by comparison with those that focus exclusively on a disease or a behavioral model. See M. D. Griffiths, "The Cognitive Psychology of Gambling," *Journal of Gambling Studies* 6, no. 1 (1990): 31–42; C. Sylvain, R. Ladouceur, and J. M. Boisvert, "Cognitive and Behavioural Treatment of Pathological Gambling: A Controlled Study," *Journal of Consulting and Clinical Psychology* 65, no. 5 (1997): 727–32; T. Tonneatto, "Cognitive Psychopathology of Problem Gambling," *Substance Use and Misuse* 34, no. 11 (1999): 1593–1604.

11. Some examples are S. G. Sullivan, R. McCormack, and J. D. Sellman, "Increased Requests for Help by Problem Gamblers: Data from a Gambling Crisis Hotline," *New Zealand Medical Journal* 110, no. 1053 (1997): 380–83; C. MacDougall, "Problem Gambling Helpline: Annual Narrative Report, 1997–1998," Nova Scotia Department of Health, 1998; M. Griffiths, A. Scarfe, and P. Bellringer, "The U.K. Telephone Gambling Helpline: Results of the First Year of Operation," *Journal of Gambling Studies* 15, no. 1 (1999): 83–90.

Chapter 7

E-Gambling

In theory, there should be no need for a chapter devoted to the formulation of public policy for gambling using the new electronic technologies of the Internet, interactive television, and cell phones, collectively known as e-gambling. Whatever theoretical considerations are appropriate to the development of good public policy for regulating gambling at physical, "land-based" venues such as casinos, betting offices, and lottery ticket sales points should be applied straightforwardly to the regulation of commercial gambling activities that take place using personal computers, television sets, and telephones.

Thus if it is a good idea to require suppliers of land-based gambling services to demonstrate that they are honest, competent, and possessed of adequate financial resources, then the same requirement should be imposed on suppliers of e-gambling services. If regulators need to lay down the specifications for physical gambling machines, then they should do the same with virtual machines. If special measures are needed to protect the young and vulnerable in relation to gambling at casinos or racetracks, then the same or similar protections should be put in place for gambling on-line. Moreover, government should secure for the population as a whole an equitable proportion of the gross gambling revenues in the form of taxes or tax equivalents.

New delivery systems for gambling services do not by themselves alter the moral or social principles that should inform good gambling policy. What they alter, however, and have the potential to alter dramatically, are the practical, political, and economic realities. Consequently, in thinking about how governments should respond to the fact that gambling services are among the large range of goods and services that can now be supplied by Internet-related technologies, this chapter will concentrate mainly on how e-technologies affect the range not of what it is desirable for governments to do but of what it is possible for them to do.

The most fundamental difficulties arise from two features peculiar to e-gambling. The first is that the new communications technologies make it possible for people to gamble anywhere in the world and, in particular, in the privacy of their own homes. The second is that e-gambling services can not only be consumed anywhere in the world; they can also be supplied from nearly anywhere in the world.[1]

Each of these considerations raises a major difficulty in applying general social principles to the regulation of e-gambling. Because gambling can be carried out in the privacy of people's homes, governments—at least in liberal democracies—are likely to feel an especial reluctance about trying to regulate the pleasures that people may choose to indulge in there. Because e-gambling can be supplied to citizens from outside the jurisdiction of the national state, governments—even the U.S. government—may also feel some compunction if they try to legislate about what commercial activities may be pursued by the citizens of other sovereign states. In both cases, there will be serious practical problems of enforcement to the extent that government needs to police either or both what happens in the privacy of people's homes and on the soil of foreign countries.

Bearing this in mind, let us now see how far policies and practices developed for the regulation of land-based gambling can be applied to e-gambling.

GENERAL GAMBLING POLICY AND E-GAMBLING

It is sensible to begin by considering to what extent e-gambling can be accommodated within the principles of good policy and good regulation that have been established for land-based gambling. For this purpose, we need to remind ourselves of the five basic positions with respect to government policy and gambling that we identified in the introduction, namely:

- Gambling is immoral and should be banned
- Gambling is dangerous and should be contained and discouraged
- Gambling is a more or less normal part of the entertainment industry and should only be subject to special regulation to the extent that it is relevantly different from other forms of entertainment
- Gambling is a good way of raising taxes and tax equivalents in support of good causes
- Gambling is a good way to promote tourism and so earn dollars from the citizens of other jurisdictions by exporting legal gambling services to them

People who believe that gambling is immoral and should be prohibited will, of course, also believe that Internet and other forms of e-gambling should be prohibited. They may take the view that this is especially important in the case of e-gambling, which people do not even have to leave their homes to engage in, and it is especially difficult to prevent children from engaging in. The same is true of people who believe that gambling is undesirable—like cigarette smoking—primarily because of the harm it does to those who engage in it and that the only really good reason for not banning it completely is that this would lead, as in other cases of prohibition, to an extensive and by definition unregulated (and untaxed) illegal industry.

People whose conception of good public policy is founded on either of the first two positions share the conviction that there should be less gambling than there would be if governments did not seek to prevent people from doing what they would otherwise choose to do regarding gambling. For them, therefore, the questions for public policy in relation to e-gambling all relate to the practicality of enforcing total prohibition or at least severe restriction.

It is sometimes thought that these practical difficulties are insuperable, that policing a ban on e-gambling would be either technologically impossible or prohibitively expensive. This, however, is only a half-truth. E-gambling relies on the cooperation of bankers, and governments could make it illegal for banks to supply credit and debit card services to merchants whose business is gambling. Government could also, for example, make it illegal for citizens to gamble on the Internet—as currently it is not even in those parts of the United States most supportive of banning Internet gambling or in jurisdictions such as the U.K. where the supply but not the consumption of Internet gambling services is illegal. They could enforce this by random raids on private homes and by rewarding neighbors or family members who report illegal gambling activity. As these examples show, however, the moral rather than the material costs of enforcing prohibition are likely to be regarded as excessive, and it is this combination of doubtful moral justification and difficulty of practical implementation that makes it difficult to generate the political will to support the prohibition of e-gambling.[2] Governments do, of course, seek to overcome these difficulties in the case of narcotics: they do so, however, with spectacular unsuccess even though there is a wider consensus favoring prohibition. They are also likely to continue to do so with greater success in the cases of Internet child pornography, on the one hand, and, on the other, of Internet material that facilitates terrorist activity. In these cases, the requisite political will exists both domestically and internationally to make effective action possible.

In general, however, the argument that e-gambling should be prohibited or as thoroughly restricted as possible runs into the same powerful objections that, as we have already seen, tend to command majority support in liberal democracies against prohibitionist arguments applied to land-based commercial gambling. Does this mean that e-gambling should be treated as just another part of the entertainment industry and that its availability should be regulated and restricted only to the extent necessary to prevent fraud and to protect the vulnerable?

It is sometimes alleged that the reason why e-gambling should be prohibited is precisely that it is not in fact possible to enforce regulations that would accomplish what regulations accomplish with respect to land-based gambling, for example, preventing minors from gambling or affording adequate player protection. This argument is not persuasive: in principle, it is easier to regulate e-gambling than land-based gambling, since in the former case, but not the latter, there is an automatic record kept of every electronic transaction made. One consequence of this is that it is easier to identify patterns of excessive or addictive behavior and to intervene by automatically switching a problem player to a responsible gambling site.[3] It is also easier to require players to set advance limits to their losses on a daily or monthly basis, after which the site will refuse to accept further bets. It is also at least as easy for regulators to carry out anonymous spot inspections of games, or to set up sting operations to ensure, for example, the integrity of the games or compliance with anti-money-laundering regulations, when gambling services are delivered electronically as it is when gambling takes place on land.

The only area where e-gambling is more difficult to regulate than land-based gambling is that of player identification, and this causes particular worries to those who want to prevent minors from gambling. The commonest way of addressing this issue is to require that copies—perhaps certified copies—of documents such as birth certificates, passports, or similar identity documents be faxed or mailed to the gambling company before a player is allowed to play. To verify addresses, players can be required to send copies of a utilities bill. This is what is increasingly done by banks to comply with the international anti-money-laundering requirement that banks know their customers. With regard to children there is the further safeguard that they will need a credit card, telephone account, or other credit facility to gamble electronically, and most children will not have much access to this kind of credit. It is, of course, true that parents can circumvent these requirements on behalf of their children and that children can steal documents and credit cards. However, parents can already buy their children lottery tickets, and children can already defraud their parents and others to purchase goods and services whether on the Internet or at conventional outlets such as ATMs if they secure the relevant smart cards and PIN codes.

The really important point for policy makers to grasp about gambling on personal computers and other devices is that all the bad things they may fear and deplore about e-gambling are already likely to be occurring with at least as great a frequency while Internet gambling is illegal as they would if it were legal and well regulated.

At present there are estimated to be about 1,200 Web sites offering virtual gambling mostly regulated in Caribbean countries, led by Antigua. It would be wrong to sneer at these so-called Third World jurisdictions and assume that they are necessarily incompetent or corrupt. On the contrary, the governments of these jurisdictions should be credited with having shown considerable entrepreneurial initiative and having pioneered an activity that more-developed countries are now seeking to imitate. Moreover, some of the existing sites are operated by respectable international gambling companies, which cannot afford to jeopardize their reputations by being associated with government corruption. Most important, if the present situation had resulted in epidemics of compulsive, fraudulent, or underage gambling, those opposed to e-gambling would presumably have found out. No such evidence has been forthcoming. Be that as it may, the choice for governments in developed countries is not what to do given that there is at present no e-gambling available to their citizens, and that it might therefore be possible to maintain that happy situation. The choice is what to do given that there is a great deal of e-gambling already happening that, whether well regulated or not, is not currently regulated by them. Consequently, they have no effective control over the way their citizens gamble in cyberspace, and they derive no public benefits from this activity.

Faced with this situation, governments in developed countries seem to be ambivalent.[4] On the one hand, they believe that, especially in the aftermath of the huge expansion of gambling in the 1990s, they now have enough commercial gambling, at least for the time being. On the other hand, they seem to regard the costs of trying to stop people from gambling electronically as being too high in terms of violations of individual liberty. The same thinking informs government reluctance to clamp down on the availability of pornography on the Internet, except in the case of child pornography.

Given this ambivalence, public policy about e-gambling is likely in the end to come down on the side of legalization and regulation for the two main reasons that it does so with respect to land-based gambling: first, that it is better to have an industry that you regulate yourself than one that is supplied by foreigners or criminals who are difficult to control; second, if governments must regulate gambling anyway, they might as well secure some advantages from it—especially economic ones—for their own citizens.

This is why public policy about e-gambling does not concern itself only with finding the right balance between respecting individual freedom and minimizing potential harm to consumers. As with all forms of gambling, there are potentially large sums of money involved, and government policy will to a large extent determine who gets it, including how much the government itself gets. Once societies have come to the conclusion that commercial trading in a commodity whose consumption was once prohibited on grounds of immorality should be legalized, the question of how much of the earnings from that trade should accrue to government becomes crucial. It is this consideration, at least as much as public health considerations, that determines the character of all gambling regulation, including the regulation of Internet gambling.

In the case of Internet gambling, as with land-based gambling, the first thoughts of governments when contemplating the economic advantages they might secure through a legal gambling industry are about the possibility of export earnings by attracting the gambling dollars of foreigners. The first jurisdictions to legalize e-gambling, most notably Antigua, were those that saw an opportunity to develop what would essentially be a cyber-tourism business that would provide new investment, new earnings, and new employment. Hitherto, by far the largest market for these Internet casino services has been the United States, so other jurisdictions are effectively exporting cyber-gambling services to the United States, whose own gambling businesses cannot supply them. As we have seen, it makes a huge difference to what constitutes good gambling policy whether it is anticipated that the majority of gamblers will come from within the jurisdiction or from outside of it. When Monte Carlo and Las Vegas legalized gambling, their objective was to become the principal resort on their respective continents, to which gamblers would flock from all the neighboring states where casinos were illegal. These jurisdictions and others that have imitated them, therefore, regulated gambling to secure the maximum benefits from a new form of tourism.

Now, if governments wish to regulate gambling to attract tourists, they have the power to do a number of things to make their jurisdiction more attractive to potential visitors compared to competing destinations around the world. Four are particularly important:

- Influencing the comparative costs and conditions of doing business so as to attract hoteliers and other tourism businesses to their jurisdiction
- Ensuring that the infrastructure in terms of roads, railways, harbors, and airports is of a high standard and efficiently operated
- Minimizing bureaucratic hassle for visitors entering the country by making it easy for them to get visas, pass though customs, et cetera
- Ensuring that the environment is healthy, clean, and safe for tourists

These four functions of government in relation to the tourism industry have their analogues in the Internet gambling business. Thus governments in the Caribbean, the states of Australia (though not, it seems, the federal government), Gibraltar, the Isle of Man and Alderney in the U.K., South Africa, parts of Canada, and elsewhere explicitly wish to attract Internet gambling companies to their jurisdiction, and so they seek to

- Keep taxes comparatively and competitively low and licensing conditions simple (this does not necessarily mean they are easy to comply with: the governments typically want to attract gambling companies with established track records and deep pockets)
- Adopt regulations that make it easy for players to access the sites they regulate
- Ensure that the essential communications infrastructure has adequate capacity and is efficient and reliable
- Offer various degrees of player protection, because this will attract players to sites located under their jurisdiction

In general, there are two main questions that global gaming companies will ask when choosing among jurisdictions where to locate their Internet business.

- How low is the cost of doing business, including especially licensing and taxation costs?
- How much customer confidence will be generated by the fact that our business is regulated by this particular government? In other words, how much commercial advantage attaches to be regulated in this jurisdiction rather than another?

They will also ask the subsidiary questions:

- How good is the IT infrastructure, or how good can it be made?
- How much use can we make of local labor?
- How congenial will this jurisdiction be as a place for our nonlocal employees (especially our executives) to spend time?

As with tourism, then, when governments address the question of how to license and regulate e-gambling, they are competing with other jurisdictions for valuable export earnings. In general, they will be seeking to offer low costs (and taxes) in combination with a regulatory dispensation that offers a high degree of player confidence. In this way, they will hope to induce companies offering e-gambling to base themselves in their jurisdiction, employ their locals, and pay their corporation taxes.

Unfortunately, the strategy of trying to design a regulatory environment that is maximally attractive to big e-gambling companies is not likely to prove viable over the long term. The reason is the same as that which prevented many individual jurisdictions in the United States from sustaining the economic benefits of legalizing land-based gambling, namely, competition between jurisdictions. Just as individual states were persuaded to legalize casinos and lotteries to prevent the gambling dollars of their citizens from flowing out to their neighbors, so whatever one jurisdiction does to attract the world's e-gambling business will be matched and, in the first instance, bettered by competing jurisdictions. The result is that the customers for gambling services become no longer foreigners but locals, resident within the jurisdiction. And the consequence of that, of course, is that any public policy benefits will come from redistributing wealth rather than from new foreign earnings.

In the end, what is likely to happen is that governments will increasingly enter into agreements with one another, so that eventually an internationally agreed set of regulations will be established, and whatever taxes are levied will accrue to the governments under whose jurisdictions the individual gamblers fall. This is particularly likely to happen as it becomes clearer that e-commerce generally needs international regulation. Some of this need will be associated with the kind of activities where everyone agrees that international regulation and enforcement are necessary—child pornography, terrorist activity, fraud, money laundering, trading in drugs, and so on.

However, international regulation of e-commerce, including e-gambling, is perhaps at least as likely to be driven by commercial needs. One of the reasons why the "new economy" has so far failed to take off is that at present it is almost impossible to make sustainable profits out of the majority of e-businesses. This is because it is not presently possible to patent commercially good e-commerce ideas. Companies that set up a good e-business are therefore likely to find themselves competing with others who have simply copied their business plan and are perhaps undercutting them on price. In other words, most e-businesses are subject to the laws of near-perfect competition, with low barriers to entry and with no fees paid for intellectual property, that is, for using the original business idea. This drives the price of goods and services offered via the Internet down to the absolute minimum at which it is worth anyone's while to supply them.

In any event, as the e-gambling business grows, the need for international regulation will become more and more apparent and pressing. It may also be true that until there is good international regulation, it will be difficult for the business to grow to anything like its full potential.

There is one other important commercial consideration that governments sometimes need to consider when contemplating the legalization of e-gambling. This consideration tells with some governments more forcefully than others and concerns the impact that the introduction of legalized e-gambling may have on the existing land-based industry. Governments will be under lobbying pressure from the existing industry if that industry believes that its interests will be gravely imperiled by the legalization of e-gambling. More crucially, governments will find this consideration irresistible if the public, through its government, has a significant stake in the profitability of the land-based industry. This happens whenever a significant share of gambling revenues is earmarked for funding public interest capital projects or public services. It happens most damagingly from a government's point of view whenever land-based gambling operations employ significant numbers of people. In this connection, it is obviously relevant that Internet gambling is much less labor intensive than land-based gambling.

At least part of the reason why e-gambling has not been legalized in the United States is that the large Nevada-based gambling companies were initially able to lobby successfully against e-gambling because they feared it would have a detrimental effect on their earnings from land-based operations. In the U.K., the impulse to legalize Internet gambling was first sparked by the fact that government was losing significant tax revenues from betting because bookmakers were offering bets from call centers and over the Internet from jurisdictions, especially Gibraltar, where there was no betting tax. More generally, jurisdictions tend to protect the monopoly of their state lotteries by a combination of interstate agreements, bans on advertising, and exploiting the natural advantages of being a local, rather than a foreign, lottery. It must be only a matter of time, however, before lottery products are delivered over the Net or via cell phones that can outcompete state and national lotteries on price—that is, they will offer more and bigger prizes or cheaper tickets—and also perhaps on the attractiveness of the good causes they support.

From a government's point of view, even more important than protecting revenues to the public purse will be protecting its electoral support. Consequently, the decisions government makes about legalizing e-gambling will be shaped by a perennial concern with how the treatment of gambling matters will be perceived by electorates, especially by voters who are opposed to gambling. The federal government of Australia, whose individual states successfully pioneered the legalization and regulation of e-gambling outside the Caribbean, has recently imposed a moratorium on e-gambling, responding to a general backlash against gambling among Australians and believing that there are votes to be gained by proclaiming itself against introducing a casino into every Australian home, conveniently forgetting the fact that there are already some 1,200 casinos located in every home that has access to the Internet. In the United States, the continuing legislative struggles at state and federal level are now predominantly driven not by existing vested interests in the gambling industry but by antigambling lobbies.

These economic reasons—little prospect of sustained export earnings, insignificant tax benefits, threats to existing employment, and so forth—combine with the purely political reason that there is no serious public demand from consumers to have a legalized and regulated e-gambling industry while at the same time there are pressure groups that are fairly passionately opposed to such legalization. Consequently it is not surprising that governments have—to the great disappointment of would-be suppliers—proceeded slowly in deciding what to do about e-gambling.

This situation would obviously change if e-gambling products and services become much more popular with consumers. Is this likely to happen? The e-gambling industry, which has for rather longer than was originally predicted remained in a fledgling state, claims that it is only a matter of time before e-gambling becomes as big as, or bigger than, land-based gambling. All sorts of predictions about the growth of e-gambling have been made and revised over the past decade, most of them unduly optimistic, and all of them highly speculative. The truth is that how large the market for e-gambling turns out to be at any given point in the future depends on factors about which we are presently ignorant. One of these is precisely what governments around the world will decide to do about e-gambling. Another is how soon and how effectively new technologies will be able to deliver both new and traditional gambling products. Perhaps the most difficult of all to predict is how consumer tastes will develop. Estimates are regularly put out about how the industry will grow, and some of the numbers are mouthwatering—as they are intended to be. The fact is, however, that the future of e-gambling remains uncertain, and quantification of its likely value is consequently too difficult to be useful.

Even so, I believe that some speculations are more plausible than others, and for what they're worth, I conclude by offering some of my own speculations, since ultimately what constitutes good public policy in relation to e-gambling will be shaped even more by what consumers actually want than by what suppliers would like them to want. In particular, I offer two predictions about what will become possible for e-gambling, and I then make some suggestions about how governments, consumers, and suppliers are likely to react to these new possibilities.

First of all, it seems likely that advances in technology and in e-commerce generally will make it attractive to consumers, for example, to use their cell

phones (and to be debited on their phone account) to gamble on keno-type numbers games whenever they feel like it, or to participate using their telephony, especially cell phones, in cheap international daily lotteries, perhaps supporting
popular international causes—children with AIDS, land mine removal, starvation in Africa. Here the attraction is, in the first case, the pleasure of cheap, simple play that adds the prospect of winning money to the pleasure of playing the
kinds of games that are already built into cell phones and laptops; in the second,
the pleasure of dreaming about becoming fabulously, life-changingly rich by
staking only a small amount of money at very long odds.

Second, it seems probable that betting of all kinds will become increasingly
available via the new technologies. Of course there is nothing new in principle
about placing bets over the telephone. What is new is the ease and, especially,
the cheapness of international communications that make it easy for bookmakers to trade with clients based anywhere in the world. Because the pleasures of
betting are closely linked to the pleasure of watching the events being bet on, it
seems likely that growth here will at first focus on interactive television. Eventually, presumably the technologies of the cell phone, the television, and the
personal computer will become fully integrated, at which time it will in principle be possible to make bets, play games for money, and participate in lotteries
from anywhere that it is possible to take one's integrated, personal, all-purpose
communicator.

Governments will not relish this potential anarchy. They will certainly want to
regulate all these gambling activities both to prevent fraud and excessive and addictive gambling and to protect their own lottery and other gambling revenues.
Moreover, they will be able to do so because of their power to control all financial
transactions. E-gambling and e-commerce generally cannot function without
banks, and banks have to do what governments tell them to do. Governments
would, perhaps, not be able to do much—at least to the extent that government
remains subject to democratic sanctions—if their attempts to limit e-gambling
were widely unpopular with both consumers and suppliers. Strong regulation,
however, is likely to be welcomed by both gambling companies and their customers because, as with the early days of the lotteries, racing, and casinos, there
is a huge potential for cheating. If e-gambling is to globalize the market for individual gambling products, it will be imperative to ensure that the lotteries are not
rigged, the sporting events not fixed, and the games not crooked.

Assuming, then, that governments are able to ensure that gamblers get as
fair a deal when e-gambling as they do when engaging in well-regulated land-
based gambling, what will gamblers choose to do? Will they still want the
glamor and glitz of going to a casino in the company of other gamblers, or will
they prefer the convenience of staying at home to gamble in cyberspace? Or
will they have blown their entire stake playing interactive bingo while waiting
for a bus or sitting in a traffic jam?

My own view on this matter is the following. The most plausible way of
thinking about the future of e-gambling, at least initially, is by analogy to

home videos. The ability to watch movies at home obviously creates a huge increase in convenience. Also, since there is no need for suppliers to cover the costs of renting theaters, movies can potentially be supplied more cheaply. On the other hand, watching a movie at home, even when the technical quality is as good as can be found in a cinema, has a different feel to it; and, in fact, even though people know that they can watch videos more cheaply at home, they still choose in large numbers to go out to see films in the theater. There seems to be something distinctive about the experience of "going out" for entertainment rather than "staying in" to enjoy the same product. This applies to meals, which people would often prefer to eat in a restaurant even if they can get the same gastronomic products delivered to, or prepared in, their home. In fact, what has happened with videos is that they have not killed off the market for theaters, and still less have companies that deliver meals to your home killed off the market for dining in restaurants. I suspect that the same will turn out to be true of home-based gambling, to the extent that it is entertainment, and not an activity that is pursued quasi-professionally, and where price is decisive. On the whole, the home video industry has ensured that people see more films overall without significantly denting the popularity of going out to a movie as a form of "going out" entertainment.

If this is so, one should see e-gambling as essentially part of the home entertainment business, whose future will be closely allied to the future of that whole industry. Presumably, like the rest of the entertainment industry, growth will be closely related to increases in the amount of time and money that people have to spend on recreation. Even when people can gamble at home with greater ease than at present, I would still expect there to be a large number of people who will prefer, either regularly or occasionally, to go out to a casino or other venue where they can play the games of their choice or bet on sporting and other events as they watch them. As long as, and to the extent that, going out to gamble remains an attractive option when people want to go out to have fun, the land-based industry will continue to flourish. On the other hand, gambling is predominantly an activity that is popular with the less affluent, and there is some reason to think that the popularity of all types of gambling—especially machine gambling—will decline if affluence in the developed world continues to spread and higher levels of education are more widely achieved throughout society.

This relates to the kind of gambling that is likely to be popular as home entertainment. Already it is significant that at virtual casinos, machine gambling is far less popular than table games, a trend that is the reverse of the situation at land-based casinos. It may also be expected that people who have grown up playing TV and computer games will want to play adult gambling games that require a higher degree of intellectual or manual dexterity than is offered by fruit machines.

How will suppliers of gambling services react to these changes and the threats and opportunities they present? I believe that from the point of view of a gambling company, the worst thing about the gambling business is the possibility that players might win, and the company might lose. This goes against the heroic image of bookmakers or casino owners as people who win because they pit their superior skill and courage against the players. This image arose when professional suppliers of gambling services saw themselves, and usually started out as, professional gamblers. Nowadays the most attractive forms of gambling business to be in are those where the risk of losing is eliminated: parimutuel betting, lotteries, and slot machines where what is paid out is set as a fraction of what is paid in.

As e-gambling develops, the incentives to suppliers only to deal in forms of gambling where their earnings are guaranteed will grow. This is partly because their clients will be anonymous, and personal judgments will therefore be harder to make about how much, for example, a high roller is likely to lose at blackjack and how reliable he or she will be in covering losses. Mostly, however, it is because the possibilities of cheating increase hugely with e-gambling. The effect of this will be that betting exchanges where the gambling company simply puts bettors in touch with each other may become more popular in the world of e-gambling and more lucrative than traditional bookmaking. Similarly, companies supplying gambling games in cyberspace may increasingly seek to charge a fee for arranging the games rather than relying on house advantage to make their profits. Already, playing poker, bridge, and other games of real skill with real people over the Internet is one of the most popular uses of the Internet, and as in land-based casinos, the house at these Internet sites simply takes a fee for organizing the games.

All in all, it seems to me quite likely that the future of e-gambling will mirror the history of land-based gambling. From an essentially anarchic business, e-gambling will develop into a highly regulated one. From an industry that began by seeking to attract customers from outside of the jurisdiction where it is regulated, e-gambling will come to service customers who live within the jurisdiction. From one that was originally treated as exotic, e-gambling will come to be integrated into the general entertainment industry. I also suspect that e-gambling may develop from an industry that was thought to be capable of generating exceptional tax revenues to one that is taxed normally.

If something like this turns out to be so, the future of e-gambling will reflect the future of gambling generally within the home entertainment industry, and e-gambling's fortunes will be linked to the future of entertainment generally. These considerations suggest a solidly prosperous future for e-gambling, if not the sensational one that has from time to time been predicted. This is because the general global prospects for the entertainment industry must be exceptionally good. On the other hand, it is far from clear how successfully gambling will compete with other sectors of the entertainment industry (movies, sports, bars, restaurants, music, books, etc.) for the public's entertainment dollars—and this is true whether the entertainment is being offered in their own homes or at venues to which people go out. Perhaps the sheer boredom that the prospect of especially the more mindless forms of gambling inspires in many people will spread to the great majority of the population and both spell an end to the gambling boom of the last twenty-odd years and ensure that the oft-predicted e-gambling boom never takes place. But perhaps it won't, and the popularity of mechanical gambling will hold steady or even increase. In that case, e-gambling could well become the dominant and most lucrative form of commercial gambling, enabling people to gamble on their game of choice whenever and wherever they felt like it.

NOTES

1. A useful account of some of the main legal difficulties that arise out of the present uncertain situation in the United States are discussed in S. Philippsohn, "Landmark Cases of Internet Gaming," *Gaming Law Review* 3, nos. 5–6 (1999): 329–33.

2. Compare, however, B. P. Keller, "The Game's the Same: Why Gambling in Cyberspace Violates Federal Law," *Yale Law Review* 108, no. 7 (1999): 1569–1609. Keller argues that new law is not needed to prohibit Internet gambling, so the political will does not need to be mustered to secure prohibition. However, the political will would still need to be mustered in support of enforcement, and this is unlikely to be forthcoming if it requires serious invasions of privacy rights.

3. Mark Griffiths, however, argues that there may be problem-gambling issues specific to the Internet to the extent that the delivery system itself enhances the addictiveness of the games. See Griffiths, "Gambling on the Internet: A Brief Note," *Journal of Gambling Studies* 9, no. 4 (1996): 387–99.

4. Governments tend to worry about the perception that they are licensing too much gambling and that voters will not like the thought of authorizing casinos in the home. Academics who do not have to worry about popular (mis)perceptions overwhelmingly favor a policy of legalizing and regulating. See, for example, T. Bell, "Internet Gambling: Popular, Inexorable, and (Eventually) Legal," *Policy Analysis* 336 (1995); and M. P. Kailus, "Do Not Bet on Unilateral Prohibition of Internet Gambling to Eliminate Cyber-Casinos," *University of Illinois Law Review* 3 (1999): 1045–81; and for the U.K., J. Harris, "The Case for Regulating Internet Gambling in Great Britain," *Gaming Law Review* 3, nos. 5–6 (1999): 335–440.

Chapter 8

Gambling and Morality

We saw in chapter 3 that the question of whether gambling should be legalized is a separate issue from the question of whether gambling is immoral. We also saw that a strong case can be made for thinking that even if gambling is immoral, it should not be made illegal; and moreover, we saw that much of this strong case is itself a moral case. It is a moral case because it is based on considerations about the principles that should determine and constrain the conduct of governments. With respect to allowing people to gamble, the most important of these moral principles is that (except in the case of preventing harm to innocent third parties) governments should treat their citizens as autonomous adults entitled to decide for themselves how to live their lives, even if this means that many of them will make bad choices from the point of view of both their own best interests and what morality requires. Any other policy is paternalistic and morally indefensible.

In this view, the argument for prohibition is itself morally defective even if it is true that gambling is an immoral activity. Nevertheless, because views about the morality of gambling play such a substantial, if often unacknowledged, part in shaping people's views about what public policy should be regarding gambling, we need to directly consider the question "Is gambling immoral?"[1] In other words, if it were agreed, on the purest libertarian grounds, that the state should do absolutely nothing to try to prevent or discourage people from gambling as much as they like, would there still be any good reasons why you and I should decide on moral grounds that gambling should play little or no part in the way we conduct our daily lives? Many people are tempted to dismiss this question by saying that there is no general answer; it is a matter of taste or personal choice; no one has the right to tell anyone else whether he or she should or shouldn't gamble, just as no one has the right to tell anyone else what he or she should eat or drink, or to whom he or she should or shouldn't make love. One reason for not dismissing questions about the morality of gambling so quickly is that people who make these kinds of permissivist claim usually accept that it is, however, perfectly all right to advise people about what it would be prudent for them to do, for example, on health grounds, and this may itself shade into moral counseling. A still stronger reason for considering the question of how people in general should conduct their lives in relation to gambling regardless of what the law forbids or permits is that this question becomes inescapable when we consider what we should teach children about gambling. Should we take an essentially puritanical view and tell them, "Gambling is bad. Don't do it"? Or should we adopt a fundamentally permissivist approach and say, "There's nothing wrong with gambling. Gamble as much as you please"? Or should we say something in between?

It will be helpful to anchor this discussion by locating it within the context of reasoning about the role that pleasure generally and pleasures of various particular sorts should play in our lives. This is a fundamental issue in moral philosophy, and I propose to discuss it in relation to the two types of ethical theory that are usually—though often rather too facilely—discussed by contemporary moral philosophers as being the principal competing theories in the field.[2] The two types of theory have imposing names: "deontological" theories, which ground morality in doctrines of absolute and objective duties and rights; and "utilitarian" theories, according to which moral questions are to be settled by ascertaining which course of action will be most conducive to securing human interests and promoting human happiness. I will consider these views in turn and argue that neither of them is decisive in showing that gambling is necessarily immoral, but both have some substantial moral force that we should consider when thinking about how to live our own lives and about what to teach our children about gambling. Moreover, I will argue that where they are most persuasive, each of these kinds of moral reasoning leads to the same conclusion about the role that gambling should play in people's lives.[3]

DUTY-BASED (DEONTOLOGICAL) THEORIES

Deontological arguments derive their name from the Greek word for obligation. In more modern times, this kind of ethical reasoning has primarily been associated with the eighteenth-century German philosopher Immanuel Kant, especially his doctrine of the "categorical imperative," according to which morality is about those rules of conduct that we have an absolute duty to obey, regardless of whether we have any desire to obey them and whether they are in our interests. For example, we have an absolute duty to keep promises. We also have an absolute duty to respect the autonomy of other people and not to treat them merely as means to our own ends.

Typically, Kant based his arguments about what we have an absolute duty to do and to refrain from doing on a consideration of what we can rationally de-

sire. The criterion he proposes for determining the nature of our moral obligations is that we should only act in ways such that we can rationally wish the
principle underlying our action to become a universal law or a law of nature.
Thus, he thought, one could not rationally desire that the world should be a
place where all people told lies or broke promises whenever it suited them. This
seems plausible to the extent that there does seem to be something very like a
piece of self-contradiction in asserting, "It would be a good thing if people always told lies when they felt like it" or "Everyone should break their promises
if they think they will gain thereby." It also seems plausible to claim that there
would be something not just bad but mad about someone who asserted without
any further explanation that it is just or right for blue-eyed people to be paid
much more than brown-eyed people for doing the same job.

According to Kant, we have a moral duty to do what we can rationally will to
become a universal law, and a duty to refrain from doing what we cannot so
will. People sometimes deploy Kantian reasoning to support the view that it is
morally wrong to gamble. In particular, they argue that this is a morally wrong
way of treating money. Thus the whole point of gambling is to distribute property randomly: to make some people richer who have done nothing to deserve
it and others poorer simply as a consequence of chance. Allied to this is the
thought that gamblers are people who want something for nothing. A Kantian
might then argue that one could not rationally desire a world in which what
people possess bears no relation to what they deserve in terms of their natural
endowments, the talents they cultivate and deploy, their industry, and their
general contribution to the welfare of society.

One objection to this line of reasoning would be a sort of socialist argument
that pointed out that, as a matter of fact, property in society has mostly been
and mostly still is distributed according to accidents of birth. It might then be
further argued that it would be much fairer and perhaps less divisive if instead
of allowing people to inherit wealth (and otherwise benefit materially from fortunate accidents of birth), differences in at least unearned wealth should be determined entirely by an actual lottery rather than the so-called lottery of life.
From a purely Kantian point of view, it would not obviously be irrational to desire that the world become a place in which economic inequalities are randomly
distributed.

A more down-to-earth objection to the Kantian antigambling argument is to
deny that gambling is all about wanting something for nothing. On the contrary, it may plausibly be argued, gambling is merely a pastime in which some
people take pleasure and for which they are willing to pay in the form of the
losses they incur because the odds are set, to a modest degree, against the player
and in favor of the house. Surely there is nothing irrational about the principle
that people should be able to spend their own time and money on entertainments of their own choosing.

Of course, people who advocate the puritan view that we have a duty to deny
ourselves pleasure generally and the pleasure of gambling in particular do not

most commonly appeal to considerations of what we can rationally desire. The view that all indulgence in worldly pleasures is immoral is more closely associated with the kind of religious asceticism that is a feature of all major faiths rather than with philosophical rationalism. The key notion in these religious views is the alleged duty of self-denial. This religious asceticism has a secular counterpart in the views of people who ascribe to political commitment the same importance as others ascribe to religious faith: the pursuit of private pleasure distracts from the work of establishing the ideal society, however conceived. An interesting, if eccentric, puritan view about gambling is to be found in Freud's claim that gambling is really a substitute for masturbation and, as such, characteristic of impaired mental health and an impediment to achieving the Freudian ideal of full genitality.

At the heart of the notion that we have duties of self-denial that make many forms of dissipation, including gambling, immoral is the idea of stewardship. In the religious version, the claim is that our minds and bodies, our time and talents, as well as whatever material resources we possess, are all gifts of God.[4] We are the stewards of these gifts and should not squander or abuse them. Rather, we should put them to noble use in the service of God and of our fellows. The secular version of the stewardship argument typically appeals to the notion that we have a duty to deny ourselves in order to promote the well-being of others. We may thus be urged to use our gifts and resources for the good of society as a whole, and this allegedly requires that we not engage in sterile forms of self-indulgence but use our time and energies in socially useful work. Sometimes it appeals to our alleged obligations to future generations, including, most obviously, our own children. In this view, indulgence in certain forms of pleasure (of which gambling is one) constitutes a dereliction of our duties of stewardship because the seductive pleasure in question distracts us from our duty to engage in more constructive pursuits that in some way make the world a better place.

In its simplest and strongest form, however, this kind of deontological argument appeals not to the notion of our duty to others but to the idea of our duty to ourselves. If this life is all we have, we owe it to ourselves not to fritter it away, for example, by wasting our time and money gambling. The claim here is that we would be squandering our gifts if we devote ourselves to pleasures that are unworthy in themselves. Thus, indulging in certain forms of sexual pleasure, or perhaps any form of sexual pleasure, is thought to be (mildly or seriously) degrading or disgusting, and similar sentiments underlie the view held by some people that gambling and the places where it takes place are (mildly or seriously) squalid or offensive.

Whether our perspective is predominantly religious or humanistic, it is easy to make sense of what people have been getting at in their hostility to drugs, gambling, and promiscuity. In each case, a plausible argument can be made for the view that loveless sex is not a right use of the body, that consigning one's property to chance is improper stewardship of one's possessions, and that altering one's state of mind with chemicals is an abuse of one's mind. Arguments of this kind will never be decisive, but that does not mean they are without rational force. And the force of these stewardship arguments is to alert us in what may be an extremely salutary way to the dangers of squandering our lives. It does not, however, support the view, nor is it usually taken as supporting the view, that any particular pleasures are in themselves wrong, including gambling.

On the contrary, against puritanism one can cogently argue that pleasure is always a good and, as such, always a good prima facie reason for action. Thus if there is anything morally wrong about indulging in any alleged vice, this cannot be a function of the character of the pleasure it offers, let alone of the fact that it offers pleasure at all. It is indeed difficult to see how gambling or anything else could rationally be adjudged immoral merely on the grounds that people enjoy it. Like any other activity in which people take pleasure, if gambling is immoral, this must be because of its propensity for corrupting character or otherwise doing damage to those who engage in it or to others. In the case of all pleasures, this must be primarily an empirical issue, and in the case of gambling, the empirical evidence seems to be that most gambling does not do most gamblers more harm than good.

INTEREST-BASED (UTILITARIAN) ARGUMENTS

The question of whether gambling does more harm than good is central to utilitarian arguments about gambling. The most general form of the utilitarian position is that we should do whatever will most contribute to the greatest happiness of the greatest number of people, when all count for one and none for more than one. In the view of Jeremy Bentham, one of the founding fathers of utilitarianism in England, this principle should be our guide both in determining our personal ethics and in determining what the content of the law should be. It might therefore be thought that whether we should gamble ourselves and whether the law should permit, encourage, or forbid us to gamble are both questions to be settled by determining which course of action will as a matter of fact lead to the greatest amount of happiness in the world or the least amount of unhappiness. As we have seen, however, John Stuart Mill, the philosopher whose name is most closely associated with classical utilitarianism and whose book of that name remains a seminal text for utilitarian ethics, took the view that gambling is an activity that, like consensual fornication or self-intoxication, cannot legitimately be banned on the grounds of the damage these activities do to the people who engage in them. In other words, even if we knew that gambling in the long run leads to more human misery than human felicity, that would still not justify prohibition. Mill thought this because he thought that a society in which government prevented people from exercising free choice in matters that affect only themselves would, for all sorts of reasons, be a society whose political arrangements were not ultimately conducive to the greatest happiness of the greatest number of people. Thus we cannot outlaw gambling on the grounds that it is harmful to the gambler because the unhappiness that we thereby prevent gamblers from inflicting on themselves is outweighed by the greater overall unhappiness that we cause by frustrating people's desire to live as seems good to them—a freedom that, Mill thinks, is a chief ingredient of human happiness.

But the fact that an activity ought not to be banned does not mean that it is morally right or even morally neutral to engage in it. In fact, Mill clearly thought that the traditional vices, including gambling, are indeed immoral, and consequently people should eschew them and encourage others to eschew them, even though indulgence in them may do no harm to anyone else.

According to utilitarianism, it is presumably true that if an activity such as gambling affords me some pleasure, this means that I should engage in it, other things being equal, if to do so will indeed add to the sum total of human happiness at least by the amount of my enjoyment: there is always, therefore, a prima facie reason for doing what you think will make you happy, that is, what you currently want. However, prima facie reasons can be overridden, and with respect to pleasures such as gambling and drinking, the most obvious utilitarian consideration that would override the case for self-indulgence is the likely effect on others. This is particularly clear in cases where people neglect the interests of, and otherwise cause misery to, their families through their drinking, gambling, or sexual self-indulgence. But Mill claimed that there is an additional utilitarian consideration that supports an ethic of self-denial in relation to "the vices" (such as drinking, gambling, and fornication) and relates only to their effect on the happiness of the drinker, the gambler, and the fornicator themselves. This is that fornicating, gambling, and drinking are "lower pleasures" that should be abstained from in favor of "higher pleasures" such as enjoying works of great art.[5]

As it stands, this qualitative distinction between lower and higher pleasure is unconvincing. Apart from the difficulty of measurement, it is far from clear that the vices would always fail Mill's own test. This test consists of asking moral or hedonic experts who have experience of both higher pleasures such as reading poetry and lower pleasures such as playing pinball which of the two activities affords them the greater pleasure. Mill thought that in this test, poetry would emerge unambiguously as a "higher" pleasure than pinball and, in general, that mental pleasures would fare better than bodily pleasures, that high culture would be preferred to popular culture, and even that a life of self-sacrifice would be preferred to a life of self-indulgence. Unfortunately for puritans, however, it is far from clear that applying this test produces the empirical result that they desire. Many people will tell you that they get just as much pleasure from watching football as from going to the opera. Many who thoroughly appreciate Picasso's paintings nevertheless rate the pleasures of fornication even more highly. (Perhaps Picasso himself did.) And, alas, it is not uncommon for people to regret, after it is too late, having been persuaded to pursue a life of self-denial in the name of virtue.

I think the truth, as far as Mill is concerned, is that the moral theory of utilitarianism does not yield the particular moral code he wished to endorse. He shared with more conventional and Christian Victorian moralists a substantial degree of puritanism, at least in relation to traditional vices. Though an uncompromising atheist, he was as deeply committed as any of his Christian contemporaries to an ethic of service, from which the pursuit of "lower pleasures" was inevitably a distraction. He was also clearly committed to a conception of human dignity that inclined him to think of some activities not only as being of an inferior order of pleasurableness but also as being inherently ignoble.

Given these convictions, it is understandable that Mill would regard the pursuit of lower pleasures, and particularly pursuing such pleasures to the point where they are clearly vices, as a distraction not only from a life devoted to the welfare of others but also from a life that nourishes the fundamental need of individuals for a sense of their own dignity and for feelings of self-respect.

However, it remains true that the puritanical view that considers as vices forms of enjoyment that, at least in many cases, do no harm either to those who indulge in them or to others is not easily derived from a straightforward utilitarianism any more than from Kantian arguments about absolute duties. But perhaps we can reach a more persuasive conclusion on these matters by considering the older form of utilitarianism that is at the heart of Greek ethics but is also at the basis of all moral systems that derive from religious creeds or secular belief systems such as Marxism and psychoanalysis.

The fundamental tenet of this kind of theory is that the answers to ethical questions are to be found by discovering the best kind of life that a human being can lead. Here the best kind of life is understood as the one that is most conducive to true inner well-being, to self-fulfillment, to our flourishing as human beings, or simply to the highest kind of happiness of which we are capable—all of which are interpretations of the Greek concept of *eudaimonia*, literally, spiritual or psychological well-being.

The great strength of such theories is that they make all ethical judgments ultimately a matter of enlightened self-interest and thus render the facts about human nature and human experience crucial for determining how we should live. In technical terms, it is analytic (true by definition) that one should live the best possible life of which one is capable, and it is also analytic that the best possible life is the one that is most conducive to *eudaimonia*.

If this line of reasoning is to be helpful in answering the question "Is gambling immoral?" we need to ask the question that is asked by the Greeks in a self-consciously philosophical way and to which all religions and secular ideologies offer (usually dogmatic) answers, namely, "What is the role of pleasure generally and of individual pleasures specifically in the life of a truly happy person?"

At this point, I want to claim that in general, the view of Aristotle is superior to the views not only of later religious puritans but also of other secular philosophers in both the ancient and the modern worlds. For Aristotle, pleasure is indeed an important part of the best kind of life that a human being can lead, as is wealth. A life in which there is no fun can no more be accounted a happy or successful or fulfilling life than a life of grinding poverty.

But pleasure, like money, is not the only ingredient in a truly happy and ful-filling human life, nor is it the most important ingredient. And indeed a life that is exclusively devoted to the pursuit of either pleasure or money will not be a happy one. Hence the famous doctrine of the golden mean, which in this case would require finding the right median course between the opposing vices of an excessive asceticism, on the one hand, and of hedonistic overindulgence, on the other.

Obviously, for many people, gambling will not be an important source of pleasure in their lives. But for those who do derive significant pleasure from gambling, what Aristotle defends regarding pleasure generally seems to be a sensible view to take regarding gambling. This is the Delphic injunction "Noth-ing in excess."

The virtue of temperance that this maxim recommends is one that it is highly plausible to see as an essential ingredient in living the best kind of life of which we are capable, especially with respect to the commonest sources of pleasurable recreation. Not only does temperance obviously avoid the dangers of addiction, but it is also not unreasonable to suppose that in moderation it fos-ters a life that is better than one of total abstinence. Thus it may in fact be the case that more people who drink in moderation, have temperate sex lives, and even enjoy the occasional game of chance have lives that are not only more en-viable but also more admirable than those who eschew all such pleasures and all play. Their obvious advantage over both the hedonist and the ascetic is that their wants are tempered to their ability to satisfy them. Consequently, tem-perate individuals do not find themselves in the condition of permanent tanta-lization that Schopenhauer believed to be our natural lot. A less obvious advantage may be that they are psychologically healthier and more balanced than those who either deny or indulge themselves excessively, with the conse-quence that they are more, not less, able to discharge their higher obligations of performing useful work and cultivating creative human relationships.

At least this is a way I can imagine we might talk to our children about "adult pleasures" with honesty and helpfulness.

CONCLUSION

In considering what role, if any, gambling should play in our lives, it seems implausible to appeal directly either to considerations of absolute duty or to considerations of the consequences for human happiness. The results are too uncertain. Nevertheless, I think there is something profound and important about both the Kantian ideas about the duties of stewardship and Mill's conception of an ethic of service. Moreover, I think that what is profound and morally important about both these views as far as traditional vices are concerned is similar and relates to the effect of gambling on human character. I want to conclude, therefore, by considering how gambling may indirectly affect our disposition and ability to live both virtuously and happily. What qualities of character does gambling require and reinforce?

The worst that might be said about gambling is that its effects on character are baleful because it tends to make people more stupid, weak-willed, self-absorbed, feckless, and insensitive than they otherwise would be. This line of reasoning does not apply with exclusive or particular force to gambling. Similar charges about the deleterious effects on character may be leveled against many of the other activities—playing solitaire, watching soap operas, and so forth—with which human beings divert themselves in their moments of leisure in the interval between birth and death.

Moreover, in the case of gambling, we need to seriously consider the view that gambling may actually be good for the character. Perhaps gambling accustoms us to sit more loosely than we otherwise would toward money and material possessions, and such a stance may be morally desirable. Perhaps, too, gambling inculcates the virtues of courage, equanimity, and graciousness in adversity and good fortune alike. After all, the supreme poet of traditional Victorian virtue and values, Rudyard Kipling, asserted that you will attain to his ideal of moral perfection not only

> If you can meet with triumph and disaster
> And treat those two impostors just the same

But also

> If you can make one heap of all your winnings
> And risk it on a turn of pitch and toss
> And lose, and start again at your beginnings
> And never breathe a word about your loss.[6]

It would be pleasantly perverse to conclude with the suggestion not only that gambling is generally good for the moral character but also that gambling for very high stakes is particularly likely to develop moral heroism. The truth of the matter, however, is almost certainly much duller. This is that for the vast majority of people who engage in it, gambling has no significant impact on their moral character at all.

If this is so, then it looks as if the truth about gambling is that the lives of those who gamble regularly are not likely, for the most part, to be much better or much worse from a moral point of view than the lives of those who never gamble. Nor are people who gamble likely to be much more or less happy or more or less useful. Consequently whether people gamble is not a morally important question, and gambling itself is a morally trivial issue.

This is, of course, not to deny that it is far from morally trivial if people devote too much of their time, talents, energies, and resources to activities that *are* morally trivial. And that includes according too large a part in one's life to gambling, even if one is not addicted to it.

NOTES

1. Surprisingly little has been written on this specific issue in contrast to the question of whether gambling should be legal. The following articles are germane: Valerie C. Lorenz, "Gambling," in *Encyclopedia of Applied Ethics* (San Diego: San Diego Academic Press, 1998); Lisa Newton, "Gambling: A Preliminary Enquiry," *Business Ethics Quarterly* 3, no. 4 (1993): 405–18; Jeffrie G. Murphy, "Indian Casinos and the Morality of Gambling," *Public Affairs Quarterly* 12, no. 1 (1998): 119–36; C. Singer, "The Ethics of Gambling," in *Gambling in Canada: Golden Goose or Trojan Horse?* ed. C. Campbell and J. Lowman (Burnaby, B.C.: School of Criminology, Simon Fraser University, 1989).

2. For a discussion of moral theories (including those discussed here) which is anything but facile or shallow and has endured so well because it combines great conceptual incisiveness with rich insight into social and psychological contexts, see Alasdair MacIntyre, *A Short History of Ethics* (London: Routledge and Kegan Paul, 1967).

3. The claim that there is in general much less substantive difference than is usually supposed between deontological theories and utilitarian ones is argued with great force, clarity, and elegance in R. M. Hare, *Moral Thinking* (Oxford: Oxford University Press, 1982).

4. A fine compendium of antigambling arguments from a religious point of view is to be found in W. Douglas MacKenzie, *The Ethics of Gambling*, 4th ed. (London: Sunday School Union, 1899).

5. The relevant discussion of lower pleasures is in chapter 2 of J. S. Mill, *Utilitarianism*, 4th ed., ed. and annotated by Roger Crisp (1871; Oxford: Oxford University Press, 1998).

6. Rudyard Kipling, "If," in *Rudyard Kipling's Verse, 1885–1918* (London: Hodder and Stoughton, n.d.), 645.

Appendix

Reforming Gambling Law in the United Kingdom: A Case Study

The regulation of gambling in the U.K. is at present being overhauled. The process began in early 2000 when the U.K. government set up a review body under the chairmanship of Sir Alan Budd to review all aspects of U.K. gambling law, with the notable exceptions of the national lottery and of gambling taxes. This body reported in July 2001. Its recommendations were then published for consultation with all interested parties, and the responsible government department, the Department of Culture, Media, and Sport (DCMS), published a response document entitled *A Safe Bet for Success* in March 2002, in which the government declared its intention of implementing the bulk of the Budd proposals. Subsequently the Parliamentary Select Committee responsible for matters pertaining to culture, media, and sport invited interested parties to make submissions to it and held three sessions at which those who had made submissions could be questioned by the committee. The report of the committee was published in July 2002. In the same month there was a parliamentary debate in the course of which the responsible minister, Richard Caborn, emphasized that the consultation process would continue and that on some issues the government had not yet made up its mind.[1] The earliest this process will be completed with the passing of a new act of Parliament and the establishment of a new regulatory authority is 2004, assuming that a bill can be drafted by the end of 2003 and that it passes the process of parliamentary scrutiny in time to be signed into law in 2004.

This furnishes a fascinating and instructive opportunity to observe gambling policy in the making. Because the process is not yet complete, however, it is impossible to judge how wise and effective the regulatory dispensation will finally turn out to be. Much depends on what the U.K. government decides about the aspects of policy that have not yet been finalized. My strategy in this appendix will therefore be to describe and discuss what has been agreed so far, to set out options for what remains to be done, and to express my own hopes and fears.

THE PRESENT SITUATION

Gambling in the United Kingdom is at present mainly governed by an act of Parliament passed in 1968. This act was passed to address the fact that the earlier act of 1960, which had substantially liberalized gambling law in the U.K. and mainly focused on off-course betting, had inadvertently resulted in the proliferation of several thousand small casinos and the fact that the American Mafia was showing signs of wanting to penetrate the U.K. gambling business. It is also true that the philosophy underpinning the legalization of gambling in the U.K. in the 1960s was very much that gambling is an undesirable activity that government is compelled to tolerate but which it should only make available under strictly controlled circumstances to those (somewhat inadequate) citizens who insist on indulging in this vice. Certainly, government should do nothing to encourage gambling or to enable commercial organizations to encourage it. On the other hand, because government was focused on potential evils relating to table games, including bingo, and because playing small-stakes machines at amusement parks was a well-established and popular part of British vacationing, government treated this form of gambling more or less as harmless entertainment. In 1993 Parliament also implemented a recommendation of the 1978 Royal Commission chaired by Lord Rothschild and authorized a national lottery whose purpose would be to raise money for good causes, which was to have a monopoly on the right to offer big prizes, and whose operator was to be selected by a bidding process.

The result of all this is that the U.K. has one of the most peculiar gambling industries in the world. Some aspects of the U.K. industry are not especially peculiar in the context of Europe, though they would be highly controversial in the jurisdictions in the United States. Thus there are outlets for private bookmakers ("betting shops") in every neighborhood, and there is a monopoly national lottery, run for profit by a private company, which has largely replaced betting with private companies on football pools. As in other countries, it is legal for U.K. citizens to gamble on the Internet with foreign companies that may be subject to light or indeed no regulation, but it is illegal for highly regulated U.K. companies to supply casino gambling services over the Internet because the gambler is not physically present. However, it is in the area of casino games, and especially machine gambling, that U.K. law is decidedly and uniquely peculiar.

On the one hand, all casinos must be private clubs and may only be located in towns that had populations of more than 125,000 in 1969. Customers may not enter a casino until twenty-four hours after their application for membership of that particular casino club has been received. Casinos may be open only between 2 P.M. and 6 A.M. Before mid-2002 they were not allowed to serve liquor at the tables or offer live entertainment. Credit cards may not be used to gamble, and casinos may not advertise. To open a new casino, you must apply for a license from the local court and prove that there is a demand for more casino gambling in the area than is presently being met by existing casinos.

Most significant of all, in a casino there may not be more than ten machines paying out a maximum prize of £2,000.

On the other hand, the U.K. is the only country in the world where the law allows children of any age to gamble on slot machines (currently called "amusement with prizes" machines, where the maximum prize is £8), not only at traditional seaside resorts but also at the slot machine arcades that abound in urban areas. There are also large numbers of machines with a maximum prize of £25 (prohibited to children) located in clubs and pubs around the country, as well as in venues such as fast-food outlets, taxicab offices, and highway service stations, and again in urban arcades, which are quite frequently called casinos. All told, there are an estimated 250,000 small-prize gambling machines in the U.K. All this is supervised by two regulatory bodies—the National Lottery Commission and the Gaming Board of Great Britain. The Lottery Commission is responsible, in addition to regulating the operating company, for adjudicating the bidding process and for promoting the work of the lottery in maximizing contributions to good causes. The Gaming Board is mainly responsible for issuing licenses to gambling companies and their employees and ensuring their compliance with regulations. Significantly, they have the power to withhold or revoke licenses with no reason given and no appeal, but they have no law enforcement powers. They also have no responsibility for, or power to act in relation to, problem gambling.

THE CURRENT PROPOSALS

It was against this background and at the most creditable urging of the Gaming Board that the government decided in 2000 to set up a review body under the chairmanship of economist, academic, and former civil servant Sir Alan Budd. Apart from the chair of the Gaming Board, members were drawn from a diversity of professions, and none had special knowledge of gambling. The review body received evidence from a large number of individuals and organizations, most notably the Gaming Board.

There is a direct link from the submission of the Gaming Board to the review body, the Budd Report, and the DCMS response document that results in both the philosophy and the concrete proposals of all three bodies being on all the most substantive issues identical. The shared philosophical assumption is that government needs to regulate gambling for three purposes only:

- To keep crime out of gambling
- To ensure that the games are honest
- To protect children and other vulnerable persons

Otherwise, the provision of gambling should be left to market forces.

In practice this means that government intends to abolish all of the following:

- Permitted areas
- The twenty-four-hour rule
- The demand test
- The prescription of uniform opening hours
- The ban on live entertainment
- The ban on serving liquor at gambling tables
- The ban on using credit cards
- The ban on advertising
- The ban on unlimited numbers of unlimited-prize machines
- The absence of a right of appeal against decisions by regulators
- The ban on U.K.-based companies' supplying of interactive gambling services (instead they are to be licensed, regulated, and authorized to use a kite mark indicating that they operate with the approval of, and under regulation by, the U.K. government)

On the other hand, there is a commitment to much stronger measures to deal with underage and problem gambling. Government will not extend ambient gambling, and were it not for the power of existing vested interests, gambling machines would have been taken out of many of the venues such as pubs and clubs that are not primarily intended to be gambling venues. Of particular significance, the government proposes that industry should develop a voluntary scheme for contributing some £3,000,000 ($4,500,000) per annum for funding research into gambling behavior and problem gambling and for contributing to the prevention and treatment of problem gambling.

WHAT REMAINS TO BE DONE

There is no doubt that the *Gambling Review Report* (GRR) and the Government Response Paper that largely endorses it are in many respects excellent documents: their conclusions are eminently reasonable, informed by credible empirical judgments and based on moral and political principles that enjoy a high degree of public acceptability. In particular, gamblers will enjoy greater freedom, but problem gambling will also be much more effectively addressed. Less obviously, their recommendations offer a way of getting from a status quo that is, in many ways, unsatisfactorily restrictive, but in which legitimate vested interests have become entrenched, to a more open and commercially normal dispensation in which those legitimate interests are not unduly disturbed. It is not easy to see how this difficult feat could be accomplished other than along the lines of the current recommendations.

Furthermore, the conclusions of the report converge to a large extent with what both the industry and the regulators agreed in wanting to see, and if the

GRR's recommendations were to be adopted in their entirety, there would be much satisfaction and little serious dissatisfaction within the existing industry, among those who would like to get into the industry, within the regulatory community, among the gambling public, and even among those who are professionally concerned about problem gambling. Moreover, implementing the report would almost certainly bring about a significant growth in the gambling industry that would yield some benefit to the Treasury in the form of new and unresented tax revenues. There could also be some worthwhile enhancement of the tourism industry. All in all, implementing the GRR by an appropriate combination of legislative and administrative action would constitute a creditable contribution to the modernization and better regulation of commercial activity generally in the U.K. and to the more rational governance of the gambling industry in particular.

However, in one crucial area there is serious cause for concern to the extent that government has not yet formulated a clear policy. This is the area of licensing new casinos. By far the most profound consequence of the contemplated changes in U.K. gambling law will be the potential introduction into the U.K. of casinos where many forms of gambling and other entertainment are offered, but where the dominant activity is the playing of unlimited-prize gambling machines that may be present in unlimited numbers. I follow the Gaming Board in referring to this form of gambling as "international-style" casino gambling and the venues where it takes place as "international-style" casinos. This reflects the fact that almost everywhere else in the world, a casino is understood to be a place where the dominant activity is unlimited-prize machine gambling. This is in sharp contrast to the U.K., where a casino is essentially a place where table games are played. Relatedly, international-style casinos tend to be large and patronized by a mass market, whereas in the U.K. "domestic" casinos are small private clubs catering to rather small and rather specific social groups. For these reasons, it is imperative that government understand that in removing the limits on the number of gambling machines that may be housed in a casino and the size of prizes that the machines may offer, government will be introducing a wholly new kind of gambling business into the U.K., which, moreover, is likely to dominate the industry both financially and in terms of public perception. In fact, government will be doing something no less dramatic than what it did when it introduced the national lottery.

The introduction of international-style casinos into the U.K. has the potential to grow the gambling industry considerably and to redistribute market share within it away from all other forms of gambling and toward casinos. This process carries with it the opportunity to secure some significant social and economic benefits over and above the benefits that accrue to the suppliers and consumers of gambling products, and to the public though the generation of normal tax revenues. It also has the potential for increasing the risks of excessive and pathological gambling and of contributing to the less easily identified social ills that might be broadly classified under the heading "cultural degradation" or "damage to the social environment." Overall, the effect of introducing these large new casinos into the U.K. will be to recirculate a great deal of money, and the decisions that government makes about what gambling companies and their customers may, may not, must, and must not do will to a large extent determine who benefits, and how much, from this process of recirculation, and at whose expense.

Whether and how the general public and particular sectors of it benefit from the introduction of international-style casino gambling depends crucially on how many such casinos the government allows to be developed and, in particular, on whether government adopts a policy favoring the emergence of a large number of small casinos or a small number of large ones. The answer that government gives to these questions also has a crucial bearing not only on the question of how the economic benefits flowing from the introduction of new casinos will be shared but also on the question of how great the negative social impacts of introducing new casinos will be and on whom the costs will fall.

So far, the government, following the Budd Report, has recognized the need to prevent an undesirable proliferation of big-prize gambling machines and has indicated that these may only be housed in venues licensed as casinos.[2] It has also recognized the need to prevent an undesirable proliferation of new casinos. It is, therefore, reviewing the GRR recommendations that the area allocated to the playing of table games in a new casino be at least two thousand square feet, and that the number of machines permitted in a casino be eight times the number of tables, unless the number of tables is eighty or more, in which case there will be no limits on the number of machines permitted. The government is reviewing these numbers because it recognizes that they will in fact permit the emergence of very small casinos offering international-style casino gambling, and the government is anxious not to see the emergence of gambling sheds full of slot machines and little else. On the other hand, the government is reluctant to make the limits so high that the 120-odd existing casinos, which are very small by international standards, could not qualify for casino licenses.

What is remarkable about the U.K.'s thinking so far about the introduction of international-style casinos is that it has apparently not yet considered what it wishes to do in relation to taxation. Taxation in one form or another is, after all, at least in jurisdictions where most of the gamblers will be locals rather than foreigners, the principal way in which governments secure benefits for their citizens from the introduction of international-style casino gambling. In particular, the U.K. government seems not yet to have seriously considered doing what is done in almost all other jurisdictions, namely, limiting either the total number of new casinos that may be licensed or the number of places where they may be licensed within a particular gambling catchment area. Most governments prescribe limits to the number and locations of casinos because they wish to contain the negative social impacts on, and maximize the economic benefits to, the area. We have explored at some length in chapters 4 and 5 the various ways in which these goals can be accomplished. The U.K. government, however, appears only belatedly to be thinking about the possible role of casinos in the economic regeneration of regions and of the possible negative political consequences of permitting far more casinos to be established than the public will want.

Instead, the U.K. government has hitherto taken the view, originally propounded by the Gaming Board, that it can safely be, and ought to be, largely neutral on the question of how many new casinos there should be and where they should be located. Provided gambling is kept crime free and honest, and provided the young and otherwise vulnerable are adequately protected, then the provision of commercial gambling services should be left to market forces.

There are, of course, perfectly respectable reasons for leaving the supply of casino gambling largely to market forces. Most prominent among these reasons are the following:

- Leaving it to market forces will get the best deals for gamblers
- If gambling is just another part of the entertainment business, it should be treated as such, and the number of establishments selling gambling services should not be prescribed
- Decisions about how gambling should be taxed should be made centrally by the Treasury, and central government should also decide how these taxes are spent
- Treating the licensing of casino premises more or less like the licensing of bars and pubs is simple

It is probable that these reasons weighed substantially with the free-market-oriented economist and former Treasury official Sir Alan Budd, who also took the view that it was not up to either the review body or the government to try to foresee and shape the commercial activity that would follow from implementing the report's recommendations. What is certain is that everyone in government is determined to compel both the existing industry and any future new entrants into the industry to subject themselves to the processes of normal, healthy commercial competition.

A consequence of this commitment to healthy commercial competition, however, is that government has been inclined to take the view that if the operation of market forces leads to the emergence of a large number of relatively small casinos, then either that is not a bad thing, or if it is a bad thing, it is not the kind of bad thing that government should try to anticipate and forestall.

I will seek to demonstrate why I think the present proposals will lead to a situation in regard to casino gambling that the government will regret and the general public will dislike. Meanwhile it is clear that what the U.K. government still has to do is twofold:

- To find ways of preventing a proliferation of new casinos, which would be widely unpopular and bad in terms of problem gambling and the general social environment
- To decide what taxation policy it will adopt with respect to gambling generally, and what economic benefits, if any, it will seek to secure for the general, as opposed to the gambling, public from introducing international-style casinos

The situation that the government will regret will be one where there are many small casinos that bring no economic benefits to the area where they are located. The alternative strategy that I would recommend is to ensure that there are only a few big *new* casinos that bring substantial economic benefits to their region.

ANTICIPATING THE CONSEQUENCES OF CURRENT THINKING

To the extent that the U.K. government has taken the view that market forces should determine what kind of new casinos emerge and in what quantity, they have thought it neither necessary nor appropriate nor perhaps even possible to try to anticipate what the landscape of casino gambling in the U.K. would look like if left to market forces. I do not think this position is tenable. It is possible both to foresee what market forces will produce and to evaluate, in the light of this foresight, what the advantages and disadvantages of a free market in international-style casino gambling will be. Moreover, it is essential that government anticipate the consequences of its decisions if these are to accord with its general political principles and its specific policy objectives in facilitating the introduction of new casinos into the U.K. Specifically, if left to the combination of market forces and planning controls as originally envisaged by the government, the introduction of international casino gambling in the U.K. will result in an unacceptably large number of new small casinos. This situation will be brought about through the combined operation of two general facts about the gambling business.

The first is that unlimited-prize machine gambling is an exceptionally profitable business. The average casino machine will earn about $30,000 per annum in gross gambling revenues and will have very small costs. This means that everyone will want to get into this business, which in the proposed U.K. context means that everyone will want a casino license.

The second fact is that gamblers will not travel farther than they must to reach a venue where they can engage in their preferred form of gambling. In the case of the new casinos we are considering, this is principally going to be unlimited-prize machine gambling. They will travel farther than their nearest venue to avoid one that they regard as unsafe or uncongenial, or to get to a venue where the odds are better (and therefore the cost of gambling cheaper). However, most gambling venues will be more or less equally safe and congenial, and the prices will be more or less the same. This means that people will gamble at the casino nearest to where they live or, in a smaller number of cases, where they work. To some extent, they will travel somewhat farther to reach a larger casino because they perceive it as offering more glamour and glitz. However, in a competition for customers between a larger and glitzier casino (with, say, more than one thousand machines) and a smaller but nearer casino (with, say, fewer than two hundred machines), convenience will typically trump glitz. A related point is that big casinos offering a wide variety of other entertainment (live shows, theme parks, classy restaurants, the proximity of good shopping, and so forth) may well attract more visitors from a wide area than a more conveniently located casino offering little more than well-priced basic gambling opportunities. However, while it is true that the other attractions may bring more visitors to the site of the big casino, it is unlikely that these visitors will choose to spend their gambling pounds at the casino. Instead they may actually do less gambling because they prefer to spend their money on the other attractions. Be that as it may, what is certain is that if the smaller casino has lower costs and can therefore offer better prices, it will certainly outcompete the larger casino.

Taken together, these two facts make it near certain that under the currently proposed U.K. regulations there will be a huge proliferation of small casinos. This is simply because in such circumstances, investors will prefer to invest in small, no-frills casinos that have lower costs than in large casino developments with higher costs and therefore higher risks.

EVALUATING "MANY-SMALL" VERSUS "FEW-BIG"

In considering whether to adopt a policy of "many-small" or "few-big," the U.K. government will be primarily concerned to minimize the negative impacts of liberalization. The most important of these are the following:

- *Problem gambling.* The single development most likely to increase the risk of problem gambling is the location of large numbers of high-prize machines in venues that are easy to get to and therefore create a widespread temptation to engage in impulse gambling.

- *Crime.* The kinds of crime that may increase with an inadequately regulated casino industry range from fraud and money laundering to mugging. Many small casinos are more difficult to regulate than a few large ones, where inter alia the owners of the casinos will contribute policing to ensure the safety of their patrons and will be ultra-nervous about being caught out in any improper behavior lest they lose their valuable operator's license.

- *Protecting the social environment.* Those who are opposed to the spread of all forms of gambling and especially of casino gambling are likely to argue not only that gambling is morally corrosive and psychologically dangerous but also that it leads to a deterioration in the quality of community life, which most people in the community would not agree to if they were accorded a democratic right to express informed consent.

In choosing between many-small and few-big with respect to new casinos, the arguments for minimizing negative social impacts all tell in favor of few-big. This is not so in the case of the arguments about maximizing economic benefits to the public, where, if public benefits were the only consideration, the issue might be adjudged finely balanced. Indeed, if the only consideration was maximizing the monetary value of the contribution that casino gambling makes to the public purse, the argument would favor many-small and a high rate of gambling tax, as is the practice in most of Europe.

There are, however, two essentially political rather than economic arguments why government would be well advised to consider forgoing the marginal additional tax revenue that many-small brings.

The first is that if government simply allows small casinos to proliferate, so that the number increases by, say, a factor of 12 or 15 to 1,500 or 1,800 with an average of one hundred machines each, then there will be no *visible* public benefit. It may be that the gambling taxes that are accruing to the central government are paying for a minute portion of whatever improvements are taking place in the health or education services. But the voting public will not be aware of this, and it will cut no ice with them to point it out if there is a backlash against gambling and voters start to focus on the damage apparently being caused by increases in problem gambling and the perceived degradation of the social environment.

The second political consideration that should make government extremely cautious about leaving the determination of the number and location to private entrepreneurs and local authority planners derives from the price inelasticity of demand for gambling services. Because demand for gambling, like demand for alcohol (but not for soft drinks), is not particularly sensitive to price, profitability depends crucially on the degree to which gambling operations are exposed to competition. In a free market, less competition means higher prices and larger profits. Consequently, in the proposed U.K. environment where the amount of competition will be drastically dependent on planning processes, the difficulty of keeping the planning process free of corruption will be immense.

The third political reason why government should avoid allowing a situation in which too many new casinos are licensed too quickly is simply that, while it is always easy to relax regulations and increase the availability of commercial gambling opportunities, it is extremely difficult to cut back the supply if it is decided that, for whatever reason, there is too much gambling. This is because powerful and legitimate vested interests are likely to have been established, and will have become legally and politically difficult to frustrate, and, moreover, will have a moral claim to be protected.

To summarize, then. The principal arguments in favor of many small casinos are that they are maximally convenient for customers; they probably lead to slightly higher gambling spending and therefore to higher potential gambling taxes; they avoid the inconvenience of tendering processes; and they facilitate access by new entrants to the market. The principal arguments in favor of few big casinos are that they reduce the risks of impulse gambling and therefore of problem gambling; they are easier and less expensive to license and regulate; they are less likely to provoke a backlash from those who dislike gambling on cultural grounds; they can bring substantial developmental benefits; and they are highly conducive to focusing economic benefits in particular areas or on disadvantaged communities. The disadvantages of each strategy are the converse of the advantages of the alternative.

PREDICTING AND PRESCRIBING THE FUTURE

The reason why government is in a quandary now about whether to adopt a policy that favors the emergence of many small new casinos in the U.K. or a few large ones is not just because the government originally thought that it didn't need to and indeed ought not to. It is also because government thought that, as a matter of fact, adopting the new proposals would not lead to the emergence of an undesirable number of new casinos. This, I believe, is probably a mistake. It is a mistake based on the belief that if the number and location of new casinos were mostly left to the combined judgment of commercial operators and local planning authorities, the results would be quite acceptable from a public interest point of view. In its evidence presented to the Parliamentary Committee, the Gaming Board estimates that the number of casinos might increase to 450 from 123. I think, by contrast, that just for a start, at least 500 of the 700-odd bingo clubs that operate today will be seeking a casino license so that they can operate around-the-clock big-prize machine gambling. Why would they not want such a license? Then there would be leisure centers, racetracks, Internet cafés, the larger arcades, as well as new purpose-built casinos, all of which would need a casino license to be able to cash in on the lucrative big-prize, linked-jackpot machine market.

Government has also—mistakenly, in my view—hitherto thought that it could not limit the number of new casino licenses without either affording unfair protection from competition to the existing industry, or alternatively without doing unacceptable damage to the legitimate aspirations and interests of the existing industry. Finally, in my view, government has, also wrongly, so far thought about new big casinos only in terms of the one already highly developed and highly publicized project to make the rather run-down seaside resort of Blackpool into an Atlantic City–type of casino destination resort. This would require a monopoly on the supply of international-style casino gambling in the area, and government has rightly taken the view that it would be unfair to single out Blackpool for windfall economic development or the company proposing to develop Blackpool for monopoly profits. However, government seems also and erroneously to have concluded that therefore nothing should be done to enable public authorities at the national, regional, or local level to grant a degree of exclusivity to international-style casino projects in the interests of harnessing unlimited-prize machine gambling to securing developmental benefits in the regions where the new casinos will be sited, or to funding good causes.

It seems clear to me that what government could and should do, with respect to new casinos, is to foster the development of a small number of large ones, which will bring substantial economic benefits to the areas from which the gambling customers come. What these benefits should be will probably be best determined at least to a significant extent by the appropriate local bodies, among which Regional Development Authorities are likely to have a particularly important role. Once a decision has been made in a region about what the public benefits to be secured should be, determining the number of new casino projects to be authorized will follow automatically. The commonest way of determining who gets the licenses is through a competitive tendering process that may be like an auction or may be more like an architectural competition—the so-called beauty contest method.

However, it also seems clear to me that government is presently reluctant to use competitive tendering as a way of ensuring that the industry is exposed to the rigors of commercial competition. In this case, a possible alternative is to stipulate a minimum quantum of capital expenditure for new casinos, of which, say, 30 percent must be invested in public interest projects approved by the relevant local, regional, and national authorities. Combined with a suitably large minimum size for casinos, this would probably be enough to secure the benefits of "few-big."

As far as the existing industry is concerned, existing casinos would gain some advantage in being protected from competition, but they would not enjoy any automatic right to expand or to transfer existing licenses to new and larger premises. Bingo companies would also retain protection of their existing business but would be denied the windfall profits that would accrue to them if they enjoyed the automatic right to convert their present premises into casinos. In the first instance, the industry might complain. But when they reflected that under a many-small scenario they would probably face European-style tax rates of up to 80 percent, they might agree that a national policy of forgoing tax to encourage investment was a wise one.

Clearly these are fundamentally matters for taxation policy. It is much to be hoped, therefore, that the Treasury will soon apply its mind to these issues. What is certain is that whether the U.K. winds up with a well-regulated gambling industry depends not only on how successful regulation is in minimizing negative social impacts but also on how successful it is in securing positive economic benefits. The U.K. government must adopt one of three policies depending on whom they wish to benefit by introducing international-style casino gambling:

1. Casino gamblers should not be treated any differently from other consumers of leisure products; consequently casino gamblers should be taxed no differently from, say, cinemagoers.

2. Casino gambling can make an exceptional contribution to the national exchequer; consequently casino gambling should be set so as to raise the maximum revenue without fostering an illegal industry.

3. Casino gambling can be harnessed to various kinds of local economic development by requiring casino projects to include capital investment that generates particular public benefits.

The first of these policies benefits consumers of gambling services; the second confers small benefits on everyone equally; the third benefits the communities where casino projects are located. I would expect industry to favor the first policy, civil servants to favor the second, and elected politicians to favor the third.

As with everything else to do with gambling, the prizes are large, and the competition for them is predominantly political in that it is a matter of persuading government that what it *should* do is what it is in your interests for government to do. I hope that the elected politicians come to understand where their true best interests lie, because that way benefits are maximized to the general public.

Other jurisdictions, especially in the United States, where there is set to be yet another wave of new casino authorizations, would do well to keep a close eye on what the U.K. government finally decides.

NOTES

1. The key documents are the *Gambling Review Report* (the Budd Report), Gambling Review Body, Department of Culture, Media, and Sport, Cm 5206, July 2001; *A Safe Bet for Success*, Department of Culture, Media, and Sport, Cm 5397, March 2002; *The Government's Proposals for Gambling: Nothing to Lose?* 3 vols., House of Commons Culture, Media, and Sport Committee (London: Stationery Office, July 2002).

2. There is, however, a danger here in that government, responding to huge pressure from social clubs, many of them party political clubs, has overruled Budd and is proposing to allowing machines in clubs to have jackpots of £250.

Bibliography

Adams, Charles. *For Good or Evil: The Impact of Taxes on the Course of Civilization.* New York: Madison Books, 1994.

Anders, G. "The Indian Gaming Regulatory Act and Native American Development." *International Policy Review* 6 (1997).

Atkinson, Glen, Mark Nichols, and Ted Oleson. "The Menace of Competition and Gambling Deregulation." *Journal of Economic Issues* 34, no. 3, (September 2000).

Bartlett, Warwick. *First Annual Review of the Global Betting and Gaming Market, 2000–01.* West Bromwich, U.K.: Global Betting and Gaming Consultants, 2001.

Borg, Mary O., Paul M. Mason, and Stephen L. Shapiro. "The Incidence of Taxes on Casino Gambling: Exploiting the Tired and the Poor." *American Journal of Economics and Sociology* 50, no. 3 (July 1991).

Brand, Hendrik. *Gambling Laws of South Africa.* South Africa: Juta, 2002.

Browne, M. N., and N. K. Kubasek. "Should We Encourage Expansion of Casino Gambling?" *Review of Business* 18 (1997).

Buland, Rainer. "Die Einteilung der Spiele nach ihren Freiheitsaspekten." In *Homo Ludens: Internationale Beitrage des Institutes fur Spielforschung und Spielpadagogik an der Hochschule Mozarteum Salzburg.* Vol. 7. Munchen: Verlag Emil Katzbichler, 1997.

Cabot, Anthony N. *Casino Gaming: Policy, Economics, and Regulation.* Las Vegas, Nev.: UNVL International Gaming Institute.

Cabot, Anthony N., William Thompson, Andrew Tottenham, and Karl Braunlich, eds. *International Casino Law.* 3d ed. Reno, Nev.: Institute for the Study of Gambling and Commercial Gaming, 1998.

Caillois, Roger. *Les jeux et les hommes.* Paris: Gallimard, 1958.

Campbell, C., and J. Lowman, eds. *Gambling in Canada: Golden Goose or Trojan Horse?* Burnaby, B.C.: School of Criminology, Simon Fraser University, 1989.

Christiansen, Eugene Martin. "Gambling and the American Economy." *Annals of the American Academy of Political and Social Science* 556 (March 1998).

Cornell, S., J. Kalt, M. Krepps, and J. Taylor. "American Indian Gaming and Its Impacts: A Report to the National Gambling Impact Study Commission." Cambridge, Mass., 1998.

Dense, J. "State Lotteries, Commercial Casinos, and Public Finance: An Uneasy Relationship." *Gaming Law Review* 3 (1999).

d'Hautesterre, Anne-Marie. "Foxwoods Casino Report: An Unusual Experiment in Economic Development." *Economic Geography,* extra issue (1998).

Eadington, William R. "The Legalization of Casinos: Policy Objectives, Regulatory Alternatives, and Cost/Benefit Considerations." *Journal of Travel Research* 34 (1996).

———. "Contributions of Casino-Style Gambling to Local Economies." *Annals of the American Academy of Political and Social Science* 556 (March 1998).

———. "The Economics of Casino Gambling." *Journal of Economic Perspectives* 13, no. 3 (summer 1999).

———, ed. *Indian Gaming and the Law.* Reno, Nev.: Institute for the Study of Gambling and Commercial Gaming, 1990.

Fahrenkopf, F. J. "Pursuing 'An Agenda for Mature Analysis.' " *Journal of Gambling Studies* 13, no. 4 (1997): 297–300.

Findlay, John M. *People of Chance: Gambling in American Society from Jamestown to Las Vegas.* New York: Oxford University Press, 1986.

Gambino, B. "Method, Method, Who's Got the Method? What Can We *Know* about Compulsive Gamblers?" *Journal of Gambling Studies* 13, no. 4 (1997): 291–96.

Gambling Review Report. Gambling Review Body, Department of Culture, Media, and Sport, Cm 5206, July 2001.

Gazel, Ricardo. "The Economic Impacts of Casino Gambling at the State and Local Levels." *Annals of the American Academy of Political and Social Science* 556 (March 1998).

Goodman, Robert. *The Luck Business.* New York: Free Press Paperbacks, 1995.

———. *The Luck Business: The Devastating Consequences and Broken Promises of America's Gambling Explosion.* New York: Simon and Schuster, 1995.

The Government's Proposals for Gambling: Nothing to Lose? 3 vols. House of Commons Culture, Media, and Sport Committee. London: Stationery Office, July 2002.

Gray, Jeffrey. "The Concept of Addiction." Printed as annexure G to the (U.K.) Gambling Review Report, presented to Parliament by the Department of Culture, Media, and Sport, July 2001. Commonly referred to as the "Budd" Report after the chair of the review body that prepared it and on which Professor Gray served.

Griffiths, M., A. Scarfe, and P. Bellringer. "The U.K. National Telephone Helpline: Results of the First Year of Operation." *Journal of Gambling Studies* 15 (1999).

Hare, R. M. *Moral Thinking.* Oxford: Oxford University Press, 1982.

Horn, B. P. "The Courage to Be Counted." *Journal of Gambling Studies* 13, no. 4 (1997): 301–7.

Kant, Immanuel. *Kritik der Reinen Vernunft* (Critique of pure reason). 2d ed. Trans. Paul Guyer and Allen W. Wood. 1787; Cambridge: Cambridge University Press, 1998.

Kindt, J. W. "The Costs of Addicted Gamblers." *Managerial and Decision Economics* 22 (2001).

Kipling, Rudyard. "If." In *Rudyard Kipling's Verse (1885–1918).* London: Hodder and Stoughton, n.d.

Ladouceur, R., C. Jacques, F. Ferland, and L. Giroux. "Prevalence of Problem Gambling: A Replication Study." *Canadian Journal of Psychiatry–Revue Canadienne de Psychiatrie* 44 (1999).

Land, Barbara. *A Short History of Las Vegas.* Las Vegas: University of Nevada Press, 1999.

Larsen, M. D. "Gaming Industry Development: A Comparison of Three States." *Economic Development Review* 13 (1995).

Lesieur, H. R., S. B. Blume, and R. Zoppa. "Alcoholism, Drug Abuse, and Gambling." *Alcoholism: Clinical and Experimental Research* 10 (1986): 33–38.

Lieven, Charles, and Donald Phares. "Casino Gaming in Missouri: The Spending Displacement Effect and Net Economic Impact." In *Proceedings of the Ninetieth Annual Conference on Taxation.* Washington, D.C.: National Tax Association, 1998.

Lorenz, Valerie C. "Gambling." In *Encyclopedia of Applied Ethics.* San Diego, Calif.: San Diego Academic Press, 1998.

Ludovici, J. L. *The Itch to Play: Gamblers in High and Low Life.* London: Jarrolds, 1962.

MacDougall, C. *Problem Gambling Helpline: Annual Narrative Report, 1997–98.* Halifax, Canada, 1998.

MacIntyre, Alasdair. *A Short History of Ethics.* London: Routledge and Kegan Paul, 1967.

MacKenzie, W. Douglas. *The Ethics of Gambling.* 4th ed. London: Sunday School Union, 1899.

Madhusudhan, Ranjana G. "What Do We Know about Casino Taxation in the United States?" In *Proceedings of the Ninety-First Annual Conference on Taxation.* Washington, D.C.: National Tax Association, 1999.

Marshall, K. "A Sure Bet Industry." *Perspectives on Labour and Income* 8 (1996).

McGowan, Richard A. "The Ethics of Gambling Research: An Agenda for Mature Analysis." *Journal of Gambling Studies* 13 (1997).

———. *Government and the Transformation of the Gaming Industry.* Northampton, Mass.: Edward Elgar, 2001.

Mill, J. S. *Utilitarianism.* 4th ed. Ed. and annotated by Roger Crisp. 1871; Oxford: Oxford University Press, 1998.

Murphy, Jeffrie G. "Indian Casinos and the Morality of Gambling." *Public Affairs Quarterly* 12, no. 1 (January 1988).

Newton, Lisa. "Gambling: A Preliminary Enquiry." *Business Ethics Quarterly* 3, no. 4 (1993).

Nozick, Robert. *Anarchy, State, and Utopia.* Oxford: Basil Blackwell, 1974.

O'Brien, T. *Bad Bet: The Inside Story of the Glamour, Glitz, and Danger of America's Gambling Industry.* New York: Random House, 1998.

Olivier, M. "Casino Gambling on the Mississippi Gulf Coast." *Economic Development Review* 13 (1995).

Przybylski, Michael. "Does Gambling Complement the Tourist Industry? Some Empirical Evidence of Import Substitution and Demand Displacement." *Tourism Economics* 4, no. 3 (September 1998).

Rose, I. Nelson. *Gambling and the Law.* Hollywood, Calif.: Gambling Times, 1986.

Rowntree, B. Seebohm. *Betting and Gambling: A National Evil.* London: Macmillan, 1905.

Royal Commission on Gambling. Final Report. Vol. 1. London: Stationery Office, 1978.

Rubin, Max. *Comp City: A Guide to Free Las Vegas Vacations.* Las Vegas, Nev.: Huntington Press, 1994.

A Safe Bet for Success. Department of Culture, Media, and Sport, Cm 5397, March 2002.

Singer, C. "The Ethics of Gambling." In *Gambling in Canada: Golden Goose or Trojan Horse?* ed. C. Campbell and J. Lowman. Barnaby, B.C.: School of Criminology, Simon Fraser University.

Sklansky, David, and Mason Malmuth. *Gambling for a Living: How to Make $100,000 a Year.* Las Vegas, Nev.: Two Plus Two Publishing, 1998.

Skolnick, Jerome H. *House of Cards: The Legalization and Control of Casino Gambling.* Boston: Little, Brown, 1978.

Spanier, David. *Easy Money: Inside the Gambler's Mind.* 2d ed. Harpenden, U.K.: Oldcastle Books, 1995.

Steinnes, D. N. "Have Native American Casinos Diminished Other Gambling in Minnesota? An Economic Answer Based on Accessibility." *Journal of Regional Analysis and Policy* 28 (1998).

Szakmary, A., and C. M. Szakmary. "State Lotteries as a Source of State Revenue: A Reexamination." *Southern Atlantic Journal* 61, no. 4 (1995).

Thompson, W. "*Racinos* and the Public Interest." *Gaming Law Review* 3 (1999).

Vaillancourt, Francois. "Government Gambling Revenues, 1985–1995/6: Evidence from Canada, Great Britain, and Australia." In *Proceedings of the Ninety-First Annual Conference on Taxation.* Washington, D.C.: National Tax Association, 1999.

Vinje, Daniel L. "Native American Economic Development on Selected Reservations: A Comparative Analysis." *American Journal of Economics and Sociology* 55 (1996).

Walker, Douglas M., and John D. Jackson. "New Goods and Economic Growth: Evidence from Legalized Gambling." *Review of Regional Studies* 28, no. 2 (fall 1998).

Walker, I. "The Economic Analysis of Lotteries." *Economic Policy* (1998).

Wittgenstein, Ludwig. *Philosophical Investigations.* Trans. G. E. M. Anscombe. Oxford: Basil Blackwell, 1963.

Yaffee, R. A., and V. J. Brodsky. "Recommendations for Research and Public Policy in Gambling Studies." *Journal of Gambling Studies* 13 (1997).

Index

About the Author

PETER COLLINS is Professor and Director of the Centre for the Study of Gambling and Commercial Gaming at the University of Salford in the United Kingdom, and he is Executive Director of the South African National Responsible Gambling Programme.